XAML Developer Reference

Mamta Dalal
Ashish Ghoda

Published with the authorization of Microsoft Corporation by:
O'Reilly Media, Inc.
1005 Gravenstein Highway North
Sebastopol, California 95472

ISBN: 978-0-7356-5896-7

1 2 3 4 5 6 7 8 9 LSI 6 5 4 3 2 1

Printed and bound in the United States of America.

Microsoft Press books are available through booksellers and distributors worldwide. If you need support related to this book, email Microsoft Press Book Support at mspinput@microsoft.com. Please tell us what you think of this book at http://www.microsoft.com/learning/booksurvey.

Acquistion and Developmental Editor: Russell Jones

Production Editor: Kristen Borg

Editorial Production: S4Carlisle Publishing Services

Technical Reviewer: Vikas Sahni

Copyeditor: Becka McKay

Indexer: Denise Getz

Cover Design: Twist Creative • Seattle

Cover Composition: Karen Montgomery

Illustrator: S4Carlisle Publishing Services

To Nimish and to my mother, for being my inspiration and strength.

—MAMTA DALAL

I dedicate this book to my grandparents (Nayansukhray and Kumud Ghoda, Mahavir and Sarla Majmudar), parents (Jitendra and Varsha Ghoda), sister (Kruti Vaishnav), and lovely family (Pratixa, Gyan, and Anand Ghoda) whose blessings, sacrifice, continuous support, and encouragement enabled me to achieve the dream.

—ASHISH GHODA

Contents at a Glance

Contents

What do you think of this book? We want to hear from you!

Microsoft is interested in hearing your feedback so we can continually improve our
books and learning resources for you. To participate in a brief online survey, please visit:

microsoft.com/learning/booksurvey

What do you think of this book? We want to hear from you!

Microsoft is interested in hearing your feedback so we can continually improve our
books and learning resources for you. To participate in a brief online survey, please visit:

microsoft.com/learning/booksurvey

Introduction

XAML is ubiquitous today. Whether with Silverlight, WPF, WF, various XPS formats, or XML-based formats, XAML is being used in a whole lot of Microsoft platform-based technologies. Though based on XML, XAML is unlike most other markup languages, because it is strongly linked to CLR assemblies through its objects.

Microsoft originally intended XAML to be a new and much more malleable and adaptable user interface (UI) description language for the .NET Framework through a technology named Windows Presentation Foundation (formerly called WinFX). From that specific beginning, XAML has not only outgrown that original goal, but achieved far more.

Recently, WPF has begun to supersede Windows Forms as the preferred development target. XAML's support for rich web interfaces, media streaming, and data-driven Line-of-Business (LOB) applications has made Silverlight a popular application platform in the web development community. The upcoming version of the Windows operating system, Windows 8, also includes extensive support for XAML.

This book introduces you to XAML and explains its syntax and constructs. It then explores various concepts, including XAML elements, properties, data binding, and so forth. Although the book does not provide exhaustive coverage of every XAML feature, it does offer essential guidance in using the key XAML functionality; you'll gain a strong foundation for designing rich and powerful user interfaces and applications using either WPF or Silverlight.

Beyond the explanatory content, each chapter includes procedural examples and downloadable sample projects that you can explore and expand for your own projects.

Who Should Read This Book

This book is aimed at proficient developers using the .NET platform, who understand the core concepts of XAML. It is especially useful for programmers looking to work with new or existing WPF or Silverlight applications. Although most readers will have some experience with XAML, the book is also suitable for those who are new to XAML but wish to learn XAML development.

Assumptions

This book expects that you have at least a minimal understanding of .NET-based WPF and Silverlight development with C# or Visual Basic. The book also assumes that you have a basic knowledge of SQL Server and XML.

If you have not yet gained familiarity with Silverlight or WPF, you might consider reading the following books:

- Ashish Ghoda's *Introducing Silverlight 4* (Apress, 2010), or Laurence Moroney's *Microsoft Silverlight 4 Step by Step* (Microsoft Press, 2010)

- Adam Nathan's *WPF 4 Unleashed* (Sams, 2010)

Who Should Not Read This Book

If you are completely unfamiliar with WPF and Silverlight, or if you're not comfortable reading and writing C# or Visual Basic code, this book is not for you. This book does not include a detailed explanation of the Model-View-ViewModel (MVVM) pattern; if you're looking for that information, take a look at:

- Raffaele Garofalo's *Building Enterprise Applications with Windows Presentation Foundation and the Model View ViewModel Pattern* (Microsoft Press, 2011)

- Gary Hall's *Pro WPF and Silverlight MVVM: Effective Application Development with Model-View-ViewModel (Expert's Voice in WPF)* (Apress, 2010)

This book also does not cover XAML for Windows 8—the timing of this edition of book precluded including that information with any reasonable hope of accuracy. However, based on our current level of information, the majority of the basic XAML concepts should remain the same for the future Windows 8 platform.

Organization of This Book

This book is divided into four sections, each of which focuses on a different aspect or set of features within XAML.

- Part I, "XAML Basics," introduces the .NET Framework and provides a quick overview of XAML fundamental concepts and classes, including object elements, attributes, properties, and events.

- Part II, "Enhancing User Experience," describes the various language features such as markup extensions, resources, and styles.

- Part III, "XAML User Interface Controls," describes the layout system and various XAML controls.

- Part IV, "Content Integration and Animation," delves into data binding, media, graphics, and animation.

Finding Your Best Starting Point in This Book

The different sections of the *XAML Developer Reference* cover a wide range of technologies associated with the Microsoft .NET Framework library and design and development tools. Depending on your needs and your existing understanding of the Microsoft .NET Framework, WPF, Silverlight, data binding, and design and development tools, you may wish to focus on specific areas of the book.

If you are	Follow these steps
New to XAML development	Focus on Parts I and III, or read through the entire book in chapter sequence. To get an overview of different XAML controls used in various samples throughout this book, read Chapters 6 and 7, which introduce layout and form and functional XAML controls.
Familiar with XAML	Briefly skim Parts I and III if you need a refresher on the core concepts. To get an overview of different XAML controls used in various samples throughout this book, read Chapters 6 and 7, which introduce layout and form and functional XAML controls. Read up on markup extensions, styles, and other features in Parts II and IV.

Most of the book's chapters include hands-on samples that let you try out the concepts covered in that chapter. No matter which chapters or parts you choose to focus on, be sure to download and install the sample applications on your system.

Conventions and Features in This Book

This book presents information using conventions designed to make the information readable and easy to follow.

- In most cases, the book includes examples that are XAML markup–based. Although you will see some minimal C# code to show the connection of the XAML to the code-behind code, the exercises rarely delve deeply into any code-behind.

- Boxed elements with labels such as "Note" provide additional information or alternative methods for completing a step successfully.

- Text that you need to type (apart from code blocks) appears in **bold**.

- A plus sign (+) between two key names means that you must press those keys at the same time. For example, "Alt+Tab" means that you hold down the Alt key while you press the Tab key.

- A vertical bar between two or more menu items (such as File | Close), means that you should select the first menu or menu item, then the next, and so on.

System Requirements

You will need the following hardware and software to complete the practice exercises in this book:

- One of the following: Windows Vista with Service Pack 2 (except Starter edition), Windows XP with Service Pack 3 (except Starter edition), or Windows 7.

- Microsoft .NET Framework 4.0 or 3.5 SP1 (4.0 is recommended)

- Silverlight 4 SDK, toolkit, and run time (including developer run time)

- SQL Server 2008 Express edition or higher (2008 or R2 release), with SQL Server Management Studio 2008 Express or higher (included with Visual Studio; Express editions require separate download)

- Visual Studio 2010, any edition (multiple downloads may be required if using Express edition products)

- Microsoft Expression Blend 4

- Computer that has a 1.6 GHz or faster processor (2 GHz or above recommended)

- Minimum 1 GB (32-bit) or 2 GB (64-bit) RAM (Add 512 MB if running in a virtual machine or SQL Server Express editions, more for advanced SQL Server editions)

- 3.5 GB of available hard disk space

- 5400 RPM hard disk drive

- DirectX 9–capable video card running at 1024 x 768 or higher-resolution display

- DVD-ROM drive (if installing Visual Studio and Expression Blend from DVD)

- Internet connection to download software or chapter examples

Depending on your Windows configuration, you might require Local Administrator rights to install or configure Visual Studio 2010 and SQL Server 2008 products.

Code Samples

Most of the chapters in this book include projects or code snippets that let you interactively try out the new material discussed in the main text. You can download all the sample code from this link:

http://go.microsoft.com/FWLink/?Linkid=233593

Follow the instructions to download the XAML_Developer_Reference_samples.zip file.

Note In addition to the code samples, your system should have Visual Studio 2010 and SQL Server 2008 installed. The following instructions use SQL Server Management Studio 2008 to set up the sample database used with the practice examples. If available, install the latest service packs for each product.

Installing the Code Samples

Follow these steps to install the code samples on your computer so that you can use them with the exercises in this book:

1. Unzip the XAML_Developer_Reference_samples.zip file that you downloaded from the book's website. (Name a specific directory along with directions to create it, if necessary.)

2. If prompted, review the displayed end user license agreement. If you accept the terms, select the Accept option, and then click Next.

Note If the license agreement doesn't appear, you can access it from the same webpage from which you downloaded the XAML_Developer_Reference_samples.zip file.

3. Attach the Northwind sample database to your instance of SQL Server 2008.

Using the Code Samples

The folder created by the Setup.exe program contains three subfolders:

- ■ **Chapters**   Example projects referenced in each chapter appear in this folder. Each chapter appears as subfolder with chapter number. Each chapter folder may include one or more sample projects related to that chapter. The chapter may contain separate projects for WPF and Silverlight. Follow the instructions given in the chapter to run the project. Some of the chapters may include one or more XAML file for individual samples. Some of these projects are incomplete, and will not run without following the steps indicated in the associated chapter.

- ■ **Snippets**   Fragmented or partial code snippets that are included in the chapter are included in text files. These can be copied and pasted into existing projects or applications and then executed.

- ■ **Sample Database**   This folder contains the SQL script used to build the sample database. The instructions for creating this database appear earlier in this Introduction.

To access the example project of a particular chapter, browse to the appropriate chapter folder in the Chapters folder, and open the project file.

Acknowledgments

Mamta Dalal:

This book is the culmination of the efforts of a number of people. Therefore, I'd like to thank the editorial and copyedit team of Microsoft and O'Reilly—in particular, our editor Russell Jones, without whom this book would not have been possible. I am also grateful to Kristen Borg, our production editor at O'Reilly; and Diane Kohnen and her amazing copyediting team. I would also like to thank my coauthor Ashish Ghoda for his valuable collaboration and strong support. Vikas Sahni, our technical reviewer, also deserves a strong vote of thanks for his feedback, which went a long way toward making this book better. I thank my parents for having believed in me and for encouraging me to nurture my skills.

I would also like to take this opportunity to thank the awesome .NET, WPF, and Silverlight communities at the MSDN forums and at Stackoverflow.com. The latter in particular has been a tremendous source of enlightenment for me. Thank you to Jeff Atwood and Joel Spolsky for having created this wonderful site.

Finally, I thank my husband, Nimish, for his constant encouragement, understanding, love, and support.

Ashish Ghoda:

Working with the Microsoft Press and O'Reilly teams and my coauthor for this book was a great experience. The support, positive attitude, and constructive feedback from the Microsoft Press editorial and production teams and from our technical reviewer—Vikas Sahni—made this project run smoothly.

My special thanks goes to Russell Jones—senior editor of Microsoft Press division—for giving me the opportunity to help write this book and for remaining confident that we could finish the book in the given time frame, despite some unexpected personal challenges faced by both Mamta and myself.

It's challenging when the authors of a work are located in different countries. Mamta Dalal, coauthor of this book, deserves full credit for her cooperation and efforts to keep the content in sync while working remotely.

With blessings from God and encouragement from my grandparents, parents, and in-laws, I was able to accomplish this task successfully. My wife, Pratixa, and two God-gifted sons, Gyan and Anand, have continued their support so that I could finish a fourth consecutive book. I thank my family for their cooperation and encouragement and for their faith in me during this difficult endeavor.

Errata & Book Support

We've made every effort to ensure the accuracy of this book and its companion content. Any errors that have been reported since this book was published are listed on our Microsoft Press site at oreilly.com:

http://go.microsoft.com/FWLink/?Linkid=233594

If you find an error that is not already listed, you can report it to us through the same page.

If you need additional support, email Microsoft Press Book Support at *mspinput@microsoft.com*.

Please note that product support for Microsoft software is not offered through the addresses above.

We Want to Hear from You

At Microsoft Press, your satisfaction is our top priority, and your feedback our most valuable asset. Please tell us what you think of this book at:

http://www.microsoft.com/learning/booksurvey

The survey is short, and we read every one of your comments and ideas. Thanks in advance for your input!

Stay in Touch

Let's keep the conversation going! We're on Twitter: *http://twitter.com/MicrosoftPress*

XAML Basics

CHAPTER 1

Introducing XAML

In this chapter:

- Windows Presentation Foundation (WPF)

- XAML—A Declarative Language for .NET Applications

- Silverlight

- The Microsoft .NET Framework

- Summary

Object-oriented and service-oriented programming models (along with language- and environment-independent features) lie at the core of the .NET Framework architecture. Since the release of .NET Framework 3.0, Microsoft has added several important components to support the unified programming and deployment model:

- **A presentation layer**   Windows Presentation Foundation (WPF)

- **A messaging and communication services layer**   Windows Communication Foundation (WCF)

- **Workflow management**   Windows Workflow Foundation (WF)

You use the Windows Presentation Foundation (WPF) framework libraries along with the XML-based *eXtensible Application Markup Language (XAML)* declarative markup language to define and develop next-generation, abstracted, dynamic, rich, and interactive user interface layers that provide data-integration capabilities and comprehensive support for multimedia, graphics, animation, and documents.

The e**X**tensible **A**pplication **M**arkup **L**anguage (XAML, pronounced *zammel*)—a declarative XML-based markup language—is at the center of the declarative user interface (UI) WPF framework. It is a language for describing an *abstracted*—externalized and decoupled—user interface layer. The current .NET Framework has extended XAML as its core user interface definition language to define user interfaces not only for WPF and Silverlight applications, but also for the custom activity libraries of WF 4.0–based workflows.

Windows Presentation Foundation (WPF)

WPF supports the development of rich and interactive Windows desktop applications that can provide sophisticated and realistic user experiences. WPF is built upon a very different architecture than Windows Forms. The key architectural differences are:

- WPF introduces a new user interface XML-based declarative markup language—XAML—that can support layout, styles, resources, and control templates to simplify and standardize management of the visual appearance of the user interface. XAML also supports properties and events that developers can handle in code-behind code to control its behavior.

- WPF provides a new presentation framework that integrates XAML for user interface design. The framework supports a unified programming model that includes data binding capabilities to develop data-driven applications as well as media integration, 2-D and 3-D vector graphics, document integration, text, and typography.

- WPF provides a set of .NET Framework libraries for the presentation core that are mainly derived from the *System.Windows* namespace. These libraries handle integration of the XAML-based user interface with the managed code-behind, including enhanced properties and events integration, such as *dependency properties* and *routed events* (topics you'll explore later in this book).

- The new Media Integration Layer (MIL) provides a rendering engine for WPF applications built upon Direct3D. The tight integration with DirectX means that WPF has high-performance rendering of the visual interface that can take advantage of hardware acceleration using the graphics processing units (GPUs) that most modern computers have, which reduces the load on the central processing unit (CPU). This is a very different approach than that taken in Window Forms applications, where the .NET Framework uses the User32 DLL to render standard Window Forms user interface elements and uses older Graphics Device Interface (GDI) to render graphics. Figure 1-1 illustrates the differences between the visual interface rendering approaches for WPF and Windows Forms applications.

More Info Visit MSDN at *http://msdn.microsoft.com/en-us/library/ms750441.aspx* to get more details on the WPF architecture.

XAML—A Declarative Language for .NET Applications

As mentioned earlier, XAML is at the center of the declarative user interface (UI) WPF framework because it implements the abstracted user interface layer. XAML is becoming a core UI definition language for .NET Framework–based applications. Using XAML, you can define and develop user interfaces for WPF and Silverlight applications and custom workflow activities for WF version 4.0.

You define and implement these user interfaces using a set of XAML controls provided as part of the WPF framework. These XAML controls are derived from a set of WPF presentation framework classes that can be hosted in either a window (WPF applications) or a page (Silverlight applications) to render the defined user interface at runtime using a XAML parser.

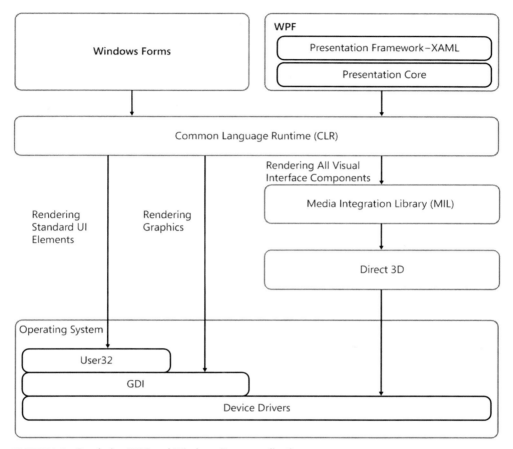

FIGURE 1-1 Rendering WPF and Windows Forms applications.

 Caution Not all XAML controls are interoperable between WPF, Silverlight, and WF applications. In addition, the XAML parsers for each platform are also different. You will need to use and set appropriate WPF, Silverlight, and WF platform specific–XAML controls and compile applications using the corresponding platform.

XAML Is Part of the Microsoft Open Specification Program (OSP)

You are probably aware that XAML is currently a Microsoft domain-specific language. To provide transparency and simplify the development of XAML applications by the broader developer community, Microsoft published the technical specification of XAML Object Mapping for WPF and Silverlight in March 2008, under its Open Specification Promise (OSP) program. Microsoft is committed to maintaining those specifications.

The XAML technical specification documentation provides details on XAML's data model for types, object hierarchies, and the techniques for mapping between XML and the object hierarchy data model. It also documents the WPF and Silverlight vocabulary of types that can be used with XAML specifications. Developers can use the WPF and Silverlight XAML technical specification documentation in conjunction with publicly available standard specifications, computer language design, and implementation art to fully understand and take advantage of XAML.

 More Info Visit MSDN at *http://msdn.microsoft.com/en-us/library/dd361847.aspx* to download the various releases of XAML Object Mapping, and the WPF and Silverlight technical specification documentation.

XAML Structure

Figure 1-2 provides a quick overview of defining a button. In the example, the button width is set to *100*, the button background color is set to *LightGray*, and the content (the button label) is set to "I am a Button" in XAML. The example also shows an identical *Button* object created in C#, with its related properties set in code.

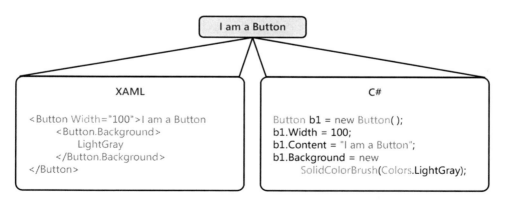

FIGURE 1-2 Defining a *Button* object and its properties in XAML and in C# code-behind.

A XAML file has a *.xaml* file extension. As shown in Figure 1-2, any XAML file consists of XML-like structured information that defines the relationships among various XAML controls. At runtime, these controls render as an object tree to create the user interface. In other words, XAML itself is an abstraction—it simply describes objects. This abstraction lets XAML serve as the UI description language for several different .NET application types (WPF, Silverlight, and WF). The properties you define within the XAML elements (such as the *Width*, *Content*, and *Background* properties of the *Button* control in Figure 1-2) control the look and feel of the particular user interface object represented by that XAML element. You can also determine how or whether a control binds with data. When you bind a control, it can display information (often from a database) unavailable at design time, and obtained only at runtime.

> **More Info** See Chapter 2, "Object Elements and Attributes," for more details on XAML syntax, XAML object elements, and attributes.

Dynamic User Interface

As shown in Figure 1-3, the key difference and advantage of using XAML—compared to building the user interface by creating and adding the controls in code-behind—is that XAML provides a declarative and separately compiled and rendered way of describing the user interface. User interface controls defined in code are described at design time and executed at runtime. In contrast, controls defined in XAML are stored separately from compiled code in .xaml files. At runtime, the XAML file is loaded and parsed by a XAML parser, and the user interface is then rendered dynamically. Thus if you change the user interface within a XAML file and redeploy it, the updated XAML content will be parsed and rendered; any changes in the user interface definition will be reflected in the user interface.

XAML's capability to develop an externalized and loosely coupled user interface enables developers to develop and modify the user interface without affecting the underlying program code and without recompiling the project for each UI change, which can significantly reduce the overall effort required for application development and testing.

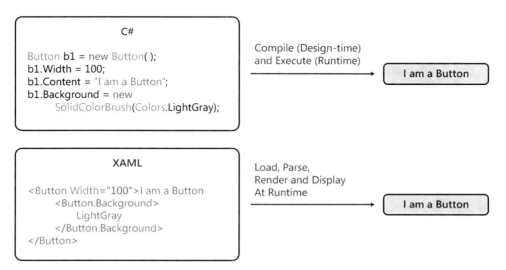

FIGURE 1-3 Defining a *Button* object with its properties in XAML and using C# in code-behind.

When working with XAML, remember that the WPF XAML parser is full-featured, whereas the Silverlight XAML parser ships with a more limited feature set. As mentioned earlier, not all XAML controls are interoperable between WPF, Silverlight, and WF applications. You will need to use the appropriate WPF, Silverlight, and WF platform–specific XAML controls and compile applications using the specific platform to which you want to deliver.

More Info Visit MSDN at *http://msdn.microsoft.com/en-us/library/cc917841.aspx* for more details on the differences between WPF and the Silverlight XAML parser.

Decouple Control Style Definitions

Applications should maintain consistency throughout to give users a predictable experience, including using the same color set, fonts, font sizes, and styles. Typically, ensuring this consistency can become quite challenging when you are using multiple controls of similar types in single or multiple XAML files within the same application, or across multiple applications. However, the WPF and Silverlight platforms help, because it provides the capability to easily externalize and decouple *style sheets*, which XAML elements can then reference from within XAML files to help maintain a consistent user experience. The approach and capability is similar to the Cascading Style Sheets (CSS) approach used in standard HTML web applications.

Figure 1-4 demonstrates how you can define a style within a XAML file as a resource or as an external resource file, and apply that style to a *Button* control.

Defining a Style

```
<Style x:Key="ButtonStyle5" TargetType="Button">
  <Setter Property="Foreground" Value="Black"/>
  <Setter Property="Background" Value="Green"/>
  <Setter Property="FontStyle" Value="Italic"/>
  <Setter Property="FontFamily" Value="Verdana"/>
  <Setter Property="FontSize" Value="16"/>
</Style>
```

Applying a Style

```
<Button Style="{StaticResource ButtonStyle5}"
    Width="115" Content="Button"/>
```

FIGURE 1-4 Defining and applying styles to XAML controls.

More Info See Chapter 5, "Resources, Styles, and Triggers," for more details on styles and resources for XAML.

Customized Design of XAML Controls

One of the biggest advantages of WPF's separation of the visual appearance of controls defined in XAML from business logic implemented mainly in code is that a designer not only controls the common styles of controls but can also alter the default look and feel of the control. For example, you might change the default look and feel of a button to make it look like a star! In WPF you can use a *ControlTemplate* to define the visual structure and behavior of a control without affecting its functionality.

Each control can exist in a number of possible states, such as disabled, having the input focus, a state where the mouse is hovering over it, and so on. A control template lets you define what a control looks like in each of these states. Sometimes this is referred to as changing the look and feel of the control, because changing the visual appearance of each state alters how a user sees and experiences a control.

Figure 1-5 demonstrates how you can define a control template to change the appearance of a *Button* control to make it look like an ellipse.

Defining a ControlTemplate

```
<ControlTemplate x:Key="ButtonControlTemplate1" TargetType="Button">
    <Grid>
        <Ellipse Margin="8,0,0,0" Stroke="#FF000000">
            <Ellipse.Fill>
                <LinearGradientBrush EndPoint="0.5,1" StartPoint="0.5,1">
                    <GradientStop Color="#FF4292F2"/>
                    <GradientStop Color="#FFC9EDF7" Offset="1"/>
                </LinearGradientBrush>
            </Ellipse.Fill>
        </Ellipse>
        <TextBlock Margin="48,19,19,14" Text="Button" TextWrapping="Wrap"/>
    </Grid>
</ControlTemplate>
```

Applying a ControlTemplate

```
<Button Margin="50" Height="56" Width="119" Content="Button"
    Template="{StaticResource ButtonControlTemplate1}"/>
```

FIGURE 1-5   Defining and applying a control template to XAML controls.

Integration with Code-Behind to Control Behavior

In general, markup languages such as HTML are mainly limited to defining the look and feel of the user interface; most markup languages cannot define the *behavior* of the user interface by controlling user interactions and defining various application actions. The typical way to implement some level of business logic within an HTML file is to use a scripting language such as JavaScript or VBScript.

In contrast to HTML, XAML was specifically developed for use with .NET Framework components. It can use the .NET Framework platform and the Microsoft design and development tools and extend its capabilities because it's not limited simply to defining the user interface. It also enables interaction by integrating XAML controls with managed code such as C# and VB .NET, and even dynamic languages such as Ruby and Python.

More Info See the article "Creating Interactive Bing Maps with Silverlight and IronRuby," at *http://msdn.microsoft.com/en-us/magazine/ee291739.aspx* for an example of how IronRuby dynamic language integrates events of XAML objects to implement required business logic.

Each XAML file for WPF, Silverlight, or WF project has a corresponding *code-behind* file, which Microsoft development tools such as Visual Studio or Expression Blend create for you automatically. However, a third file type is associated with the XAML file. Figure 1-6 illustrates the full class implementation for the MainWindow XAML file of a standard WPF project created using either Visual Studio or Expression Blend.

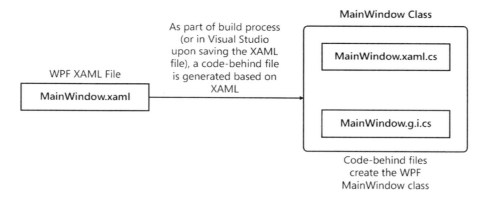

FIGURE 1-6 Full class implementation of XAML.

Note As defined on MSDN, "code-behind is a term used to describe the code that is joined with markup-defined objects, when a XAML page is markup-compiled." See *http://msdn. microsoft.com/en-us/library/aa970568.aspx* to get more information on the code-behind capabilities of XAML.

If you create a WPF application project by selecting WPF Application template in Visual Studio, you will get a default MainWindow.xaml file. If you expand the MainWindow.xaml file in the Visual Studio Solution Explorer, you will see an associated code-behind file named either MainWindow.xaml.cs file (when you create a C# WPF project) or MainWindow.xaml.vb (when you create a Visual Basic WPF project). This code-behind class is usually used to manage events and as a gateway to integrate with other application components and services to implement the business logic.

Now, open this code-behind file in the code editor. Locate the class constructor and right-click the *InitializeComponent()* method. Select the Go To Definition option from the shortcut menu. You will see that the *InitializeComponent* definition code opens a MainWindow.g.i.cs file. MainWindow.g.i.cs is a generated file based on the XAML defined in the MainWindow.xaml file. Any objects in the XAML file that have an *x:Name* cause the creation of a class member in the generated file.

The following code snippet demonstrates the default MainWindow.xaml.cs file of the WPF application and the *InitializeComponent()* method (in bold font) within the class constructor:

```
using System;
using System.Collections.Generic;
using System.Linq;
using System.Text;
using System.Windows;
using System.Windows.Controls;
using System.Windows.Data;
using System.Windows.Documents;
using System.Windows.Input;
using System.Windows.Media;
using System.Windows.Media.Imaging;
using System.Windows.Navigation;
using System.Windows.Shapes;
namespace WpfApplication1
{
    /// <summary>
    /// Interaction logic for MainWindow.xaml
    /// </summary>
    public partial class MainWindow : Window
    {
        public MainWindow()
        {
            InitializeComponent();
        }
    }
}
```

XAML defines the language features *x:Class*, *x:Subclass*, and *x:ClassModifier* directives, which (as you will explore more deeply in Chapter 2) enable integration of the XAML markup file with the code-behind partial class. You must derive the partial class defined in the root element of the XAML markup file using the *x:Class* attribute. This class usually gets defined automatically by Visual Studio, using the naming convention *<XAMLFileName.xaml>.cs* or *<XAMLFileName.xaml>.vb*, depending on which .NET language you're using. The following code snippet shows the definition of the *x:Class* attribute (in bold font) defined in the *Window* root element of the MainWindow.xaml file of the WPF application.

```
<Window x:Class="WpfApplication1.MainWindow"
        xmlns="http://schemas.microsoft.com/winfx/2006/xaml/presentation"
        xmlns:x="http://schemas.microsoft.com/winfx/2006/xaml"
        Title="MainWindow" Height="350" Width="525">
    <Grid>
    </Grid>
</Window>
```

Note Because XAML is a declarative language, it can contain data binding, state management, triggers, and so on as part of the UI definition. That means that design patterns such as the Model-View-Controller (MVC) and Model-View-Presenter (MVP) that were developed for service-oriented applications are not the best-fitting patterns for WPF-based applications. Instead, a new design pattern called the Model-View-View-Model (MVVM) pattern has been developed to define the user interface layer for XAML-based applications. Although MVVM was largely derived from the concept of MVC and MVP patterns, it differs by defining a view model that represents both a data model and behavior for views, and allows views to bind to the view model declaratively within XAML. Visit *http://msdn.microsoft.com/en-us/magazine/dd419663.aspx* to get an overview of how you can develop WPF applications using the MVVM design pattern. Also see *http://weblogs.asp.net/dwahlin/archive/2009/12/08/getting-started-with-the-mvvm-pattern-in-silverlight-applications.aspx* to get an overview on how to develop Silverlight applications using MVVM.

Inline Code

The WPF XAML namespace also supports an additional *x:Code* directive element that can contain inline programming code (in C# or Visual Basic) to implement business logic directly within the XAML file. Programming code within the *x:Code* element must be entered inside a *<[CDATA[...]]>* segment so that it will be processed as code rather than as XML by the XAML parser.

The following example implements the *Click* event of a *Button* control within the XAML file as inline code (in bold font). The code is written in C#, and is defined right next to the definition of the *Button* control, but within an *x:Code* element:

```
<Button Name="button1" Click="button1_click">Click Me!</Button>
<x:Code>
  <![CDATA[
    void button1_click(object sender, RoutedEventArgs e)
    {
        button1.Content = "Inline Code Works!!";
    }
  ]]>
</x:Code>
```

Warning Despite the existence of the *<x:code>* element, inline coding within XAML is not considered a best practice, and its use is not recommended except in special circumstances. It's defnitely not the best way to implement complex business logic. Inline code has some limitations that make implementing reusable code across a project considerably more challenging. In addition, it's more difficult to code, maintain, and support complex business logic in inline code.

The inline code must be defined within the XAML file. The scope of inline code is limited to the scope of the partial class created for that particular XAML instance.

You cannot use *using* (C#) or *Imports* (VB.NET) statements. Instead, you must fully qualify references to code entities outside the partial class.

The *<x:Code>* element must be an immediate child element of the root element of the XAML production. Moreover, although XAML itself has the advantage of abstracting the user interface definition of the application from the implementation of the business logic, inline code does not provide that abstraction, because it's defined directly within the XAML file.

> **Caution** The *x:Code* directive (and thus inline coding) is supported only by the WPF XAML parser—it is not supported by the Silverlight XAML parser. Therefore, you cannot implement inline coding in Silverlight applications. The Silverlight XAML parser also does not guarantee preservation of *CDATA* segment content.

Silverlight

Silverlight is an extension of the .NET Framework–based technology platform to develop cross-browser, cross-platform, and cross-device Rich Internet Applications (RIAs). RIAs are web applications that have features and functionality similar to traditional desktop applications, including rich and interactive user interfaces.

You can deploy Silverlight applications as plug-ins (in both in-browser and out-of-browser modes) that run in a sandboxed environment. Silverlight is built upon lightweight components of the .NET Framework that are a subset of the full WPF libraries. Silverlight applications do not require users to perform a full install of the .NET Framework; instead, users need to install only a small Silverlight plug-in on their Windows or Mac (Intel processer–based) computers, or Windows Phone 7 mobile devices.

> **Note** To install the latest version of Silverlight and get the latest information on Silverlight, visit Microsoft's official Silverlight website at *http://www.silverlight.net/getstarted/*.

Like WPF Windows applications, the declarative XAML markup language used by Silverlight is at the center of the declarative user interface (UI) framework. You can use the same Microsoft development tools (Visual Studio and Expression Blend) to define Silverlight user interfaces in XAML and you can implement business logic using standard .NET languages. However, there is a significant difference between the set of XAML controls available for WPF and those available for Silverlight. In addition, the Silverlight platform has limited .NET Framework libraries and its XAML parser as compared to the full WPF platform.

The initial versions of Silverlight (Silverlight 1.0 and 2.0 versions) were mainly targeted toward building media applications, so it focused on media integration, vector graphics, and animation. Later versions (Silverlight 3 and Silverlight 4) enhanced and streamlined Silverlight's media applications capabilities, and extended the product focus to implementing data-driven enterprise line of business (LoB) applications. Silverlight 5 version extended the LoB applications capabilities and added support for mobile applications development, as well as support for gaming and 3-D animations.

With Silverlight 5, Silverlight has reached maturity as an enterprise platform for developing and deploying media and data-driven RIAs. It supports the required security, maintainability, flexibility, scalability, and as a result, it is being adopted across a wide range of industries.

> **Note** HTML5 has extended the HTML platform capabilities to support native markup integration with multimedia (audio and video elements), enhanced user interface controls (such as calendar, date, time, email, URL, and search elements), and content integration (such as article, footer, header, and section elements). The new capabilities in HTML5 will reduce the need for custom scripting and custom plugins (such as Adobe Flash) when developing rich interactive applications. However, the implementation of the HTML5 specification is not standard. As a result, different browsers may take different approaches and render HTML5 differently. This is a challenge for developers trying to develop HTML5-based applications that provide consistent results across many different potential browser targets. Offsetting this problem is the advantage that HTML is a cross-platform technology platform supported by all modern operating systems (including operating systems such as Windows, Linux, OS X, iOS, and Android).

The Microsoft .NET Framework

When it released XAML, Microsoft also provided a set of development and designer tools to use the capabilities of XAML and the .NET Framework during the design and development process, as shown in Figure 1-7.

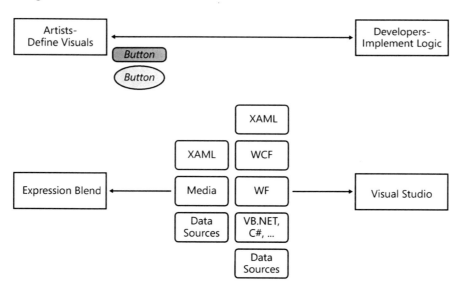

FIGURE 1-7 Separation of the design and development processes.

The WPF platform enables separation of the visual appearance of the application from the actual implementation of the business logic. In addition to Visual Studio as a development tool, Microsoft introduced Expression Blend (part of Expression Studio). Expression Blend is a tool that designers can use to create custom user interfaces in XAML. Using Expression Blend you can build sophisticated, rich, and interactive user interfaces as well as create 2-D and 3-D vector graphics and animations—all without needing a deep knowledge of XAML syntax, and also without needing any .NET language programming knowledge. This separation finally frees developers from building UI elements. Designers can work on the design while the development team starts implementing the code-behind and other application components and services. In other words, developers and designers can work in concert to implement both the UI and the actual business logic. And because Expression Blend can load and use Visual Studio projects and files directly, artists and developers can work on the same WPF, Silverlight, or WF projects, switching easily from Expression Blend to Visual Studio project and vice versa.

Before ending this chapter, it's worthwhile to provide a quick high-level overview of the key design-time and runtime components of the .NET Framework so you'll understand how they fit together.

Design-Time Components

Since .NET Framework 3.0, Microsoft has introduced the following key foundation components that support a unified programming and deployment model:

- Windows Presentation Foundation (WPF), which uses XAML to define and develop abstracted, dynamic, rich, and interactive user interface layer providing integration capabilities with data, media, graphics, animation, and documents

- Windows Communication Foundation (WCF), a service-oriented messaging system that can integrate across platforms and that supports industry-standard networking protocols

More Info See this MSDN page (*http://msdn.microsoft.com/en-us/library/ms735119.aspx*) to get more information on WCF. For an introduction to the new WCF features in .NET Framework 4.0, see *http://msdn.microsoft.com/en-us/library/dd456779.aspx*.

- Windows Workflow Foundation (WF), which provides a framework for developing workflow-driven task integration and automation

More Info Visit the MSDN page at *http://msdn.microsoft.com/en-us/library/dd489441.aspx* for more details on WF.

Runtime Cross-Platform Components

- The Common Language Runtime (CLR), the Dynamic Language Runtime (DLR) and Base Class Library (BCL) for .NET Framework components are key components of the runtime cross-platform execution engine.

  Figure 1-8 demonstrates the language-independent execution model of .NET applications developed using both static languages such as Visual Basic .NET, C#, and J#, as well as dynamic languages such as IronRuby and IronPython.

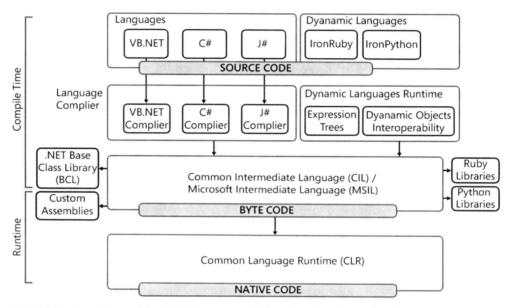

FIGURE 1-8   Execution model of .NET Framework 4.0–based applications and services.

- The Common Language Runtime (CLR) is the underlying runtime execution engine of the .NET Framework that provides a managed and secured application and services execution environment. The CLR enables abstracted development of application components and services using different languages, which get compiled to the common intermediate language (CIL) bytecode format at design time. At runtime, CLR will translate CIL bytecode to the native code using the Just-In-Time (JIT) compiler.

> **More Info**   Visit the MSDN page at *http://msdn.microsoft.com/en-us/ library/8bs2ecf4.aspx* for more details on the CLR.

- Dynamic Language Runtime (DLR) is a .NET Framework hosting model for dynamic languages, which provides a set of .NET Framework libraries and services for .NET and Silverlight that create a bridge between dynamic languages and the CLR in .NET and Silverlight.

More Info Visit the MSDN page at *http://msdn.microsoft.com/en-us/library/dd233052.aspx* for more details on DLR.

- Base Class Library (BCL) is a foundation for development of any .NET Framework–based applications or services. It is a library of classes, interfaces, and value types that provides the basic and system-level functionalities such as processing and managing XML files, integration with database, integration with file systems and connected devices, animation, graphics and media management, error and diagnostic management, integration with industry standard protocols, providing encryption mechanisms, LINQ, parallel computing, and capabilities to integrate with COM Interops.

More Info Visit the MSDN page at *http://msdn.microsoft.com/en-us/library/gg145045.aspx* for more details on BCL.

Summary

The declarative XML-based eXtensible Application Markup Language (XAML) is at the center of the WPF framework. You use XAML to define and develop abstracted, dynamic, rich, and interactive user interface layers that can integrate with data, media, graphics, animation, and documents.

Using WPF, you can develop rich and interactive Windows desktop applications that can provide sophisticated and realistic user experiences. Silverlight is a subset of WPF; you can use it to develop browser-hosted cross-platform, rich Internet applications as well as applications for Windows 7.x series mobile devices.

This chapter clearly shows that Microsoft has established a robust software and services development and delivery platform—the Microsoft .NET Framework—built upon solid core software development concepts such as object-oriented programming and language and environment independence. Together, these support the following essential attributes of software platform and services:

- **Device- and platform-independent application services**   With the introduction of Silverlight and the Dynamic Language Runtime (DLR), the .NET Framework offers broad support for development of cross-platform applications and services suitable for a broad range of development, deployment, and usage scenarios.

- **Dynamic and flexible services-focused architecture**   With the introduction of WPF, WCF, and WF and support for managed code integration, you can now develop service-oriented flexible software services using the .NET Framework deployable to both enterprise and cloud platforms.

- **Aesthetic and high-performance user interfaces**   XAML gives you the ability to define abstracted user interfaces that can support five usability dimensions:

  - Availability (can I get to it?)

  - Responsiveness (Is it fast enough?)

  - Clarity (can I figure it out?)

  - Utility (does it have what I want?)

  - Safety (is my identity and information secure?)

The next chapter, "Object Elements and Attributes," will provide a detailed walkthrough of XAML basics—all the key information you need to know to create visuals for the user interface layer of XAML-driven applications.

CHAPTER 2

Object Elements and Attributes

In this chapter:

- XAML Is XML

- Introducing the XAML Presentation Framework

- XAML User Interface Controls

- Summary

As discussed in Chapter 1, "Introducing XAML," you can use XAML with three types of applications:

- Rich and interactive Windows applications using WPF

- Rich Internet Applications (RIAs) and Windows Mobile applications using Silverlight

- Workflow activities using Windows Workflow Foundation (WF) 4.0

This is the first of eight chapters that take a deep dive into XAML and how it integrates with the .NET Framework to help you develop loosely coupled applications.

This chapter provides a detailed walkthrough of XAML basics—the key information you need to know to create visuals for the user interfaces of XAML-driven applications.

First, you'll see a brief explanation of XAML syntax and format. Later, you'll explore XAML elements and their structure, which are of key importance when defining the layout and user interface of your application. You'll explore the element attributes that control the look and feel and behavior of the elements. The chapter ends by showing examples of different types of built-in user interface XAML controls. These built-in controls support agile development through development tools such as Microsoft Visual Studio and Expression Blend.

> **Note** This chapter is purposefully kept basic—it is intended for readers who do not have a thorough understanding of XAML and who need to learn XAML from the beginning. If you are familiar with XAML and have experience developing XAML-based applications, you can skim or skip much of this chapter.

XAML Is XML

Any XAML document is a qualified XML document. Qualified XAML documents are both well-formed and valid, and can be parsed successfully by the XAML parser. XAML is structured information that defines the relationships among various XAML elements. At runtime, the .NET Framework renders these XAML elements to create the user interface for several different .NET application types (WPF, Silverlight, and WF).

The properties you define within a XAML element control the look and feel of the particular user interface object that XAML element represents. The properties also determine how or whether the displayed object or control binds with data so that it can display content available only at runtime. (Such content often comes from a database.)

XAML elements integrate with .NET code-behind through events, which makes them usable even by open source .NET-compatible code written in dynamic languages such as IronRuby and IronPython, which run on the Dynamic Language Runtime (DLR).

More Info See the article "Creating Interactive Bing Maps with Silverlight and IronRuby," at *http://msdn.microsoft.com/en-us/magazine/ee291739.aspx*.

One good way to begin working with XAML is to take a brief tour through the default XAML files that Visual Studio generates when you create a WPF, Silverlight, or WF Activity Designer Library application. (Note that these are not the only XAML files you might find in an application.)

A WPF application contains two XAML files by default—App.xaml and MainWindow.xaml files—as shown here:

App.xaml

```
<Application x:Class="WpfApplication1.App"
    xmlns="http://schemas.microsoft.com/winfx/2006/xaml/presentation"
     xmlns:x="http://schemas.microsoft.com/winfx/2006/xaml"
     StartupUri="MainWindow.xaml">
    <Application.Resources>
    </Application.Resources>
</Application>
```

MainWindow.xaml

```
<Window x:Class="WpfApplication1.MainWindow"
        xmlns="http://schemas.microsoft.com/winfx/2006/xaml/presentation"
        xmlns:x="http://schemas.microsoft.com/winfx/2006/xaml"
        Title="MainWindow" Height="350" Width="525">
    <Grid>
    </Grid>
</Window>
```

A Silverlight application contains two XAML files by default—App.xaml and MainPage.xaml—as shown here:

App.xaml

```
<Application xmlns="http://schemas.microsoft.com/winfx/2006/xaml/presentation"
             xmlns:x="http://schemas.microsoft.com/winfx/2006/xaml"
             x:Class="SilverlightApplication1.App">
    <Application.Resources>

    </Application.Resources>
</Application>
```

MainPage.xaml

```
<UserControl x:Class="SilverlightApplication1.MainPage"
             xmlns="http://schemas.microsoft.com/winfx/2006/xaml/presentation"
             xmlns:x="http://schemas.microsoft.com/winfx/2006/xaml"
             xmlns:d="http://schemas.microsoft.com/expression/blend/2008"
             xmlns:mc="http://schemas.openxmlformats.org/markup-compatibility/2006"
             mc:Ignorable="d"
             d:DesignHeight="300" d:DesignWidth="400">
    <Grid x:Name="LayoutRoot" Background="White">
    </Grid>
</UserControl>
```

WF Activity Designer Library Applications contain one XAML file by default—ActivityDesigner-Library1.xaml:

```
<sap:ActivityDesigner x:Class="ActivityDesignerLibrary1.ActivityDesigner1"
             xmlns="http://schemas.microsoft.com/winfx/2006/xaml/presentation"
             xmlns:x="http://schemas.microsoft.com/winfx/2006/xaml"
             xmlns:sap="clr-namespace:System.Activities.Presentation;assembly=
                 System.Activities.Presentation"
             xmlns:sapv="clr-namespace:System.Activities.Presentation.View;assembly=
                 System.Activities.Presentation"
             xmlns:d="http://schemas.microsoft.com/expression/blend/2008"
             xmlns:mc="http://schemas.openxmlformats.org/markup-compatibility/2006"
             mc:Ignorable="d"
             d:DesignHeight="241" d:DesignWidth="248">
    <Grid>
    </Grid>
</sap:ActivityDesigner>
```

You can create these applications using Microsoft Visual Studio 2010. See Appendix B of this book to get more details on XAML editor tools—including Microsoft Visual Studio.

By studying the preceding XAML files, you can see that XAML is simply an XML dialect; it possesses all the characteristics of XML. Like XML, XAML is case sensitive, so all element and attribute names are case sensitive.

 Important XAML is case sensitive!

Like any standard XML file, a XAML file must contain one root node. You will see many similarities in the basic XAML file structure for WPF, Silverlight, and Windows Workflow Activity Designer XAML files as well some unique features based on the targeted application type: WPF, Silverlight, or Windows Workflow Activity Designer application. To discover the differences, you need to delve deeper into the details of these files.

Root Element

Like any standard XML file, any qualified XAML file contains one root element. Based on the type of application, the related XAML file contains a different root element. However, each root element acts as a master container, which does not have any visual representation but houses different controls/elements in a structured way to build the user interface.

The root element of the XAML file of WPF-based Windows applications is *Application* for App.xaml file and *Window* for MainWindow.xaml file, as shown here:

App.xaml

```
<Application ... >
    XAML Code Goes Here
</Application>
```

MainWindow.xaml

```
<Window ... >
    XAML Code Goes Here
</Window>
```

Silverlight-based RIAs are actually plug-ins to the browser and thus the root element of the MainPage.xaml file is *UserControl* and *Application* for App.xaml (similar to WPF application), as shown here:

App.xaml

```
<Application ... >
    XAML Code Goes Here
</Application>
```

MainPage.xaml

```
<UserControl ... >
    XAML Code Goes Here
</UserControl>
```

With WF 4.0 now you can develop WPF (XAML)-based rich and interactive custom activities using the Activity Designer template in Visual Studio 2010. The *System.Activities.Presentation. ActivityDesigner* class provides base activity designer classes to develop custom activity designers by enabling design-time access to properties, and by controlling basic features such as customizing the icon that represents the activity. The root element of the XAML file of Windows Workflow Activity Designer is *<sap:ActivityDesigner>*, as shown on the next page. Note that you need to add a reference to the *ActivityDesigner* class, adding its definition to XAML by declaring a namespace (here the prefix for the namespace identifier is *sap:*), and including the *assembly* attribute:

```
<sap:ActivityDesigner
    xmlns:sap="clr-namespace:System.Activities.Presentation;
        assembly=System.Activities.Presentation"
    ...
>
    XAML Code Goes Here
</sap:ActivityDesigner>
```

XAML Namespaces

XAML namespaces follow the same syntax, concept, and scope as any other XML namespace. The key difference is that XAML namespaces define the XAML vocabulary—the elements, attributes, and the way XAML integrates with the .NET Framework class libraries.

Defining appropriate namespaces for XAML files ensures the uniqueness of element names. For example, it's possible to have two or more different element types, all named *Grid*, each of which exists in a different namespace. The different namespaces ensure that when you add elements (such as the *Grid* element in the preceding examples) to your XAML file, it identifies and renders the specific Grid element you intended, for example, the standard *Grid* control for a WPF, Silverlight, or WF application, rather than some other type of *Grid* element. The other *Grid* elements would be associated with a different namespace. The namespace prefix you define when including the namespace clearly marks each *Grid* object as unique.

As you can see in the examples, each XAML file defines XAML namespaces within its root element, starting with the XML pseudo-attribute *xmlns*. The default namespace has no prefix: it begins with only *xmlns*, but all the other namespace declarations start with *xmlns:prefix*, where *prefix* is a shorthand way to refer to the namespace later. The XAML namespace identifier itself appears after the equals sign in quotes and is either a URI or a string token in the form of a CLR namespace and some assembly information, as shown here:

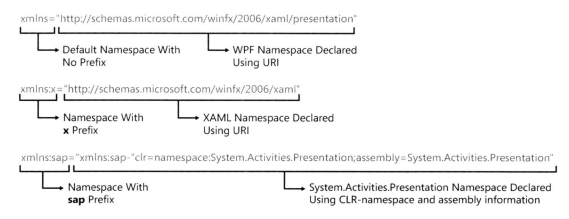

All WPF, Silverlight, and WF Activity applications contain two standard namespaces that represent the WPF and XAML classes.

The Default WPF Namespace

XAML files allow only one default namespace. The following default namespace

```
xmlns="http://schemas.microsoft.com/winfx/2006/xaml/presentation"
```

maps to the WPF namespace defined in the .NET Framework core library, which in turn references multiple CLR namespaces, such as:

- *System.Windows*

- *System.Windows.Automation*

- *System.Windows.UIElements*

- *System.Windows.FrameworkElements*

- *System.Windows.Controls*

- *System.Windows.Documents*

- *System.Windows.Shapes*

- *System.Windows.Interop*

- *System.Windows.Themes*

The default namespace declaration does not include a prefix; therefore, you don't need to include a prefix for XAML elements that are part of the libraries listed previously in your markup. To revisit the earlier example, *Grid*, with no prefix, refers to the *Grid* control defined by this default namespace. To use a different *Grid* element defined in a namespace with a *z* prefix, you'd need to write *<z:Grid>*. To get a glimpse of how much the default namespace defines, try removing it from a XAML file in Visual Studio; blue squiggly lines will appear throughout the document.

The XAML (*x:*) Namespace

The other standard XAML language namespace is typically defined with the *x:* prefix, which is mapped to the *System.Windows.Markup* class.

```
xmlns:x="http://schemas.microsoft.com/winfx/2006/xaml"
```

The *x:* namespace provides integration between the XAML instance and the .NET code-behind. Table 2-1 highlights the key capabilities enabled by the XAML (*x:*) namespace. You can get complete details of features provided by the XAML namespace at MSDN (*http://msdn.microsoft.com/en-us/library/ms753327.aspx*).

TABLE 2-1 Key Features Introduced by the XAML (:*x*) Namespace.

Attribute	Description
x:Class	A mandatory attribute that joins different pieces of a partial class together. Valid syntax for this is *x:Class="namespace.classname"* and *x:Class="namespace.classname;assembly=assemblyname"*. The XAML page generates code for a partial portion of the class, which then combines with the rest of the class code, which is a partial class file in the code-behind. If you revisit the earlier code snippet, you will notice that the *x:Class* is automatically defined in the XAML file in the root element—which is also the name of the automatically generated code-behind partial-class file (C# or VB .NET—based on your language preference settings in Visual Studio). So for the WPF application example—*WpfApplication1*, the code-behind file for *the MainWindow.xaml* file is *MainWindow.xaml.cs*, which is defined in the root element of the *MainWindow.xaml* file as shown here: *<Window x:Class="WpfApplication1.MainWindow" ... >* ... *</Window>*
x:Key	Provides a unique identifier for resources defined in XAML. These identifiers are vital for referencing resources via markup extensions. Identifiers must begin with a letter or an underscore and can contain only letters, digits, and the underscore character. You will see more information about how to use this attribute in Chapter 5, "Resources, Styles, and Triggers."
x:Name	Provides a way to give an identifier to an object element in XAML for accessing via the code-behind. This is not appropriate for use with resources. (Use *x:Key* instead.) Many XAML elements have a *Name* property also, and although *Name* and *x:Name* can be used interchangeably, only one should be set at a time. Identifiers must begin with a letter or an underscore and can contain only letters, digits, and the underscore.
x:Null	This attribute corresponds to null in C# (or Nothing in VB .NET). You can it use as a markup extension (*{x:Null}*) or through a property element (*<x:Null/>*).

Warning As described in this MSDN article (*http://msdn.microsoft.com/en-us/library/ cc917841.aspx*), the Silverlight XAML parser supports only *x:Class*, *x:Key*, *x:Name*, and *x:Null*. In contrast, the WPF XAML parser supports additional attributes such as *x:Array*, *x:Code*, *x:Type*, *x:ClassModifier*, *x:FieldModifier*, and *x:Uid*. Visit this MSDN page (*http://msdn.microsoft.com/ en-us/library/ms753327.aspx*) for more information about these attributes.

Additional Namespaces for Silverlight Applications

In addition to the default WPF and XAML language (*x:*) namespaces, you will see two additional namespaces defined in Silverlight applications within the root element.

The Designer *(d:)* Namespace The first additional namespace is the *d:* namespace, which enables support for design time features in Visual Studio and Expression Blend.

```
xmlns:d="http://schemas.microsoft.com/expression/blend/2008"
```

The XAML designer namespace *d:* for Silverlight contains design-time attributes that apply only while you are designing the application. The attributes provide designers and developers with design-time control while using the Microsoft Visual Studio and Expression Blend design surface.

The *d:DesignHeight* and *d:DesignWidth* attributes control the height and width of the Silverlight user control at design time without affecting the height and width of the application at runtime.

It's very useful to be able to use a set of sample data to populate your application interface at design time so that designers can see and test how the user controls and the applications will behave using representative data values. The designer namespace provides a set of attributes that you can use with data-bound user controls to bind them to sample data at design time. At runtime, the controls use the *DataContext* to set the data source; at design time, the *d:DataContext* attribute defines the data context. Similarly, the *d:DesignSource* attribute defines the design-time data source.

Among other attributes that function as part of the *d:DataContext* and *d:DataSource* declaration, the *d:DesignData* attribute defines the XAML file used as a sample data file, and *d:DesignInstance* defines the type using a *d:type* attribute, used as a data source to bind with the controls. You can use *d:IsDesignTimeCreatable* to specify whether the designer should be able to create an instance of your type or create a designer-generated substitute type. The *d:CreateList* attribute, part of the *d:DesignInstance* markup extension, specifies that the design instance is a list of the specified type when it has a value of *true*.

> **More Info** For additional information on the design of *d:* namespace attributes, see this MSDN link: *http://msdn.microsoft.com/en-us/library/ff602277.aspx*. For an example of how to use sample data for the Silverlight application at design time, see *http://msdn.microsoft. com/en-us/library/ff602279.aspx*.

The Markup Compatibility *(mc:)* Namespace The second additional namespace, *mc:*, supports markup compatibility mode for reading XAML.

```
xmlns:mc="http://schemas.openxmlformats.org/markup-compatibility/2006"
```

The *mc:Ignorable* attribute specifies which XML namespaces defined in a markup file the XAML parser should ignore at runtime. For example, the *mc:Ignorable* attribute is associated with the *d:* designer namespace for Silverlight and WF applications. In the earlier Silverlight application and WF activity examples, it's set to the *d* prefix of the designer namespace within the root element by default. The attribute specifies that the XAML parser should ignore all the design-time attributes at runtime.

You can also use the *mc:ProcessContent* attribute to inform the parser about element content that it *should* process at runtime—even if that element's immediate parent is set to be ignored at runtime because of an *mc:Ignorable* attribute.

> **More Info** For additional reference material on the markup compatibility *mc:* attribute, see this MSDN page: *http://msdn.microsoft.com/en-us/library/aa348909.aspx*.

The Silverlight SDK *(sdk:)* Namespace The Silverlight Software Development Kit (SDK) provides extended capabilities for developing Silverlight applications. It includes a set of additional controls, including *DataGrid*, *DatePicker*, and *Calendar,* as well as additional .NET Framework libraries such as *System.Xml.Linq.dll.*

Silverlight version 4 or later support the *XmlnsDefinition* attribute, which declares the namespaces for custom assemblies. This lets you declare the Silverlight SDK using a URI format rather than a string token (the syntax that consists of a CLR namespace and the required assembly information). If you add any controls from the Silverlight SDK library, Visual Studio adds the following additional Silverlight SDK namespace (*sdk:*) to the root element of that XAML file automatically:

```
xmlns:sdk ="http://schemas.microsoft.com/winfx/2006/xaml/presentation/sdk"
```

The Silverlight Toolkit *(toolkit:)* **Namespace**   The Silverlight Toolkit provides even more Silverlight controls, such as *DockPanel*, *WrapPanel*, *DataForm*, *Label*, and related source code and themes that support Visual Studio 2010 and .NET 4.0. The Silverlight controls part of the toolkit uses open-source licensing.

With Silverlight version 4 or later, when you use any controls from the Silverlight toolkit, Visual Studio adds the following additional Silverlight toolkit namespace (*toolkit:*) to the root element of that XAML file automatically:

```
xmlns:toolkit ="http://schemas.microsoft.com/winfx/2006/xaml/presentation/toolkit"
```

Additional Namespaces for WF Activities Application

You have already seen that the WF activity designer needs a reference to the *ActivityDesigner* class namespace, referenced with the *sap:* prefix. A Windows Workflow Activity Designer application also contains the Designer (*d:*) and Markup Compatibility (*mc:*) namespaces by default, just like Silverlight applications. The additional namespace is described here.

The *System.Activities.Presentation.View (sapv:)* Namespace

```
xmlns:sapv="clr-namespace:System.Activities.Presentation.View;
    assembly=System.Activities.Presentation"
```

Adding a reference to the *sapv:* namespace lets developers create view elements and provides access to commands and view state, user selections, and the *ExpressionTextBox* control. The *ExpressionTextBox* is a XAML control that lets users edit expressions in an activity designer.

Default User Interface Element

You may have noticed the presence of a *Grid* element in the example WPF, Silverlight, and WF XAML files shown earlier. The *Grid* element is a layout control; in fact, it's the default UI element that appears within the root element of MainWindow.xaml, MainPage.xaml, and ActivityDesigner1.xaml file.

```
<Grid … >
   XAML code goes here
</Grid>
```

One XAML rule is that you can have only *one* UI element for each XAML file. However, as you will see in the examples in this chapter and throughout this book, the *Grid*-type layout user control can contain multiple child elements, so you can use it as a base layout control for building complex and rich user interfaces.

Introducing the XAML Presentation Framework

The *System.Windows* namespace provides a wide set of feature-rich WPF and Silverlight presentation framework classes.

WPF and Silverlight Presentation Framework

As discussed earlier, the WPF and Silverlight .NET Framework libraries are not exactly the same. WPF provides full-featured .NET Framework 4.0 libraries to support the development of rich and interactive client applications using XAML as a presentation layer. You need to install the full .NET Framework and WPF application and related components and services on the target computer to run any WPF application successfully. As a result, WPF applications have full control of and can integrate with machine resources and other installed application components. However, this requirement introduces a restriction: you can run WPF applications only on the Windows platform. (WPF applications cannot run on Mac OS or Linux.)

In contrast, the Silverlight .NET Framework is a lightweight subset of the WPF libraries. It also contains lightweight .NET Framework libraries that support the development of media-rich applications that run in a sandboxed environment. This small package makes Silverlight a suitable cross-platform, application-delivery environment, which users can run by installing a Silverlight plug-in for their particular operating system, including Windows, Mac, and Linux.

Figure 2-1 shows the presentation framework objects hierarchy for WPF applications.

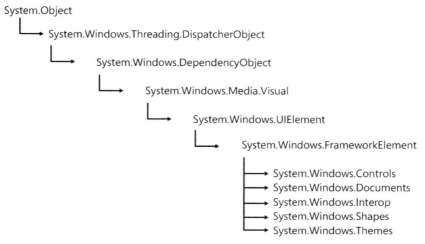

FIGURE 2-1 WPF Presentation framework object hierarchy.

Figure 2-2 shows the presentation framework object hierarchy for Silverlight applications.

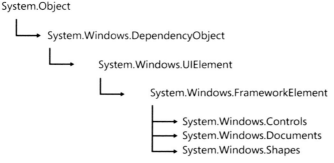

FIGURE 2-2   Silverlight presentation framework objects hierarchy.

As you can see from Figures 2-1 and 2-2, both the WPF and Silverlight presentation frameworks derive from the *System.Windows.DependencyObject* class. The *DependencyObject* class is responsible for providing property system services. The property system processes the values of object properties (with the support of *GetValue* and *SetValue)* and also provides notification services when property values change. You'll see more about this class and the dependency property system later in this chapter and in Chapter 3, "XAML Properties and Events," which discusses attributes and properties.

The *System.Windows.UIElement* class derives from *DependencyObject*. It functions as a base class for object elements that can appear or be interacted with in a user interface. It handles keyboard, mouse, and stylus input; provides focus support; and provides basic layout support for building an interactive and animated visual representation of the application.

The *UIElement* class is part of the *PresentationCore.dll* assembly of .NET Framework 4 for WPF applications. In contrast, in the Silverlight .NET Framework, the *UIElement* class is included in the System.Windows.dll.

The *System.Windows.FrameworkElement* class derives from *System.Windows.UIElement*. It extends the layout support, data binding capabilities, and adds the ability to build a logical tree of object elements. It also provides object-lifetime events, and defines the *Style* property, which you can use with the *Control* and *ContentControl* classes.

Revisit Figures 2-1 and 2-2 and you will notice that some key XAML UI object element classes— such as *System.Windows.Controls*, *System.Windows.Documents*, and *System.Windows.Shapes*—are common for WPF and Silverlight platforms, whereas *System.Windows.Interop* and *System.Windows. Themes* are available only to the WPF platform.

The *System.Windows.Controls.Control* class is the base class for the majority of object elements/ controls in the complete WPF and Silverlight control set. It uses a *ControlTemplate* to define the appearance of the control. This class provides properties to set the background and foreground colors of a control, configure the appearance of text within the control, and enable control templating. You will learn more about styles and templating in Chapter 5.

With this basic understanding of the building blocks of the WPF and Silverlight presentation framework, the next step is to understand how to define object elements in XAML to build a user interface.

Defining User Interfaces with XAML

To begin building a user interface in XAML, Figure 2-3 shows a basic example Silverlight application that lets users enter an email address and vote for their favorite vacation location.

Vote for your favorite vacation location

Your Email Address: [   ]

vacation location:
- ( ) Hawaii
- ( ) Switzerland
- ( ) Italy

[Vote]

FIGURE 2-3 Sample XAML-based screen output.

The following XAML code snippet creates the UI shown in Figure 2-3:

```xaml
<UserControl x:Class="SilverlightApplication1.MainPage"
    xmlns="http://schemas.microsoft.com/winfx/2006/xaml/presentation"
    xmlns:x="http://schemas.microsoft.com/winfx/2006/xaml"
    xmlns:d="http://schemas.microsoft.com/expression/blend/2008"
    xmlns:mc="http://schemas.openxmlformats.org/markup-compatibility/2006"
    mc:Ignorable="d"
    d:DesignHeight="300" d:DesignWidth="400">
    <Grid
        x:Name="LayoutRoot"
        Background="White"
        Height="250"
        Width="350">

        <Grid.Resources>
            <Style
                x:Key="HeaderFontStyle"
                TargetType="TextBlock">
                <Setter
                    Property="FontFamily"
                    Value="Times New Roman"/>
                <Setter
                    Property="FontSize"
                    Value="20"/>
            </Style>
            <Style
                x:Key="LabelFontStyle"
                TargetType="TextBlock">
                <Setter
                    Property="FontFamily"
                    Value="Arial"/>
                <Setter
                    Property="FontSize"
                    Value="14"/>
            </Style>
        </Grid.Resources>

        <Grid.RowDefinitions>
            <RowDefinition Height="35"/>
```

```xml
            <RowDefinition Height="35"/>
            <RowDefinition Height="Auto"/>
            <RowDefinition Height="Auto"/>
        </Grid.RowDefinitions>
        <Grid.ColumnDefinitions>
            <ColumnDefinition Width="Auto"/>
            <ColumnDefinition/>
        </Grid.ColumnDefinitions>

        <TextBlock HorizontalAlignment="Center"
                Text="Vote for your favorite vacation location"
                Grid.Column="0"
                Grid.Row="0"
                Grid.ColumnSpan="2"
                Margin="5"
                Style="{StaticResource HeaderFontStyle}"/>
        <TextBlock VerticalAlignment="Top"
                HorizontalAlignment="Right"
                Grid.Column="0"
                Grid.Row="1"
                Margin="5"
                Style="{StaticResource LabelFontStyle}">
                Your Email Address:</TextBlock>
        <TextBox VerticalAlignment="Top"
                Grid.Column="1"
              Grid.Row="1"
              Margin="5"/>
        <TextBlock VerticalAlignment="Top"
                HorizontalAlignment="Right"
                Grid.Column="0"
                Grid.Row="2"
                Margin="5"
                Style="{StaticResource LabelFontStyle}">
                vacation location:</TextBlock>
        <StackPanel
            Grid.Column="1"
            Grid.Row="2"
            Margin="5">
            <RadioButton x:Name="radioButton1"
                    GroupName="group1"
                    Content="Hawaii"/>
            <RadioButton x:Name="radioButton2"
                    GroupName="group1"
                    Content="Switzerland"/>
            <RadioButton x:Name="radioButton3"
                    GroupName="group1"
                    Content="Italy"/>
        </StackPanel>
        <Button Content="Vote"
                Grid.Column="1"
                Grid.Row="3"
                Width="100"
                Margin="10"
                HorizontalAlignment="Left"
                Click="Button_Click"/>
    </Grid>
</UserControl>
```

That's a lot of code for such a simple application. As you can see, the XAML is a standard XML file, but one with a specific structure as defined in Figure 2-4.

```
<UserControl x:Class="SilverlightApplication1.MainPage"
    xmlns="http://schemas.microsoft.com/winfx/2006/xaml/presentation"
    xmlns:x="http://schemas.microsoft.com/winfx/2006/xaml"
    xmlns:d="http://schemas.microsoft.com/expression/blend/2008"
    xmlns:mc="http://schemas.openxmlformats.org/markup-compatibility/2006"
    mc:Ignorable="d"
    d:DesignHeight="300" d:DesignWidth="400">
```
Root Element

```
<Grid
    x:Name="LayoutRoot"
    Background="White"
    Height="250"
    Width="350">
```
Root Layout Control

```
<Grid.Resources>
    <Style
      x:Key="HeaderFontStyle"
      TargetType="TextBlock">
      <Setter
        Property="FontFamily"
        Value="Times New Roman"/>
      <Setter
        Property="FontSize"
        Value="20"/>
    </Style>
    .......
</Grid.Resources>
```
Static Resource Dictionary

```
<Grid.RowDefinitions>
    <RowDefinition Height="35"/>
    ....
</Grid.RowDefinitions>
<Grid.ColumnDefinitions>
    <ColumnDefinition Width="Auto"/>
    .....
</Grid.ColumnDefinitions>
```
Grid Layout Control Definition (Rows and Columns Definition)

```
<TextBlock HorizontalAlignment="Center"
        Text="Vote for your favorite vacation location"
        Grid.Column="0"
        Grid.Row="0"
        Grid.ColumnSpan="2"
        Margin="5"
        Style="{StaticResource HeaderFontStyle}"/>
    ......
</Grid>

</UserControl>
```
Additional XAML controls Defining User Interface

FIGURE 2-4 XAML structure.

Here's a quick breakdown of the various sections within the XAML file shown in Figure 2-4:

- The XAML file starts with a root element, which is *UserControl* for Silverlight and *Window* for WPF applications.

- Each XAML element must contain only a single node within the root element. However, you can include multiple child nodes within that single node to build the user interface. To meet this requirement, you will usually have a XAML layout control element (the *Grid* object element in this example) as the root node. Beneath that, you build a hierarchical tree of object elements. See Chapter 6, "Layout and Positioning System," to gain a more detailed understanding of the different layout and positioning controls available.

- To maintain consistency when setting up object element attributes, you can define *static resources* (which are similar to the Cascading Style Sheet (CSS) classes used in HTML), in a XAML file. In Figure 2-4, the static resources are defined at the *Grid* control-level scope, and define a font style. Using defined styles for object elements simplifies your code and helps keep such things as font attributes consistent across controls.

  Revisit the App.xaml file for WPF and Silverlight applications. You can define application-level resources within the *Application.Resources* element.

 More Info See Chapter 5 for a more detailed understanding of resources and styles. Note that defining styles and resources is optional.

- Depending on the type of the layout control you use, you may need to define additional attributes for the layout control to determine its scope. For the *Grid* layout control, for example, you need to define the number of rows and columns in the grid, and its *Height* and *Weight* attributes. Again, the exact attributes you need to define depend on the layout control used and your application requirements. As an example, you do not need to define any additional attributes if you use a *Canvas* layout control.

- Layout controls can contain nested child object elements. This example includes several nested object elements as children of the *Grid* layout control that define the user interface, including *TextBlock*, *TextBox*, *StackPanel*, *RadioButton*, and *Button* controls. You'll see more about these controls later in this chapter.

  The controls used in this example are common for both Silverlight and WPF. However, the root elements for the two platforms are different. To test this, you can copy the XAML code for the *UserControl* element in this Silverlight example and paste it into the *Window* root element of the WPF application default XAML file. When you compile the application, you will see a user interface similar to that shown in Figure 2-3, but it runs as a WPF desktop application rather in a browser like the Silverlight example.

From the preceding explanations and the structure presented in Figure 2-4, you can deduce that:

- A XAML file consists of series of structured object elements (controls), which are defined and declared as namespace within the root element.

- Each object element contains a set of attributes. By defining these attributes you can control the appearance and content of the control.

- The nested structure of the definition of the object elements defines the location of the control within the user interface layout.

Object Elements

XAML user interface controls are object elements. Each control represents a CLR type defined in the .NET presentation framework library (primarily derived directly or indirectly from the *FrameworkElement* class). In XAML, you declare these controls through the default namespace or as a custom assembly. (The reference library is actually mapped through the namespace declaration.)

As you saw earlier, the object element syntax is similar to any other standard XML element. You write these object elements in one of the following ways. When an element has no content, only attributes, you can use the empty element syntax, which requires only one tag that ends with a forward slash and the closing bracket:

Empty Element Tag Syntax:

```
<ObjectElementName … />
```

As another example, here's a *TextBox* element that uses the empty element tag syntax:

```
<TextBox … />
```

Alternatively, you can use separate opening and closing tags.

Open/Close Tag Syntax:

```
<ObjectElementName … >
  …
</ObjectElementName>
```

When an element has content (not just attributes), you must use the open/close tag syntax. The following *TextBlock* element example uses separate open and close tags, enclosing its content between the tags:

```
<TextBlock … >
        Your Email Address:
</TextBlock>
```

An element may contain child elements rather than content between its tags. The following *StackPanel* example uses separate opening and closing tags and contains *RadioButton* elements as child elements between the tags:

```
<StackPanel … >
            <RadioButton … />
            <RadioButton … />
            <RadioButton … />
</StackPanel>
```

If you revisit Figure 2-4, you'll notice that the XAML file contains only valid elements in a hierarchical structure that follows the definition of the namespaces within the XAML file. As mentioned earlier, the namespaces also allow the XAML instance to interact with .NET Framework libraries and custom assemblies at runtime.

XAML elements in a XAML file must follow a defined hierarchical order to create a qualified, well-formed XAML file that will compile, render, and function properly at runtime. When XAML is compiled and parsed at runtime, the result is an object tree with a *UserControl* object as its root for Silverlight applications, or a *Window* object as the root for WPF applications.

Visual Studio provides a view of the object logical tree through the Document Outline feature at design time. Figure 2-5 shows the Document Outline window (the left-hand window in the figure), displaying the object tree for the example application shown in Figure 2-3.

FIGURE 2-5 Design Time XAML objects tree view as Document Outline window within Visual Studio 2010.

Object Element Properties

Just as the XAML parser maps XAML namespaces to CLR namespaces and assemblies, and object elements to CLR types, it maps object element attributes to properties or events.

In addition, you can reference *attached properties* and *routed events* (also called attached events) that are attached to an element using the attribute syntax. Attached properties and routed events are not declared in the mapped CLR type for an object element; they're specific to XAML. Chapter 3, discusses attached properties and routed events in more detail.

You can set object element properties in any of the following four ways:

- Attribute Syntax
- Property Element Syntax

- Content Element Syntax

- Collection Syntax

Attribute Syntax   The syntax for setting object element attributes is similar to any other standard XML element. You include XAML element attributes within the start tag to define mapped properties or events using this syntax:

```
<ObjectElementName AttributeName="Value" EventName="Value" … />
```

Note that you place attributes in the opening tag even for elements that have both open and close tags:

```
<ObjectElementName AttributeName="Value" EventName="Value" … />
  …
</ObjectElementName>
```

There are a few ground rules for setting up attributes and their values that are mapped to object properties and events:

- To set properties using the attribute syntax within XAML, the mapped CLR-type properties must be defined as *public* and must be writable.

- To set events using the attributes syntax within XAML, the mapped CLR-type events must be *public* and must have a public delegate.

- Object elements can contain zero or more valid attributes and events.

- All required attributes must be defined within the start tag of the object element.

- Attribute values must be a string representation of the value type.

- Attributes must be separated by white space (not by commas).

The *Grid* and *TextBlock* elements from the earlier example illustrate the different types of attributes.

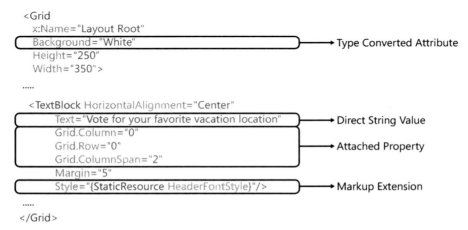

```
<Grid
  x:Name="Layout Root"
  Background="White"          → Type Converted Attribute
  Height="250"
  Width="350">
…..

  <TextBlock HorizontalAlignment="Center"
    Text="Vote for your favorite vacation location"   → Direct String Value
    Grid.Column="0"
    Grid.Row="0"                → Attached Property
    Grid.ColumnSpan="2"
    Margin="5"
    Style="{StaticResource HeaderFontStyle}"/>   → Markup Extension
…..
</Grid>
```

As you can see in the preceding image, you can define attribute names in two ways:

1. Define just the property name. *Background*, *Height*, and *Width* are defined directly as attributes for the *Grid* object. This means that the *Grid* object exposes these properties as both *public* and writable. The *Text*, *Margin*, and *Style* for the *TextBlock* element object are defined similarly.

2. Define as attached properties. The *Grid.Row*, *Grid.Column*, and *Grid.ColumnSpan* properties set within the *TextBlock* element define the row and column of the parent *Grid* object in which the *TextBlock* element will appear. These properties are defined as *attached properties* for the *Grid* object and can be set within other child elements. This feature is specific to XAML; it's not a feature of standard XML files.

 More Info See Chapter 3 for more about attached properties.

Attribute values are always strings, but as you can see in the preceding example, the XAML parser parses these values in three ways, based on the property type and the way you define the string value of the property:

Markup extension A markup extension is a special syntax used to specify property values that require interpretation. The interpretation itself depends on which markup extension is used. A markup extension uses this syntax: { (opening curly brace), followed by the markup extension name, optionally followed by parameters to the markup extension, and ending with } (a closing curly brace). Markup extensions are specific to XAML, enabling resources, data binding, and template binding.

This example uses a markup extension to bind the *TextBlock* element's *Style* property to defined static resource named *HeaderFontStyle*:

```
<TextBlock ...
        Style={StaticResource HeaderFontStyle}/>
```

Type converter Some properties require a specific type of object rather than a simple string value. This feature is specific to XAML. Based on the property type, the XAML parser must determine how to convert the string representation to a new object instance. You declare this property with an attribute *TypeConverter* for the XAML parser to parse the value properly.

In our example, we have set the *Background* property of the *Grid* object element to *"White"*. In XAML, the *Background* property is of *Brush* object type. So here the XAML parser will create a *SolidColorBrush* object instance to set the background with the solid white color.

You can explicitly define *TypeConverter* attributed properties using property element syntax rather than attribute syntax, as discussed in the next section.

Direct conversion The XAML parser converts string representations of property values that are not markup extensions or type-converted directly to the property type value or to appropriate enumeration values.

In the example, the *Grid* object element has *x:Name*, *Height*, and *Width* properties. The *TextBlock* object element has *Text* and *Margin* properties—all are examples of direct conversion.

The next logical question is: How does the XAML parser determine and prioritize the processing of an attribute value? As shown in Figure 2-6, markup extensions (either the attribute value starts with an opening curly bracket, or the object element is derived from *MarkupExtension*) get the highest priority. When a property is not a markup extension, the next priority is to check whether the attribute value requires type conversion; if so, the parser performs the appropriate type conversion. Finally, the XAML parser performs direct string conversions.

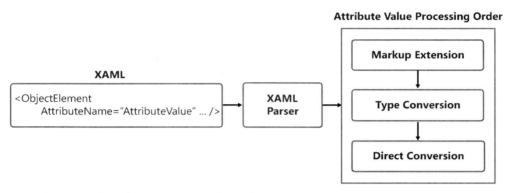

FIGURE 2-6 Precedence for processing attribute value.

To set events using the attributes syntax within XAML, the mapped CLR-type events must be public and must have a public delegate. As shown in the following example, the *Button* control object has a public *Click* event, which is set as a *Button_Click* declaratively, using attribute syntax. When a user clicks the button, the application will call the code-behind class's *Button_Click* method.

```
<Button Content="Vote"
        Grid.Column="1"
        Grid.Row="3"
        Width="100"
        Margin="10"
        HorizontalAlignment="Left"
        Click="Button_Click"/>
```

The attribute syntax also supports keyboard and mouse events, called *routed events* (attached events). The following example shows the *MouseLeftButtonDown* event set as *Grid_MouseLeftButtonDown* for the *Grid* element:

```
<Grid
    x:Name="LayoutRoot"
    Background="White"
    Height="250"
    Width="350"
    MouseLeftButtonDown="Grid_MouseLeftButtonDown">
```

You will learn more about events and routed events in Chapter 3.

Property Element Syntax   You can set properties using property element syntax, where you represent a property using the object element–like syntax shown here:

```
<ObjectElementName … >
    <ParentObjectElementName.PropertyName>
        Value
    </ParentObjectElementName.PropertyName>
</ObjectElementName>

   or

<ObjectElementName … >
    <ParentObjectElementName.PropertyName>
        <ObjectElementName AttributeName="Value"/>
    </ParentObjectElementName.PropertyName>
</ObjectElementName>

   or

<ObjectElementName … >
    <ParentObjectElementName.PropertyName>
        <ObjectElementName … >
            <ObjectElementName AttributeName="Value"/>
                …
        </ObjectElementName>
    </ParentObjectElementName.PropertyName>
</ObjectElementName>
```

Earlier you saw how to set the type-converted *Grid Background* property to *White* using attribute syntax:

```
<Grid
    x:Name="LayoutRoot"
    Background="White"
    Height="250"
    Width="350">
```

In XAML, the *Background* property is actually a *Brush* object type, so the XAML parser creates a *SolidColorBrush* object instance to set the background to a solid white color. You could define this property using property element syntax instead, in one of the following ways:

```
<Grid … >
    <Grid.Background>
        White
    </Grid.Background>
</Grid>

   or

<Grid … >
    <Grid.Background>
        <SolidColorBrush Color="White"/>
    </Grid.Background>
</Grid>
```

The first approach still uses the *Background* property as a type-converted property; again, the XAML parser will create a *SolidColorBrush* to set the background color. In contrast, the second approach explicitly sets the *Background* property to a *SolidColorBrush*, creating that as a child element of the *Background* property and setting its *Color* property to *White* using attribute syntax.

There are a few ground rules for setting up object element properties using property syntax:

- Properties that can be set up using attribute syntax can also be set up using the property element syntax.

- When using property syntax, the XML element used as the property value must be a child element of the object element.

- The property element name must be in the format *ParentObjectElementName.PropertyName*, where *ParentObjectElementName* is the name of the parent object element (*Grid* in the example) and *PropertyName* is the name of the property (*Background* in this example) that you want to set for the parent object. *ParentObjectElementName* and PropertyName must appear as a single term, separated by a period (.).

  Note that in standard XML, a term such as *ParentObjectElementName.PropertyName* is treated as a single element name containing a period (.), whereas the XAML parser treats the period as a separator between the object name and its property name.

- The property object element must not contain any other properties as an attribute.

Content Element Syntax   If the object property is declared as a *ContentPropertyAttribute*, which is usually of type *string*, you can set it using content element syntax, where the content (the property value) appears between the object element's opening and closing tags as shown here:

```
<ObjectElementName>
    value
</ObjectElementName>
```

   or

```
<ObjectElementName … >
    value
</ObjectElementName>
```

The example sets the *Text* property of the *TextBlock* object element using content element syntax:

```
<TextBlock VerticalAlignment="Top"
        HorizontalAlignment="Right"
        Grid.Column="0"
        Grid.Row="1"
        Margin="5"
        Style="{StaticResource LabelFontStyle}">
        Your Email Address:
</TextBlock>
```

Note that although content element syntax is supported in WPF and Silverlight version 4 and later, it is not supported in the earlier Silverlight 2 and 3 versions.

Collection Element Syntax   When a property type implements *IList*, *IDictionary*, or an *Array*-type collection, you use the collection element syntax to define a collection of one or more object elements as child elements:

```
<Grid.RowDefinitions>
    <RowDefinition Height="35"/>
    <RowDefinition Height="35"/>
    <RowDefinition Height="Auto"/>
    <RowDefinition Height="Auto"/>
</Grid.RowDefinitions>
```

In the preceding example the *RowDefinitions* property of the *Grid* object implements *RowDefinitionCollection*, which contains one or more *RowDefinition* object elements, defined above as child elements.

Similarly, in the full example, *Grid.ColumnDefinitions*, *Grid.Resources*, *StackPanel*, and *Style* use collection element syntax.

XAML User Interface Controls

As you saw earlier in this chapter, XAML user interface controls are represented in XAML as object elements. Each object element represents a CLR type, defined in the .NET presentation Framework library (mainly derived directly or indirectly from the *FrameworkElement* class, which is declared in XAML in the default namespace) or a custom assembly (mapped through a namespace declaration).

The .NET presentation framework library provides a standard set of rich XAML user interface controls. These are mainly derived from *System.Windows.Controls*, *System.Windows.Documents*, and *System.Windows.Shapes* classes, and are common to both WPF and Silverlight platforms. In contrast, *Windows.Interop* and *System.Windows.Themes* are available only to the WPF platform.

It's worth emphasizing the point that Silverlight is a subset of WPF. There are substantial differences in the total number of standard controls available for WPF and Silverlight and in their features. Some controls are common to both WPF and Silverlight; others are unique controls available only in one platform or the other.

Based on the features and functionality these controls provide, you can group them into six categories, which can help you understand them in an organized way:

- Layout and positioning controls

- Form controls

- Functional controls

- Image and media controls

- Graphics and animation controls

- Data-handling and information-management controls

Note that these are not official Microsoft categories; they're simply a logical grouping based on control features and functionality. Other authors and experts might equally well group these standard controls into different categories.

Layout and Positioning Controls

System.Windows.Controls.Panel is a base class that provides a set of layout and positioning controls that range from the very basic to advanced. These controls act as a main or sub container for group of user controls so that you can arrange them in specific positions and in a particular order to build a meaningful user interface.

As shown in Figure 2-7, *Canvas*, *StackPanel*, *Primitives.TabPanel*, and *Grid* are key layout and positioning controls for Silverlight and WPF. Figure 2-8 shows *DockPanel*, *WrapPanel*, and *Primitives. ToolBarOverflowPanel*, which are additional standard controls for WPF only. Note that *WrapPanel* and *DockPanel* controls are present in the Silverlight toolkit, and these controls will be included as standard Silverlight controls in future releases.

 More Info See Chapter 6 for more detailed information and examples on layout and positioning controls.

Form Controls

Handling and processing user input is a basic requirement of all Windows and web applications. Microsoft provides a rich set of standard XAML controls that support a variety of user input and interactions, including:

- The *TextBox*, *RichTextBox*, *AutoCompleteBox*, and *PasswordBox* controls in Silverlight, and the *TextBox*, *RichTextBox*, *PasswordBox*, and *StickyNoteControl* controls in WPF handle and process text input.

- *SpellCheck* and *SpellingError* provide a real-time spelling checker and spelling error notification scheme for text-editing controls such as *TextBox* and *RichTextBox* control. At the time of this writing, the spelling check and spelling error indication features are available only for WPF applications.

- *Calendar* and *DatePicker* controls handle date-related input in a user-friendly fashion, providing a consistent user experience for displaying and selecting calendar-related information. Silverlight SDK includes these controls for the Silverlight platform.

- *Button*, *RepeatButton*, *CalendarButton*, and *CalendarDayButton* are a common set of button controls that provide basic as well as specialized features (such as a *CalendarButton* that displays a calendar within the button) for building rich and interactive UI in WPF and Silverlight applications with little effort. Silverlight provides an additional *HyperlinkButton* button that displays a hyperlink within the button control.

- *ToggleButton* is a base class for *CheckBox* and *RadioButton* controls, which basically switch from one state to another (*checked*, *unchecked*, and *indeterminate*), letting you provide multiple ways to select individual items and choose an item from a group (*RadioButton*).

More Info See Chapter 7, "Form and Functional Controls," for more detail about form controls.

Functional Controls

Functional controls provide a different set of features that make the user interface cleaner and more usable; control and monitor an application's behavior; and interact with file systems to access and save files, print information and content, and generate custom child windows.

Making the User Interface Cleaner and More Usable

You can use the same types of techniques you have probably been using in your Windows Forms and/or ASP .NET applications, but using XAML lets you do so in a more manageable and controlled way. Here are some examples:

- You can associate a *Label* control with any control to display related text. This control exposes different features in WPF and Silverlight applications. In WPF you can associate an access key with the label text. Such an association is not available in Silverlight, but you can use the label as a *validator* for the control (for example, if the associated control is a required field). The *Label* control in Silverlight is available as part of the Silverlight toolkit. If you do not need an access key for WPF or validation for Silverlight, you can use a *TextBlock* control instead, described next.

- The *TextBlock* control, arguably one of the most-used controls in XAML, is like a label in that it displays non-editable text. Unlike *Label*, it has extended features that provide rich text formatting using inline elements such as *Bold*, *LineBreak*, *Underline*, and *Italic*.

- Use the *Border* control to create a border that may include a special background to surround the content.

- The *PopUp* control displays content in a pop-up window. When used correctly, it can significantly improve the usability of your applications. You can use the *PopUp* control along with a group of other controls to create a right click–enabled shortcut menu in Silverlight.

- The *ToolBarPanel* (for WPF), creates a toolbar that holds toolbar items.

- For WPF applications, you can use the *Menu* and *ContextMenu* controls to create a menu containing a group of items that control event-based features and functionality exposed by the application and its content.

Controlling and Monitoring Application and Content Behavior

It is critical to position and size controls so that they fit properly in the available display area. At the same time, you want to be able to support oversize content and display information in a usable manner. It is also important to have a visual control that manages the behavior of the application, the application's controls, and the content. WPF and Silverlight provide a set of standard XAML controls that feature such capabilities.

- *ScrollBar*, *ScrollViewer*, and *Slider* controls are useful for displaying oversize content in a well-managed and controlled fashion. You can set the range of the display as well as manage slider values to control the behavior of the both the control(s) and their content.

- The *ProgressBar* control provides a visual indication of progress during a lengthy operation or process.

- WPF provides a *StatusBar* control that can display items and information about the application itself, an ongoing or available operation, and/or some process status. The *StatusBar* is a horizontal bar typically placed at the bottom of an application window. You can include a *ProgressBar* control as part of your status bar to show real-time progress.

- The *Thumb* control is a control that users can drag. Thumb controls typically control the behavior and/or appearance of an application or control. For example, the *ScrollBar* control is a combination of two *RepeatButton* controls and a *Thumb* control. In the *Scrollbar*, the *Thumb* control represents a current value within the control's range. Users can drag it in one direction or another to select a particular value within the defined range.

Dialog Boxes

The ability to display default dialog boxes that interact with the file system and connected devices is essential for providing a consistent and integrated way of implementing these features in line-of-business (LoB) applications. In addition, you will need to create custom dialog boxes in a majority of enterprise LoB applications. WPF and Silverlight both provide support for displaying default dialog boxes—such as an open or save file dialog box and a print dialog box—and for implementing custom dialog boxes.

- The *OpenFileDialog*, *SaveFileDialog,* and *PrintDialog* classes facilitate calling these default modal dialog boxes from code-behind. Note that the print dialog box implementation differs somewhat between WPF and Silverlight. The *PrintDialog* control is part of the *Systems.Windows.Controls* library in WPF. In Silverlight, you use the *Print* method of the *System.Windows.Printing* namespace to open a print dialog box.

- You use the *System.Windows.MessageBox* class to show a modal message box window from code-behind. However, the Silverlight implementation of this class is limited. By default, it creates an OK button message box. You can customize the title of the window and add a Cancel button to the window. In contrast, WPF supports both Yes-No and Yes-No-Cancel button options in addition to OK and OK-Cancel. WPF also supports various message box images (*None, Hand, Question, Exclamation, Asterisk, Stop, Error, Warning*, and *Information*).

- There are separate implementation for WPF (for Windows applications) and Silverlight (for Web applications) to create custom dialog boxes. In WPF you will have to use the *System.Windows.Window* class to create the custom modal window. In Silverlight you will need to use *System.Windows.Controls.ContentControl.ChildWindow* class to create the custom modal windows.

> **More Info** See Chapter 7 to get more detailed information about functional controls.

Data Handling and Information Management Controls

Data-driven applications require integration with different types of data and external processes and represent them in different ways. XAML contains a set of controls that support data binding with different data sources and can display a wide range of data types:

- Controls such as *ListBox*, *ComboBox*, *TabControl*, and *TreeView* present and process lists of items.

- The *DataGrid* control can display and process items in a tabular format, in spreadsheet-like rows and columns.

- The *DataForm* control displays and processes individual items in a form format.

- The *DataPager* control lets you implement data paging easily so that users can navigate through large data sets.

- To display a summary of validation errors when a user updates data and submits those changes in a form, you can use the *ValidationSummary* control.

> **More Info** See Chapter 8, "Data Binding," for more detailed information about data handling and information management controls.

Image and Media Controls

WPF and Silverlight both provide rich support for working with images and media (audio and video).

The *Image* XAML control lets you place an image on the user interface. You can load and display several different common formats of image files using this control: The WPF version of the *Image* control supports bitmap (.bmp), Graphics Interchange Format (.gif), Joint Photographics Experts Group (.jpeg), Portable Network Graphics (.png), Tagged Image File Format (.tiff), Microsoft Windows Media Photo (.wdp), and icon (.ico) formats, whereas the Silverlight 4 version of the *Image* control supports only .jpeg and .png format.

The *MediaElement* control provides a control surface for integrating media (audio and/or video) in WPF and Silverlight applications.

The *MultiScaleImage* control is available only for Silverlight. This control can render multi-resolution images, which users can zoom in on and pan across. This control enables Silverlight's DeepZoom feature.

 More Info See Chapter 9, "Media, Graphics, and Animation," for a deeper understanding of the image and media controls.

Graphics and Animation Controls

Silverlight and WPF development platform are both intended for delivering rich and interactive applications. Graphics and animations play a vital role in supporting the complex visual effects required by such applications. Using XAML's graphic capabilities, brush, and storyboard controls, you can easily develop 2-D and 3-D graphics and complex animated applications.

XAML's graphics features make it easy to create interesting surfaces. In addition, both WPF and Silverlight controls can be completely re-skinned, resized, and transformed to generate complex and interesting visual effects.

- The *System.Windows.Shapes.Shape* class provides basic shape controls such as *Ellipse*, *Line*, *Path*, *Polygon*, *Polyline*, and *Rectangle*.

- The *System.Windows.Media.Geometry* class provides even more 2-D geometric shape controls, including *EllipseGeometry*, *PathGeometry*, *GeometryGroup*, *LineGeometry*, and *RectangleGeometry*.

- You use *transforms* to alter an element's coordinate system; applying a transform to a root element causes it and all its child content to change appearance in a uniform and predictable way. The benefit of a transform is that the underlying elements need no knowledge of the transform—they act as if the coordinate system remains unaltered.

  You can use a *translation transformation* to change the position of an element using the *TranslateTransform* class. Other types of transformations, such as *RotateTransform*, *SkewTransform*, *ScaleTransform*, *MatrixTransform*, and *CompositeTransform* implement other 2-D visual effects.

  WPF adds support for drawing, transforming, and animating 3-D graphics. The *ViewPort3D* element holds 3-D graphics content. You can use a *ProjectionCamera* to control the projection of a 3-D model from the point of view of an onlooker, and the *PerspectiveCamera* to view a 3-D model from its vanishing point. WPF also supports 3-D geometric modeling through the *GeometryModel3D* class and the *MeshGeometry3D* class.

  In contrast, Silverlight has much more limited 3-D graphics capabilities. You can use a *perspective transformation* through the *PlaneProjection* class to create 3-D effects in Silverlight 4.

Animation is typically achieved by moving user interface objects over a specific duration along a particular pattern. If the movement is fast enough, it generates the illusion of motion—an animated effect. Using the *Storyboard* class and various types of animation such as *From/To/By* animation classes (*ColorAnimation*, *DoubleAnimation* and *PointAnimation*) and keyframe animation classes (*ColorAnimationUsingKeyFrames*, *DoubleAnimationUsingKeyFrames*, *PointAnimation*, and *ObjectAnimationUsingKeyFrames*), you can produce a wide range of smooth, realistic animations.

 More Info Chapter 9 contains much more detail about the graphics and animation controls.

Summary

A qualified XAML file is a well-formed and structured XML file that defines the relationships among various object elements. The XAML parser can render these elements at runtime to create the user interface of several different .NET application types (WPF, Silverlight, and WF). At the time of rendering, the XAML parser maps XAML namespaces to CLR namespaces and assemblies, it maps object elements to CLR types, and it maps object element attributes to properties or events.

The .NET presentation Framework library provides a standard set of rich XAML user interface controls. There are substantial differences in the total number of standard controls available for WPF and Silverlight and in their features. Although some controls are common to both WPF and Silverlight, others are unique controls available only in one platform or the other. This chapter provided an overview of layout and positioning controls, forms and functional controls, image, media, graphics and animation types controls, and data-handling and information-management controls.

The next chapter, "XAML Properties and Events," will cover different types of properties and events you can set for XAML object elements and perform code-behind integration to implement different types of application features.

CHAPTER 3

XAML Properties and Events

In this chapter:

- XAML Properties
- XAML Events
- Summary

As discussed in Chapter 2, "Object Elements and Attributes," declaring an object element in XAML maps it to the corresponding CLR type. The process is similar to creating an object instance of that CLR type by using the default constructor in code-behind. With that said, setting an attribute in an object element is the equivalent of either setting a property or creating an event handler for that object in code-behind. In XAML you can also use the attribute syntax to define *attached properties* and *attached events*, which are properties and events not actually defined in the mapped CLR type.

This chapter explores the different types of property and event systems available as part of WPF and Silverlight frameworks.

XAML Properties

The WPF property system extends the functionality of .NET CLR property and provides plumbing for the following:

- Gaining access to object properties
- Processing the values of object properties (with the support of *GetValue* and *SetValue)*
- Providing notification services when property values change
- Defining and mapping resources, styles, and templates
- Performing validation and data binding
- Implementing animation

Dependency Properties

Supported By	
WPF	Yes
Silverlight	Yes

Quick Summary	
Definition	Extended CLR properties backed by the WPF property system—*DependencyProperty*—that can process property values based on different sources such as data bound values, animation values, template resources specified in the XAML, styles, or local values. Dependency properties can also handle property change notifications.
Naming Convention	The name of the dependency property field is always the name of the property with the suffix *Property* appended. For example, for a *Width* dependency property implemented in WPF, the class would have a dependency property field name of *WidthProperty*.
Can You Create Custom Dependency Properties?	Yes
MSDN Reference	For WPF: *http://msdn.microsoft.com/en-us/library/ms752914.aspx* For Silverlight: *http://msdn.microsoft.com/en-us/library/cc265148.aspx*

Microsoft .NET Framework 3.0 and later versions provide a system called *dependency properties* for the WPF, Silverlight, and WF platforms. Like regular .NET properties, the main focus of dependency properties is to manage object state by performing property value resolution and property value change notification. The key difference between regular .NET properties and dependency properties is that unlike storing a local property value in an instance variable for a regular .NET property, the dependency property doesn't store the value locally; instead, it uses the dependency property framework to determine the property value when required, providing a value change notification service when the value changes. You register dependency properties along with a defined set of rules for value resolution and change notification in the central dependency property registration repository, which is managed by the dependency property framework.

Defining a Dependency Property

You define a dependency property with the *DependencyProperty* type, using the *public static* and *readonly* identifier keywords. This field is registered to the dependency property system and then wrapped by a .NET property by defining *Get* and *Set* access using the *DependencyObject.GetValue* and *DependencyObject.SetValue* methods.

The WPF and Silverlight property systems are built upon dependency properties. The *FontSize* property of the *System.Windows.Controls.Control* class of WPF and Silverlight framework is an example of a dependency property, one that you use for many XAML controls. The *FontSize* property is defined in the *Control* class as a dependency property, as shown here:

```
public static readonly DependencyProperty FontSizeProperty;
```

The definition of the dependency property follows a specific naming convention. The name of the field is always the name of the property, with the suffix *Property* appended—in this case

FontSizeProperty. It is then wrapped by a .NET property—in this case the *FontSize* property—using the *GetValue* and *SetValue* methods to process the dependency property's value.

```
public double FontSize
{
    get {
            return (double) this.GetValue(FontSizeProperty);
        }
    set {
            base.SetValue(FontSizeProperty, value);
        }
}
```

Using this approach, developers can get and set dependency property values exactly as they do regular .NET properties—but the property still provides all the features and advantages of the dependency property system. In the following XAML code snippet, the *FontSize* and *Text* properties are dependency properties, set like regular .NET properties.

```
<TextBlock x:Name="sampletextblock"
        Text="Text goes here..."
        FontSize="12"/>
```

You can also get and set dependency properties as regular .NET properties in code-behind, as shown here for the *sampletextblock TextBlock* control.

```
//Get Dependency Property in code-behind
sampletextblock_text = sampletextblock.Text;
sampletextblock_fontsize = sampletextblock.FontSize;
//Set Dependency Property in code-behind
sampletextblock.Text = "Text goes here...";
sampletextblock.FontSize = 12;
```

Two dependency property framework classes—*DependencyProperty* and *DependencyObject*—are critical for implementing the dependency property system in WPF and Silverlight.

The *DependencyProperty* Class

The *System.Windows.DependencyProperty* class handles registration of a dependency property backed by a CLR property. The property value can be set through data binding, with animation values, or from template resources specified in XAML. The template resource can be defined as styles or can be defined as local values.

You can retrieve the dependency property identification and other related information using the following key properties of the *DependencyProperty* class:

- **DefaultMetadata**   Gets the default metadata for the dependency property.

- **Name**   Gets the name of the dependency property.

- **OwnerType**   Gets the object type, which has either registered with the dependency property system or added itself as the owner of the property.

- **PropertyType**   Gets the type of dependency property value.

- **ReadOnly**   Returns a Boolean *true* when the dependency property is read-only; otherwise returns *false*.

- **ValidateValueCallback**   Gets the value validation callback for the dependency property. It returns *null* when the dependency property does not have a registered validation callback.

You can register and define identification, metadata, and dependency property notification using methods provided by the *DependencyProperty* class. Some of the key overridden methods are:

- **AddOwner()**   Add an owner for the dependency property.

- **GetMetadata()**   Retrieve metadata for the dependency property.

- **OverrideMetadata()**   Override metadata for the dependency property.

- **Register()**   Register a dependency property.

- **RegisterReadOnly()**   Register a read-only dependency property.

- **RegisterAttached()**   Register a dependency property as an attached property.

- **RegisterAttachedReadOnly()**   Register a dependency property as a read-only attached property.

 Note See the "Attached Properties" section on page 62 for more information about attached properties.

The *DependencyObject* Class

The *System.Windows.DependencyObject* class is a base class. Instances of *DependencyObject* can host dependency properties and attached properties. As discussed in Chapter 2, both the WPF and Silverlight presentation frameworks derive from the *DependencyObject* class. (See Figure 3-1.) As a result, the majority of the object elements in XAML for both WPF and Silverlight support dependency properties.

The *DependencyObject* class provides *GetValue* and *SetValue* methods to get and set dependency property values and the *ClearValue* method to reset the dependency property value to its default value.

 More Info Visit MSDN at *http://msdn.microsoft.com/en-us/library/system.windows .dependencyobject.aspx* for more information about the *DependencyObject* class.

Creating a Custom Dependency Property

Microsoft recommends that you create a custom dependency property only when you want to create a property that can process values that come from different sources, such as data binding, animation, template resources specified in the XAML, styles, or local values—*and* when you potentially need to handle property change notification. If you do not need these features, you should use a custom .NET property backed by a private field instead.

WPF Presentation Framework Objects Hierarchy

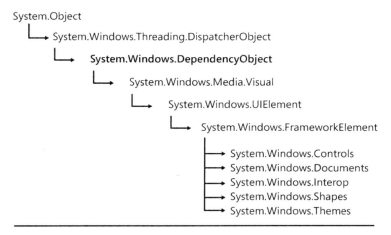

```
System.Object
    └──→ System.Windows.Threading.DispatcherObject
            └──→ System.Windows.DependencyObject
                    └──→ System.Windows.Media.Visual
                            └──→ System.Windows.UIElement
                                    └──→ System.Windows.FrameworkElement
                                            ├──→ System.Windows.Controls
                                            ├──→ System.Windows.Documents
                                            ├──→ System.Windows.Interop
                                            ├──→ System.Windows.Shapes
                                            └──→ System.Windows.Themes
```

Silverlight Presentation Framework Objects Hierarchy

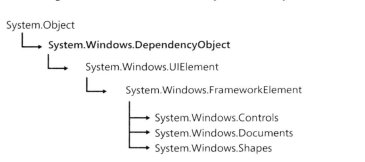

```
System.Object
    └──→ System.Windows.DependencyObject
            └──→ System.Windows.UIElement
                    └──→ System.Windows.FrameworkElement
                            ├──→ System.Windows.Controls
                            ├──→ System.Windows.Documents
                            └──→ System.Windows.Shapes
```

FIGURE 3-1 WPF and Silverlight presentation framework objects are derived from the *DependencyObject*.

You need to follow some specific steps to create a custom dependency property.

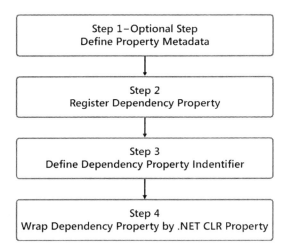

```
Step 1–Optional Step
Define Property Metadata

        ↓

Step 2
Register Dependency Property

        ↓

Step 3
Define Dependency Property Indentifier

        ↓

Step 4
Wrap Dependency Property by .NET CLR Property
```

- *Step 1*   This is an optional step. Create dependency property metadata. You'll see how to do this in the next example.

- *Step 2*   Register the dependency property name with the dependency property system. You need to specify an owner type and the type of the property value, and optionally specify property metadata.

- *Step 3*   Define the *DependencyProperty* identifier as a *public static readonly* field in the owner type.

- *Step 4*   Wrap the dependency property with a .NET CLR property using the *GetValue* and *SetValue* methods to process the dependency property's value.

You can create a custom dependency property within your WPF or Silverlight project's code-behind file for any XAML file, or you can create a custom class that inherits from the *DependencyObject* class.

More Info   See this MSDN page: *http://msdn.microsoft.com/en-us/library/ms753358.aspx* for more information on creating custom dependency properties for the WPF platform. See *http://msdn.microsoft.com/en-us/library/cc903933.aspx* for information on creating custom dependency properties for the Silverlight platform.

Create a custom dependency property in the XAML code-behind file   The following example is a WPF application with the project name WpfApplication1. This example creates a custom dependency property named *SSN* in the code-behind for the MainWindow.xaml file, in MainWindow.xaml. cs. The goal of this example is to create a custom dependency property named *SSN* of type *string* that contains the default value *000-00-0000*. The code also validates a string in the SSN (Social Security Number) format using a regular expression as part of the custom dependency property change notification service. After validation it displays a message box when the entered value does not match the format, and sets the property back to the default value.

Here's the complete code for that code-behind file. The code in bold text is related to adding the custom dependency property and setting the data context to bind this property within XAML controls:

```
using System;
using System.Collections.Generic;
using System.Linq;
using System.Text;
using System.Windows;
using System.Windows.Controls;
using System.Windows.Data;
using System.Windows.Documents;
using System.Windows.Input;
using System.Windows.Media;
using System.Windows.Media.Imaging;
using System.Windows.Navigation;
using System.Windows.Shapes;
using System.Text.RegularExpressions;
```

```csharp
namespace WpfApplication1
{
    /// <summary>
    /// Interaction logic for MainWindow.xaml
    /// </summary>
    public partial class MainWindow : Window
    {
        //Define and Register SSN Custom Dependency Property
        public static readonly DependencyProperty SSNProperty =
            DependencyProperty.Register(
                "SSN", typeof(string), typeof(MainWindow),
                new PropertyMetadata(
                    "000-00-0000",
                    new PropertyChangedCallback(
                        MainWindow.OnSSNPropertyChanged)));

        //.NET Wrapper to process SSN custom dependency property
        public string SSN
        {
            get
            {
                return (string)GetValue(SSNProperty);
            }

            set
            {
                SetValue(SSNProperty, value);
            }
        }

        //Property change notification service implementation
        private static void OnSSNPropertyChanged
            (DependencyObject ssnvalue, DependencyPropertyChangedEventArgs e)
        {
            if (!Regex.IsMatch
                ((string)ssnvalue.GetValue(e.Property), @"^\d{3}-\d{2}-\d{4}$"))
            {                                              MessageBox.Show("Not valid SSN");
                ssnvalue.SetValue(e.Property, "000-00-0000");
            }
        }

        public MainWindow()
        {
            InitializeComponent();
            DataContext = this;
        }
    }
}
```

The preceding code defines a custom SSN property within the code-behind file, above the *MainWindow* class constructor.

Following the required steps shown earlier, the code first defines the metadata—setting the default value to *000-00-000*—which helps end users understand the required format. The code also defines *OnSSNPropertyChanged* as the property change method.

You can see the *DependencyProperty* identifier defined as a *public static readonly* field named *SSNProperty* and registered using the *DependencyProperty.Register* method.

```
//Define and Register SSN Custom Dependency Property
public static readonly DependencyProperty SSNProperty =
    DependencyProperty.Register(
        "SSN", typeof(string), typeof(MainWindow),
        new PropertyMetadata(
            "000-00-0000",
            new PropertyChangedCallback(
            MainWindow.OnSSNPropertyChanged)));
```

Later the code wraps the *SSNProperty* custom dependency property in an *SSN* .NET property. Internally, the *get* and *set* process the property values using *GetValue* and *SetValue* methods, as shown here:

```
//.NET Wrapper to process SSN custom dependency property
public string SSN
{
    get
    {
        return (string)GetValue(SSNProperty);
    }
    set
        {
            SetValue(SSNProperty, value);
        }
    }
```

Caution Implementing additional business logic in the CLR wrappers for custom dependency properties will result in inconsistent results when processing dependency property values. The XAML parser omits additional logic defined in the .NET CLR property wrapper during *get* or *set* operations for custom dependency properties.

Finally the code defines the property change notification service by creating a static method named *OnSSNPropertyChanged*. The example uses a regular expression and the *IsMatch* method to check the format of the entered SSN property value. For entries that do not match the specified SSN format, it displays a message box notifying users of the problem, and resets the property to the default value.

```
//Property change notification service implementation
private static void OnSSNPropertyChanged
    (DependencyObject ssnvalue, DependencyPropertyChangedEventArgs e)
{
    if (!Regex.IsMatch
        ((string)ssnvalue.GetValue(e.Property), @"^\d{3}-\d{2}-\d{4}$"))
        {
            MessageBox.Show("Not a valid SSN");
            ssnvalue.SetValue(e.Property, "000-00-0000");
        }
}
```

Note that to use the regular expression, you have to add the *using* reference to the *System.Text.RegularExpressions* class, as shown here:

```
using System.Text.RegularExpressions;
```

At this point, you are all set to use this custom property. To bind one of the XAML *TextBox* controls to this local *SSN* custom dependency property, set the *DataContext* within the *MainWindow* class constructor, as shown here:

```
DataContext = this;
```

Access and bind a custom dependency property to a XAML control within a XAML file   Now you are all set to bind the *SSN* custom dependency property to a XAML control. This next example binds it to the XAML *TextBox* control where users enter an SSN. Here's the complete XAML code. The code in bold highlights binding the *SSN* property:

```
<Window x:Class="WpfApplication1.MainWindow"
        xmlns="http://schemas.microsoft.com/winfx/2006/xaml/presentation"
        xmlns:x="http://schemas.microsoft.com/winfx/2006/xaml"
        Title="Custom Dependency Property Example" Height="150" Width="750">
    <Grid
        x:Name="LayoutRoot"
        Background="White"
        Height="250"
        Width="650">
        <Grid.Resources>
            <Style
                x:Key="HeaderFontStyle"
                TargetType="TextBlock">
                <Setter
                    Property="FontFamily"
                    Value="Times New Roman"/>
                <Setter
                    Property="FontSize"
                    Value="20"/>
            </Style>
            <Style
                x:Key="LabelFontStyle"
                TargetType="TextBlock">
                <Setter
                    Property="FontFamily"
                    Value="Arial"/>
                <Setter
                    Property="FontSize"
                    Value="14"/>
            </Style>
        </Grid.Resources>

        <Grid.RowDefinitions>
            <RowDefinition Height="35"/>
            <RowDefinition Height="35"/>
            <RowDefinition Height="35"/>
        </Grid.RowDefinitions>
```

```
        <Grid.ColumnDefinitions>
            <ColumnDefinition Width="Auto"/>
            <ColumnDefinition/>
        </Grid.ColumnDefinitions>

        <TextBlock HorizontalAlignment="Center"
                   Text="Example: Custom Dependency Property
                       with Change Notification Service"
                 Grid.Column="0"
                 Grid.Row="0"
                 Grid.ColumnSpan="2"
                 Margin="5"
                 Style="{StaticResource HeaderFontStyle}"/>

        <TextBlock VerticalAlignment="Top"
                   HorizontalAlignment="Right"
                   Grid.Column="0"
                   Grid.Row="1"
                   Margin="5"
                   Style="{StaticResource LabelFontStyle}">
                   Social Security Number:</TextBlock>

        <TextBox x:Name="SSNTextBox"
                 VerticalAlignment="Top"
                 Grid.Column="1"
                 Grid.Row="1"
                 Margin="5"
                 Text="{Binding SSN}"/>

        <TextBlock VerticalAlignment="Top"
                   HorizontalAlignment="Right"
                   Grid.Column="0"
                   Grid.Row="2"
                   Margin="5"
                   Style="{StaticResource LabelFontStyle}">
                   Name:</TextBlock>

        <TextBox x:Name="NameTextBox"
                 VerticalAlignment="Top"
                 Grid.Column="1"
                 Grid.Row="2"
                 Margin="5"/>
    </Grid>
</Window>
```

If you've been following along, you can now compile and run the project. You will see a window with the SSN text box value set to the default: *000-00-0000*.

Custom Dependency Property Example

Example: Custom Dependency Property with Change Notification Service

Social Security Number: `000-00-0000`

Name:

Enter an SSN in an invalid format—for example, **abcd**—and you will get the invalid SSN format message box when the property changes. When you click the OK button in the message box the message box closes, and the text box value resets to *000-00-0000*.

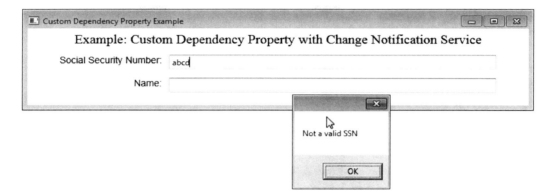

Next, enter a correctly formatted SSN—for example, **123-45-6789**. This time, you will not get the message box when the property changes, and the text box will contain the entered value.

More Info See Chapter 5, "Resources, Styles, and Triggers," for more information about resources and styling. See Chapter 8, "Data Binding," for an exploration of data binding in XAML.

Accessing a Dependency Property from Code-Behind

You access and set dependency properties from code-behind in the same way you access default WPF and Silverlight framework class properties. The following example uses the *Text* property of the *NameTextBox* text box control defined in the previous example for demonstration purposes:

```
//Demonstration of Accessing TextBox Text Dependency Property

//Set Text Dependency Property Value of TextBox Control
NameTextBox.Text = "Enter Name Here";

//Get Text Dependency Property Value of TextBox Control
string txtpropertyvalue;
txtpropertyvalue = NameTextBox.Text;
```

To prove the point, the following example uses the *SSN* custom dependency property created in the previous example:

```
//Demonstration of Accessing SSN Custom Dependency Property

//Set SSN Custom Dependency Property Value
SSN = "123-45-6789";
```

```
//Get SSN Custom Dependency Property Value
string txtpropertyvalue;
txtpropertyvalue = SSN;
```

Dependency Property Value Precedence

Dependency property values depend on varying sources, as discussed earlier.

The WPF and Silverlight dependency property system determines the value of the dependency property at runtime based on a precedence set in the dependency property framework. Figure 3-2 represents the dependency property value precedence for the WPF and Silverlight dependency property frameworks. Note that highlighted sources are supported only in the WPF framework, and thus are not applicable to the Silverlight dependency property system.

As demonstrated in Figure 3-2, animation gets higher precedence than any other value—those set as local values or set by an explicit or implicit style, theme style or style setter value, template or style triggers, inheritance, and default value. Local values are those set via an attribute or property element. Local values can also be set via data binding or a static resource, or set via explicit style—thus these all have equal precedence. As a result, if you have set a local value using any approach, setting the local value using another approach later will replace the previous value entirely. The default value has the lowest precedence and will be used only when no other source has set the value.

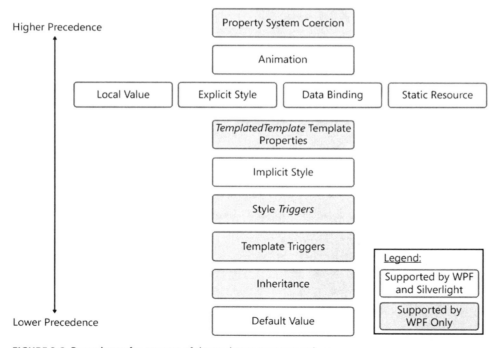

FIGURE 3-2 Precedence for sources of dependency property values.

Caution The base value for a property is *not the same* as its default value. A property's *base value* is determined by applying the sources defined in Figure 3-2, except those applied through animation. A property's *default value* is its value when no other sources provide a value. (For example, a layout container's constructor may establish a default value for a size property, and if not modified anywhere else, the default value remains untouched.)

The following XAML code snippet demonstrates how explicit style, implicit style, and default value precedence determine the *FontSize* dependency property of *Button* and *ToggleButton* controls at runtime.

```
<UserControl.Resources>
    <Style TargetType="Button">
        <Setter Property="FontSize" Value="16" />
    </Style>
    <Style x:Key="ButtonStyle" TargetType="Button">
        <Setter Property="FontSize" Value="24" />
    </Style>
</UserControl.Resources>
<StackPanel>
    <Button Content="Submit" Width="150" Height="60"  x:Name="b1"/>
    <Button Content="OK" Width="150" Height="60" x:Name="b2"
        Style="{StaticResource ButtonStyle}"/>
    <ToggleButton Content="Toggle Button Content" Width="150" Height="75" />
</StackPanel>
```

If you compile and run the project, the outcome of rendering the preceding markup will show the Submit button using the implicit style, in size-16 font. The OK button renders with a font size of 24 because the defined explicit style overrides the implicit style. The *ToggleButton* content appears in the default font size value because no other source has set the font size value.

More Info See Chapter 5 for more information on explicit and implicit styling.

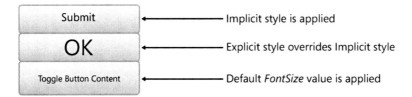

You should also notice that the *Background* property is not defined for any of the controls, and thus it renders in the default color for the background of *Button* and *ToggleButton* controls.

Read-Only Dependency Properties

WPF and Silverlight framework classes contain some read-only dependency properties, mainly used to report the state of the control. Some examples of read-only (mostly Boolean) dependency properties are:

- *IsEnabled*, a dependency property of the *System.Windows.UIElement* WPF framework class and of the *System.Windows.Control* Silverlight framework class

- *IsFocused*, a dependency property of the *System.Windows.UIElement* WPF framework class and of the *System.Windows.Controls.Primitives.ButtonBase* Silverlight framework class

- *IsMouseOver*, a dependency property of the *System.Windows.UIElement* WPF framework class and of the *System.Windows.Controls.Primitives.ButtonBase* Silverlight framework class

You can create custom read-only dependency properties for WPF framework in a similar fashion and follow the same steps that you use to create regular read/write dependency properties (as discussed earlier in this chapter). The key difference lies in how you register the property and how you wrap the CLR properties to process the dependency property value.

As discussed, you use the *DependencyProperty.Register()* method to register regular read/write properties to the dependency property system. Doing that returns a *DependencyProperty* object. For a read-only dependency property, you use the *DependencyProperty.RegisterReadOnly()* method, which returns a *DependencyPropertyKey* object. Also, instead of implementing *Get* and *Set* methods as for regular dependency properties, you need to implement only the *Get* method for read-only dependency properties.

Caution Silverlight does not support the implementation of custom read-only dependency properties.

Attached Properties

Supported By	
WPF	Yes
Silverlight	Yes

Quick Summary	
Definition	An attached property is a special type of dependency property that is specific to XAML and is not wrapped by CLR property. You use an attached property as a type of global property, defined in the parent object element, for any child object element.
Naming Convention	The property name is always the name of the property, with the suffix *Property* appended—similar to other dependency properties. For example, a *Column* attached property implemented on the *Grid* class has its attached property name set to *ColumnProperty*.
Can You Create Custom Attached Properties?	Yes
MSDN Reference	For WPF: *http://msdn.microsoft.com/en-us/library/ms749011.aspx* For Silverlight: *http://msdn.microsoft.com/en-us/library/cc265152.aspx*

Attached properties are a special type of dependency property designed solely for XAML. You can set an attached property from other object elements (usually child elements) rather than setting them in the object element where they are defined. Attached properties provide classes with dynamic extension capabilities without inheritance. They relate child objects to parent objects in a predefined specific context. Just like any other regular dependency property in WPF and Silverlight, an attached property is also defined as a *DependencyProperty*: it uses the same naming convention (the identifier field followed by *Property*) and it's registered to the dependency property system.

Why Use Attached Properties?

Attached properties are widely used by both WPF and Silverlight framework components to provide specific feature sets.

The most common use of attached properties for WPF and Silverlight is to provide a flexible and dynamic layout system. Layout and positioning controls, such as *Grid, Canvas,* and *StackPanel,* define sets of attached properties that child elements can use to define their location and positioning within the parent control. At runtime, these child elements render and position themselves to a defined location (based on the value of attached properties set for these child elements) to build an appropriate user interface.

For example, to allow the proper positioning of various elements within a grid, the *Grid* control provides a set of attached properties:

- **Grid.Column** Defines a value that indicates which column the child element content should be displayed in within a *Grid* control.

- **Grid.ColumnSpan** Defines a value that indicates the total number of columns the child element content spans within a *Grid* control.

- **Grid.Row** Defines a value that indicates which row the child element content should be displayed in within a *Grid* control.

- **Grid.RowSpan** Defines a value that indicates the total number of rows the child element content spans within a *Grid* control.

- **IsSharedSizeScope** Indicates whether multiple *Grid* elements share the size properties (if set to *true*) or not (if set to *false*—the default value). Note that this attached property is available only to the WPF *Grid* class. It's not available in the latest version of the Silverlight *Grid* class.

 More Info See Chapter 6, "Layout and Positioning System," for more information on the various layout and positioning controls available for WPF and Silverlight.

WPF and Silverlight also provide the *System.Windows.Documents.TextElement* type class with a set of attached properties, including *FontStyle, FontSize, FontFamily,* and *FontWeight.* These properties can help control the display of the content of both the parent and its child elements.

In addition, you can use attached properties to implement some common services that you can then apply to WPF and Silverlight objects.

- The *System.Windows.Controls.Validation* class of WPF and Silverlight framework provides a set of attached properties such as *Errors* and *HasError*, intended for use in data validation for the targeted element.

- Similarly WPF and Silverlight framework provide attached properties such as *Tooltip*, *Placement,* and *PlacementTarget* for the *System.Windows.Controls.TooltipService* class to display tooltips related to WPF and XAML elements.

You can also develop custom attached properties to implement similar types of features for your own purpose.

The Syntax

While setting an attached property within a child element, you need to follow the static property-like syntax and reference the parent object that actually has defined and registered the attached property—in other words, a specific named object instance. Here's an example of the syntax to set an attached property:

```
ParentObjectAttchedPropertyProvider.AttachedPropertyName
```

The attached property name must be in the format *ParentObjectAttachedPropertyProvider. AttachedPropertyName*, where *ParentObjectAttachedPropertyProvider* is the parent object and *AttachedPropertyName* is the name of the attached property that you want to set in the child element. You separate the *ParentObjectAttachedPropertyProvider* and *PropertyName* with a period.

You set an attached property using the property attribute syntax discussed in Chapter 2. The following code snippet demonstrates how you would set up an attached property that has a specific value for a child element.

```
<ParentObjectElement>
...
        <ChildElement ParentObjectAttchedPropertyProvider.AttachedProperty="Value" ... >
            ...
        </ChildElement>
<ParentObjectElement>
```

When you add child elements to the *Grid* control, you need to define the column and row where the child element should be placed. The *Grid* control provides *Column* and *Row* attached properties so that you can define the child element position.

In the following example, *Grid.Column* and *Grid.Row* are attached properties of the *Grid* layout and positioning control. These properties are defined for the *TextBox* control named *NameTextBox*. The properties let you define the specific position of that control within the parent *Grid* control (in the first column and second row of the grid in this case). The example also uses the *TextElement.FontStyle* attached property for the *Grid* control, set to *Italic*, which will set the font style of grid child elements to italic.

```
<Grid TextElement.FontStyle="Italic">
...

        <TextBox x:Name="NameTextBox"
                VerticalAlignment="Top"
                Grid.Column="1"
                Grid.Row="2"
                Margin="5"/>
</Grid>
```

Defining Read/Write and Read-Only Attached Properties

As discussed earlier, the majority of the WPF and Silverlight attached properties are built upon dependency properties systems, so just as with any other regular dependency property, to define an attached property you start by defining a *DependencyProperty* using the public static and read-only identifier field. Similar to a regular dependency property, the definition of the attached dependency property follows a specific naming convention—the name of the field is always the name of the property, with the suffix *Property* appended. However, there are some key differences in creating and registering an attached dependency property as compared to a regular dependency property:

- You use the *DependencyProperty.RegisterAttached()* method to register a read/write attached property, and the *DependencyProperty.RegisterAttachedReadOnly()* method to register a read-only attached property.

- An attached property can be set for child elements and may not be part of the related CLR namespace. As a result, attached properties cannot be wrapped by a .NET property using *Get* and *Set* as you do for a regular dependency property. Instead, you implement *GetPropertyName* and *SetPropertyName* accessors using the *DependencyObject.GetValue* and *DependencyObject.SetValue* methods to process the attached property value.

Creating a Custom Attached Property

To demonstrate creation of an attached property, we'll extend the earlier example that demonstrated creating a custom dependency property.

This example adds a *Boolean* custom attached property named *IsIdentifier*. The property value determines which user entry field acts as a unique identifier for the record. The default value of the *IsIdentifier* attached property is *false*.

You follow the same four steps discussed in the earlier section, "Creating a Custom Dependency Property," to create a custom attached property within the code-behind file for any XAML file in your WPF or Silverlight project. Alternatively, you can create a custom class that inherits from the *DependencyObject* class.

> **More Info** See this MSDN link (*http://msdn.microsoft.com/en-us/library/ms749011.aspx*) for more information on custom attached properties for WPF. See this link (*http://msdn.microsoft.com/en-us/library/cc903943.aspx*) for information on custom attached properties for Silverlight.

Create a custom attached property in the XAML code-behind file   Reopen the WPF windows application you created earlier with the project name WpfApplication1, and then open the code-behind file for the main window xaml file—MainWindow.xaml.cs.

To create the *IsIdentifier* custom attached property, you will add code immediately after the code you added to create the *SSN* named custom dependency property.

First, you need to define the metadata. In this case, the metadata defines the default value as *false* (so you won't need a property changed method).

Next, define the *DependencyProperty* identifier as a *public static readonly* field, with a *Boolean* type. Name it *IsIdentifierProperty*, and register it using the *DependencyProperty.RegisterAttached* method. Here's the code:

```
//Define and Register IsIdentifier Custom Attached Property
public static readonly DependencyProperty IsIdentifierProperty =
    DependencyProperty.RegisterAttached(
        "IsIdentifier", typeof(Boolean), typeof(MainWindow),
        new PropertyMetadata(false));
```

> **More Info** A custom attached property can have property metadata to set the default value as well as define the property change method. In the preceding example, we have set only the default value to *false*. You can also define the property change method as part of the metadata, similar to the way we discussed earlier for the custom dependency property.

Next, instead of wrapping the *IsIdentifierProperty* attached property with a .NET property using *Get* and *Set* as you did when defining the regular dependency property, add *GetIsIdentifier* and *SetIsIdentifier* accessor methods. These use the *DependencyObject.GetValue* and *DependencyObject. SetValue* methods to process the attached property value, as shown here:

```
//GetPropertyName and SetPropertyName Accessors for custom attached property
public static void SetIsIdentifier(UIElement element, Boolean val)
{
    element.SetValue(MainWindow.IsIdentifierProperty, val);
}
public static Boolean GetIsIdentifier(UIElement element)
{
    return (Boolean)element.GetValue(MainWindow.IsIdentifierProperty);
}
```

Finally, press F5 to build the solution.

Access a custom attached property for a XAML control within a XAML file   To access the custom attached property you just created within the local code-behind from XAML, you must first map an XML namespace that references the CLR namespace containing the relevant class (in this case it's the local class *WpfApplication1*) and the related assembly containing that class.

Add the local class reference to the *Window* root element (the bold text in the following code) in the *MainWindow.xaml* file of the *WpfApplication1* project, as shown here:

```
<Window x:Class="WpfApplication1.MainWindow"
        xmlns="http://schemas.microsoft.com/winfx/2006/xaml/presentation"
        xmlns:x="http://schemas.microsoft.com/winfx/2006/xaml"
        xmlns:local="clr-namespace:WpfApplication1"
        Title="Custom Dependency Property Example" Height="150" Width="750">
```

After adding the reference, you can access the *IsIdentifier* custom attached property from the XAML control. Because a Social Security Number is unique for each individual, the example uses that for the identifier field. To set that field as the unique identifier, locate the XAML *TextBox* control for SSN entry, and set the *MainWindow.IsIdentifier* attached property to *"True"*, as shown here (in bold text).

```
<TextBox x:Name="SSNTextBox"
        VerticalAlignment="Top"
        Grid.Column="1"
        Grid.Row="1"
        Margin="5"
        Text="{Binding SSN}"
        local:MainWindow.IsIdentifier="True"/>
```

Accessing an Attached Property from Code-Behind

You can set and get attached property values through code-behind in the same way you access attached WPF and Silverlight framework class properties such as *Grid.Column* and *Grid.Row*.

The following XAML code snippet adds a *TextBlock* control to the second row (1) and first column (0) of the Grid by setting the appropriate properties.

```
<TextBlock VerticalAlignment="Top"
        HorizontalAlignment="Right"
        Grid.Column="0"
        Grid.Row="1"
        Margin="5"
        Text="Social Security Number:"/>
```

To perform the identical action from code-behind, you would write:

```
TextBlock codebehind_tb = new TextBlock();
codebehind_tb.VerticalAlignment = System.Windows.VerticalAlignment.Top;
codebehind_tb.HorizontalAlignment = System.Windows.HorizontalAlignment.Right;
codebehind_tb.Margin = new Thickness(5);
codebehind_tb.Text = "Social Security Number";
codebehind_tb.SetValue(Grid.RowProperty, 1);
codebehind_tb.SetValue(Grid.ColumnProperty, 0);
LayoutRoot.Children.Add(codebehind_tb);
```

As the example shows, you use the *DependencyObject.SetValue* method to set the *Grid.Row-Property* and *Grid.ColumnProperty* attached properties. Similarly, you use the *DependencyObject.GetValue* method to retrieve the attached property value in code-behind. The following example shows how to retrieve the *IsIdentifier* custom attached property for the *TextBox* control named *SSNTextBox*, where you earlier set the *IsIdentifier* property to *true* within the XAML file.

```
Boolean IsIdentifierProperty_Value;
IsIdentifierProperty_Value =
    (Boolean)SSNTextBox.GetValue(MainWindow.IsIdentifierProperty);
```

If you step through the program in the debugger, you can see that the value returned by the *IsIdentifier* custom attached property is *true*.

XAML Events

Event handling is a notification service provided by the framework. An event is initiated by an object based on some type of action at runtime. Like any other presentation layer development technology, XAML and WPF/Silverlight framework provide event-handling capability so that you can manage user input, performing actions and processing business logic based on specific user input actions such as selecting a value or date, clicking a button, moving the mouse, or pressing a key. In addition, the event notification system lets you handle changing conditions, such as a dependency property value change notification or a validation event so that you can evaluate an entered value and generate error messages.

The object that raises the event is called the event sender; the object that consumes the event and processes it is called the event receiver. If you have worked with Windows Forms, you are probably already familiar with the way Microsoft .NET Framework handles CLR events. In Windows Forms, the same object is always the event sender and event receiver. For example, if you click a *Button* object, the *Button* object raises the event and the same object responds to process logic written in code. However, because XAML and WPF/Silverlight framework introduce a new and extended dependency property system, they also introduce an enhanced events handling and management system called *Routed Events*. You can integrate with these events through XAML, and implement logic to handle them in the code-behind.

Routed events can have one object element as event sender but one or more event receivers (including the object that raises the event), all of which can execute code in an event handler.

The Syntax

You define the event handler for a particular object event using the property attribute syntax discussed in Chapter 2. You then implement the event handler in the managed code-behind file.

The following example shows how you would define a *System.Windows.Controls.Premitives.ButtonBase.Click* event for a *Button* element in a XAML file.

```
<Button Content="SubmitButton"
        Width="100"
        Margin="10"
        HorizontalAlignment="Left"
        Click="SubmitButton_Click"/>
```

In the preceding code, the *Click* attribute name in the XAML represents the *Click* event for the *ButtonBase* class. You define the event handler method name as the string value of the *Click* attribute—in this example it's called *SubmitButton_Click*. Next, you must implement the partial class method (using the name *SubmitButton_Click*) within the code-behind file, as shown here:

```
private void SubmitButton_Click(object sender, RoutedEventArgs e)
{
    //code goes here
}
```

Routed Events

Supported By	
WPF	Yes
Silverlight	Yes

Quick Summary	
Definition	A routed event is a CLR-type event backed by the *RoutedEvent* class and processed by the WPF event system. You can define a routed event within a XAML file and implement a handler in code-behind.
	Routed events can have one object element as the event sender but one or more event receivers (including the object that raises the event) that execute the implemented code-behind event handler.
Naming Convention	There is no mandatory naming convention for routed event names. However, tunneling routed events use *Preview* as a prefix to the event name. (For example, for the *KeyDown* routed event, the corresponding tunneling routed event name is *PreviewKeyDown*.)
	Even though you can define any name for the event handler method, as a best practice, the event handler method name usually follows *<NameoftheObjectElement-EventSender>_<EventName>* naming convention. For example, the *Button* object named *SubmitButton* would have a *Click* event handler method named *SubmitButton_Click*.
MSDN Reference	For WPF: *http://msdn.microsoft.com/en-us/library/ms742806.aspx* For Silverlight: *http://msdn.microsoft.com/en-us/library/cc189018.aspx*

XAML object elements in a XAML file must follow a defined hierarchical order to create a qualified, well-formed XAML file that will compile, render, and function properly at runtime. When XAML is compiled and parsed at runtime, the result is an object tree with a *UserControl* object as its root for Silverlight applications or a *Window* object at the root for WPF applications.

As shown in Figure 3-3, routed events can do the following:

- Move upward from the element where the event was raised (the original source element) to each parent element in that branch of the object tree, continuing until it reaches the root element, or until the event is handled by setting *RoutedEventArgs.Handled* to *true* within an event handler method. Any object along the path can handle the event. This upward path is called *bubbling* and is supported in both WPF and Silverlight frameworks.

- Move downward from the root element to each subsequent child element in the object tree until it reaches the element where the event is raised (the original source element) or until the event is handled by an object in the path by setting *RoutedEventArgs.Handled* to *true* within an event handler method. This downward path is called *tunneling* and supported in WPF only; the Silverlight framework does not support tunneling. WPF input events are implemented with both tunneling and bubbling strategies.

- Specifically notify only the original source element. These events will not route upward (bubbling) or downward (tunneling). This is also called *direct routing*, and is supported in both WPF and Silverlight. Direct routing also supports class handling; thus *EventSetter* and *EventTrigger* can use the direct routing strategy.

As discussed earlier, Silverlight supports only bubbling and direct routing, whereas WPF supports all three types of routing: bubbling, tunneling, and direct. The common set of routed input events with bubbling (and optionally tunneling) that are supported on both WPF and Silverlight platforms are described in Table 3-1.

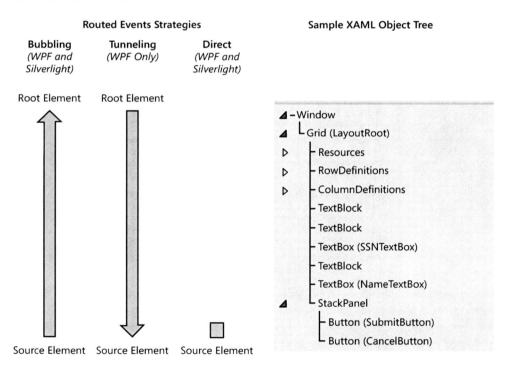

FIGURE 3-3 WPF and Silverlight platform routed events system strategies.

TABLE 3-1 Key Routed Input Events for WPF and Silverlight.

Routed Event	WPF	Silverlight
KeyDown	Bubbling and Tunneling	Bubbling
KeyUp	Bubbling and Tunneling	Bubbling
GotFocus	Bubbling	Bubbling
LostFocus	Bubbling	Bubbling
MouseDown	Bubbling and Tunneling	Not Applicable
MouseLeftButtonDown	Direct	Bubbling
MouseLeftButtonUp	Direct	Bubbling
MouseMove	Bubbling and Tunneling	Bubbling
MouseRightButtonDown	Direct	Bubbling
MouseRightButtonUp	Direct	Bubbling
MouseWheel	Bubbling and Tunneling	Bubbling
BindingValidationError	Not Applicable	Bubbling
DragEnter	Bubbling and Tunneling	Bubbling
DragLeave	Bubbling and Tunneling	Bubbling
DragOver	Bubbling and Tunneling	Bubbling
Drop	Bubbling and Tunneling	Bubbling

Note The corresponding tunneling event for the bubbling event is prefixed with the word *Preview* on the bubbling event name. Thus in Table 3-1, each corresponding tunneling event for WPF has a *Preview* prefix. For example, the *Drop* bubbling WPF event's corresponding tunneling event is *PreviewDrop*.

The following example originally appeared in a slightly different form in the book *Introducing Silverlight 4* (Ashish Ghoda, Apress, 2010). Here, the example is slightly extended to demonstrate the behavior of the bubble up routed events.

Create a WPF application project named *RoutedEvents*, and update the *MainWindow.xaml* with the following code snippet:

```
<Window x:Class="RoutedEvents.MainWindow"
        xmlns="http://schemas.microsoft.com/winfx/2006/xaml/presentation"
        xmlns:x="http://schemas.microsoft.com/winfx/2006/xaml"
        Title="MainWindow" Height="350" Width="525">
    <Grid Background="Gray"
          MouseLeftButtonDown="Grid_MouseLeftButtonDown"
          Width="350"
          Height="250" >
        <TextBlock
            Text= "Grid Control"
            FontWeight="Bold"
            Margin="5" />
        <Canvas
            Height="200"
            Width="300"
            MouseLeftButtonDown="Canvas_MouseLeftButtonDown"
            Background="Black"
```

```
                Margin="25">
        <TextBlock
            Text= "Canvas Control"
            FontWeight="Bold"
            Foreground="White"
            Margin="5" />
            <StackPanel
                Height="150"
                Width="250"
                MouseLeftButtonDown="StackPanel_MouseLeftButtonDown"
                Background="Yellow"
                Canvas.Top="25"
                Canvas.Left="25">
            <TextBlock
                Text= "StackPanel Control"
                FontWeight="Bold"
                Margin="5" />
                <TextBlock
                    Text= "'MouseLeftButtonDown' bubble up order"
                    FontWeight="Bold"
                    Margin="5"/>
                <TextBlock
                    x:Name="eventOrder"
                    Width="250"
                    TextWrapping="Wrap"/>
            </StackPanel>
        </Canvas>
    </Grid>
</Window>
```

The preceding XAML places the *Canvas* layout control within *StackPanel*, which is in turn placed within the *Grid* layout control. The *Canvas* control contains two *TextBlock* controls that display the results of bubbling routed events. Notice that each layout control defines the *MouseLeftButtonDown* routed event (in bold text in the code).

If you look at the Document Outline Window in Visual Studio 2010, you will see the related object tree: Grid → StackPanel → Canvas, as shown in Figure 3-4.

MouseLeftButtonDown Bubbling Routed Event Order

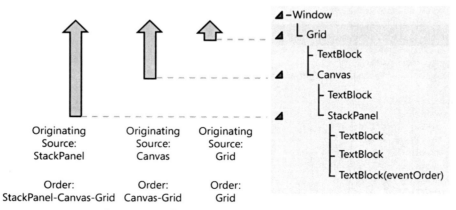

FIGURE 3-4 *MouseLeftButtonDown* bubbling routing event execution order.

Now implement the corresponding *MouseLeftButtonDown* event methods in the code-behind *MainWindow.xaml.cs* file. You can place the following code immediately after the *MainWindow* constructor.

```csharp
private void Grid_MouseLeftButtonDown
    (object sender, MouseButtonEventArgs e)
{
    eventOrder.Text += " Grid; ";
    e.Handled = true;
}
private void Canvas_MouseLeftButtonDown
    (object sender, MouseButtonEventArgs e)
{
    eventOrder.Text += " Canvas -";
}
private void StackPanel_MouseLeftButtonDown
    (object sender, MouseButtonEventArgs e)
{
    eventOrder.Text += " StackPanel -";
}
```

If you now compile and run the project, the output text depends on which control (*Canvas, StackPanel,* or *Grid*) you click; the event will bubble up to the *Grid* control and display text accordingly.

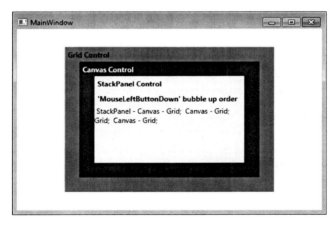

If you copy and paste the same code (XAML and code-behind) within a Silverlight project, you will receive similar output because the *MouseLeftButtonDown* event also uses bubble up routing in Silverlight.

Note If you revisit Table 3-1, you will notice that the *MouseLeftButtonDown* routed event is a bubbling event for Silverlight, but for WPF it's a direct event. However, in WPF the *MouseDown* button is a bubbling attached routed event—and it's raised together with the *MouseLeftButtonDown* event. Thus you get a similar result: the event bubbles up to the root element (the *Grid* control in this example).

The *RoutedEventArgs* Class

As discussed, a routed event can be handled by an element that did not initially raise the event. At the same time, because of its routing behavior, multiple event handlers may execute code for the event, which may not be your intention in some cases. To be able to control the behavior of routed events and execute the desired (and *only* the desired) business logic, you need two things during the execution of routed events:

1. You need to be able to retrieve the original source element that raised the event.

2. You should be able to control when to stop the routing.

The *System.Windows.RoutedEventArgs* class contains the state information and event data associated with a routed event. This information lets you manage event execution. The *RoutedEventArgs* class provides a set of properties that you use to manage the event:

- **OriginalSource**   This property returns the original source that raised the event. The *OriginalSource* property is available in both WPF and Silverlight. You use it to identify the element that actually raised the event originally rather than the element where it might be attached and executed (which could be a different element).

- **Source**   This property gets or sets the source object reference that raised the event. This property is available only for WPF; it's not available in Silverlight. In WPF you can change the *Source* in parent class code, which you might want to do when the original source is part of a composite control. For example, when a user clicks an item in a list box, the *Source* would be the selected item, not the list box. In many cases, you might want handlers further up the line to treat the source as the list box itself. In such cases, you can change the *Source* property. The selected element within the list is still available through the *OriginalSource* property. In other words, unless you change the *Source* it will contain the same object reference as the *OriginalSource*.

- **Handled**   This Boolean property (the default value is *false*) lets you control event routing logic. Setting the property to *true* makes the event invisible to any objects that might handle it along the routing path (the remaining route in the WPF object tree). As a result any remaining event handlers (except for the event handler added with the *HandledEventToo = true*) will not be invoked.

 Caution   The WPF framework *RoutedEventArgs* class contains the *Handled* property and is available to all event-base classes. However, the *RoutedEventArgs* implementation is different for Silverlight. The *Handled* property is not available for the *RoutedEventArgs* class; instead, it is available through specific event-base classes such as *DragEventArgs*, *KeyEventArgs*, *MouseButtonEventArgs*, *MouseWheelEventArgs*, and *ValidationEventArgs*.

Here's an example that implements one common scenario for using routed events. The example creates a single common event handler for multiple *Button* controls, and uses the *RoutedEventArgs* properties to manage the event. The example extends the attached property example you saw earlier in this chapter.

Reopen the WpfApplication1 WPF project and the MainWindow.xaml file. Add two buttons: a Submit button and a Cancel button. To do that, first define an additional row in the *Grid* control as shown here in bold text:

```
<Grid.RowDefinitions>
    <RowDefinition Height="35"/>
    <RowDefinition Height="35"/>
    <RowDefinition Height="35"/>
    <RowDefinition Height="35"/>
</Grid.RowDefinitions>
```

Now add a *StackPanel* control and two buttons in the newly added row, and define *Click* events (one common for both *Button* elements and one specific to a single *Button* element) within the XAML file, as shown here:

```
<StackPanel
    Orientation="Horizontal"
    HorizontalAlignment="Right"
    Grid.Column="1"
    Grid.Row="3"
    ButtonBase.Click="CommonButtonClickEvent">
    <Button
        x:Name="SubmitButton"
        Content="Submit"
        Margin="5"
        Width="100"
        Click="SubmitButton_Click"/>
    <Button
        x:Name="CancelButton"
        HorizontalAlignment="Left"
        Content="Cancel"
        Margin="5"
        Width="100"/>
</StackPanel>
```

The highlighted code defines two *Click* events for the buttons:

- A common click event named *CommonButtonClickEvent* that applies to all child elements derived from the *ButtonBase* class (by defining *ButtonBase.Click="CommonButtonClickEvent"*) at the *StackPanel* parent element level

- A click event specific to the Submit button (by defining *Click="SubmitButton_Click"*)

To finish the event handler implementation, open the code-behind file MainWindow.xaml.cs and add the following two event handler methods:

```
//Common Click Event Handler
private void CommonButtonClickEvent(object sender, RoutedEventArgs e)
{
    FrameworkElement SourceElement = e.Source as FrameworkElement;
    switch (SourceElement.Name)
    {
        case "SubmitButton":
            MessageBox.Show(e.OriginalSource + " - Common Click Event Processed");
            break;
        case "CancelButton":
            MessageBox.Show(e.OriginalSource + " - Common Click Event Processed");
            break;
    }
    //Implement your business logic here
    e.Handled = true;
}
// Click Event Handler for the SubmitButton
private void SubmitButton_Click(object sender, RoutedEventArgs e)
{
    MessageBox.Show("Submit Button Clicked");
    //Implement your business logic here
}
```

Now save the project, compile, and run it. You will see the added Submit and Cancel buttons in the application window. If you click the Submit button, here's what happens:

- First, any *Click* event specific to that element will be raised and executed (if defined). In this case, you'll get the first message box that displays the text "Submit Button Click," which is the output from the event handler method *SubmitButton_Click*.

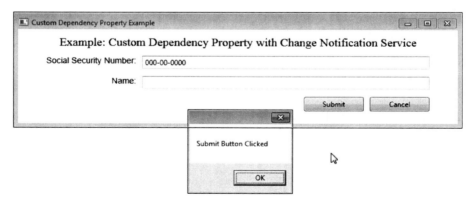

- Next, the event bubbles up to the parent object element of the *SubmitButton* control, which is the *StackPanel* element. The *StackPanel* control implements the *CommonButtonClickEvent*, so that code executes. The code also retrieves and displays the *OriginalSource* property, so you'll see a message box with the text "System.Windows.Controls.Button: Submit—Common Click Event Processed".

Because the handler sets the *e.Handled* property to *true*, the raised click event will be invisible to the remaining object tree elements.

Next, click the Cancel button. This time, you should get only one common click event specific message box that displays the text "System.Windows.Controls.Button: Cancel – Common Click Event Processed".

Finally, change the *SubmitButton_Click* event handler method and add *e.Handled = true;* as shown in the bold code here:

```csharp
// Click Event Handler for the SubmitButton
private void SubmitButton_Click(object sender, RoutedEventArgs e)
{
    MessageBox.Show("Submit Button Clicked");
    //Implement your business logic here
    e.Handled = true;
}
```

Run the project again. Now when you click the Submit button, you'll see only one message box titled "Submit Button Clicked," which is specific to the Submit button click event. Because the code now sets the event *Handled* property to *true*, the common click event handler will not be executed.

Add and Remove Event Handlers Using Code-Behind

You aren't limited to adding event handlers in XAML—you can also add object specific event handlers in code-behind by declaring a new delegate that uses the event handler method name using the += operator in C#.

Remove the attribute *Click="SubmitButton_Click"* you added earlier in the *SubmitButton* named in the XAML file. This time, you'll use the code-behind approach to implement the same event handler.

One good place to add the event is in the *Loaded* event of the existing *LayoutRoot Grid* control. Although you could do that in code-behind as well, for simplicity, define the event in XAML, as shown here:

```xml
<Grid
  x:Name="LayoutRoot"
  Background="White"
  Height="150"
  Width="650"
  Loaded="LayoutRoot_Loaded">
```

Now implement this event in code-behind, and also add the *SubmitButton_Click* event handler:

```
private void LayoutRoot_Loaded(object sender, RoutedEventArgs e)
{
    SubmitButton.Click += new RoutedEventHandler(SubmitButton_Click);
}
```

Because this alternative method simply defines the same event handler as before (*SubmitButton_Click*), you do not need to change any more code. If you run the project now you should get the same output as you received earlier.

You can also remove an event handler dynamically using the -= operator in C#;. As an example, the following code snippet removes the Submit button's *SubmitButton_Click* event.

```
SubmitButton.Click -= SubmitButton_Click;
```

Creating Custom Routed Event   You can create a custom routed event (a process similar to creating a custom dependency property) by following these steps:

1. Register the custom routed event with the WPF event system. You use the *EventManager.RegisterRoutedEvent* method to register the event, specifying the event name, routing strategy, handler type, and an owner type as parameters.

    The following is the syntax of the *EventManager.RegisterRoutedEvent* method:

    ```
    public static RoutedEvent RegisterRoutedEvent(
        string name,
        RoutingStrategy routingStrategy,
        Type handlerType,
        Type ownerType)
    ```

    The *name* parameter contains the name of the event.

    - The *routingStrategy* parameter contains the routing strategy for the event, which is a value from the *System.Windows.RoutingStrategy* enumeration, which contains *Tunnel*, *Bubble*, and *Direct* as members.

    - The *handlerType* parameter contains the type of event handler, which must be a delegate type, and cannot be null.

    - The *ownerType* parameter contains the owner class type of the routed event. This parameter cannot be null.

2. Define the *RoutedEvent* identifier as a *public static readonly* field on the owner type. The *RoutedEvent* static field name must end with the suffix *Event*, such as *<CustomRoutedEventName>Event*.

3. Wrap the routed event with .NET CLR add and remove event handler accessors.

Caution The custom routed event can be created only for the WPF framework. You cannot create custom routed event for the Silverlight framework.

The following code-snippet creates a custom routed event named *CustomSelectedText*, which follows the three steps listed previously and also raises the *CustomSelectedText* event.

```
public class MyCustomControl : Control
{
    //Define and Register CustomSelectedText Custom Dependency Property
    public static readonly RoutedEvent CustomSelectedTextEvent =
        EventManager.RegisterRoutedEvent(
            "CustomSelectedText",
            RoutingStrtegy.Bubble,
            typeof(RoutedEventHandler),
            typeof(MyCustomControl));
    //.NET CLR add and remove event handler accessors for custom routed event
    public event RoutedEventHandler CustomSelectedText
    {
        add
        {
            AddHandler(CustomSelectedTextEvent, value);
        }
        remove
        {
            RemoveHandler(CustomSelectedTextEvent, value);
        }
    }
    // Raises the CustomSelectedText custom routed event
    void RaiseCustomSelectedTextEvent()
    {
        RoutedEventArgs newEventArgs = new
            RoutedEventArgs(MyCustomControl.SelectedTextEvent);
        RaiseEvent(newEventArgs);
    }
}
```

You can call the *RaiseCustomSelectedTextEvent* method to raise the *CustomSelectedText* routed event.

Attached Routed Events

Supported By	
WPF	Yes
Silverlight	Yes

Quick Summary	
Definition	An attached routed event is a special type of routed event that is specific to XAML and *not* wrapped by .NET CLR add and remove handler accessors. The attached event is neither owned by the event sender nor by the event receiver. You can attach an attached routed event arbitrarily to any object element.
Naming Convention and syntax	The name of a *RoutedEvent* static field name is always the name of the attached routed event, with the suffix *Event* appended, similar to other routed events. For example, the *MouseDown* attached routed event on the *Mouse* class has the event identifier set to *MouseDownEvent*. To define the attached routed event in XAML, you must follow the syntax of *<Attach edEventOwnType>.<EventName>*.
Can You Create Custom Attached Events?	Yes
MSDN Reference	For WPF: *http://msdn.microsoft.com/en-us/library/bb613550.aspx* For Silverlight: *http://msdn.microsoft.com/en-us/library/cc189018.aspx*

In a procedure similar to creating a custom routed event, you can create a custom attached routed event by following these steps:

1. The first step is the same as for any other custom routed event. You need to register the attached routed event with the WPF event system. You use the *EventManager.Register-RoutedEvent* method to register the event, specifying the event name, routing strategy, handler type, and an owner type as parameters.

2. The second step is also the same as any other custom routed event. You need to define the *RoutedEvent* identifier as a *public static readonly* field on the owner type. The *RoutedEvent* static field name must end with the suffix *Event*, such as *<AttachedRoutedEventName>Event*.

3. As with attached dependency properties, you don't need to wrap attached routed events by .NET CLR add and remove event handler accessors. Instead, you need to define *add* and *remove* event handlers as utility methods:

    *   The *Add<AttachedEventName>Handler public static* method has no return value and must contain a first parameter that identifies the event and a second parameter that adds the routed event handler.

    *   The *Remove<AttachedEventName>Handler public static* method has no return value and must contain a first parameter that identifies the event and a second parameter that removes the routed event handler.

Caution You can create custom attached routed events only for WPF. You cannot create a custom attached routed event for Silverlight.

The following code creates a custom attached routed event named *MyCustomAttachedEvent*, which follows the three steps listed earlier:

```
public partial class MainWindow : Window
{
    //Define and Register MyCustomAttachedEvent Custom Attached Routed Event
    public static readonly RoutedEvent MyCustomAttachedEventEvent =
        EventManager.RegisterRoutedEvent(
            " MyCustomAttachedEvent",
            RoutingStrtegy.Bubble,
            typeof(RoutedEventHandler),
            typeof(MyWindow));
    //add and remove event handler utility methods for custom attached routed event
    public static void AddMyCustomAttachedEventHandler
        (DependencyObject d, RoutedEventHandler hander)
    {
        UIElement element = d as UIElement;
        if (element != null)
        {
            element.AddHandler(MyWindow.MyCustomAttachedEventEvent, handler);
        }
    }
    public static void RemoveMyCustomAttachedEventHandler
```

```
         (DependencyObject d, RoutedEventHandler hander)
    {
        UIElement element = d as UIElement;
        if (element != null)
        {
            element.RemoveHandler(MyWindow.MyCustomAttachedEventEvent, handler);
        }
    }
}
```

The *EventSetter* and *EventTrigger* Classes

As discussed earlier, XAML enables you to set up a common set of styles targeted to specific types of controls. But just as you can use styles and templates to set common set of properties to provide a consistent, unified look, XAML also lets you set up a common event handler that corresponds to a specific event. This event handler can perform unified actions (including the use of the *Storyboard* element to provide some types of animation) using the *EventSetter* and *EventTrigger* classes and their corresponding XAML elements.

The *EventSetter* Class

Supported By	
WPF	Yes
Silverlight	No

In XAML, the *EventSetter* represents a specific event handler that should be invoked in response to a corresponding routed event. Within the scope of the *Style*, you can set *EventSetter* as an object element in the XAML file and define the event hander for the targeted control (such as the *Click* event for a *Button* control).

Earlier in this chapter, in the section titled "The *RoutedEventArgs* Class," you saw how to set up a common *Click* event called *CommonButtonClickEvent* for the *ButtonBase* class at the *StackPanel* level by attaching the *ButtonBase.Click* in XAML to the *StackPanel* control. You can achieve the same functionality by adding a style setter at the *StackPanel* level.

Reopen the WpfApplication1 project, open the MainWindow.xaml page, and locate the *StackPanel* element in the XAML code. The *StackPanel* contains two buttons: Submit and Cancel. Remove the *ButtonBase.Click="CommonButtonClickEvent"* from the *StackPanel* element and add the highlighted portion (in bold text) from the following code. These are *StackPanel* resources that create the *EventSetter* as a style targeted toward the *Click* event of *Button* controls (in this case targeting the Submit and Cancel buttons) and process the *CommonButtonClickEvent* event handler method when a *Click* event is raised:

```
<StackPanel
    Orientation="Horizontal"
    HorizontalAlignment="Right"
    Grid.Column="1"
    Grid.Row="3">
    <StackPanel.Resources>
```

```
            <Style TargetType="{x:Type Button}">
                <EventSetter
                    Event="Click"
                    Handler="CommonButtonClickEvent"/>
            </Style>
        </StackPanel.Resources>
        <Button
            x:Name="SubmitButton"
            Content="Submit"
            Margin="5"
            Width="100"
            Click="SubmitButton_Click"/>
        <Button
            x:Name="CancelButton"
            HorizontalAlignment="Left"
            Content="Cancel"
            Margin="5"
            Width="100"/>
</StackPanel>
```

If you now compile and run the project, you should get similar results as you did before when clicking the Submit and Cancel buttons. (See the results discussed on page 74, in the section "The *RoutedEventArgs* Class.")

 Caution The *EventSetter* is applicable to only routed events and is available only for the WPF framework. Silverlight does not support *EventSetter*.

The *EventTrigger* Class

Supported By	
WPF	Yes
Silverlight	Yes

The *EventTrigger* class lets you set actions and apply animations in response to specific routed events. Event triggers make use of the *Storyboard* element to apply an animation. You can declare an *EventTrigger* within *Style* or page-level elements as part of the *Triggers* collection, or in a *ControlTemplate*.

The following XAML code snippet defines an *EventTrigger* for the *Rectangle.Loaded* event as part of the *Rectangle.Triggers* collection. The event enables you to change the color of the *Rectangle* when it gets loaded. The *EventTrigger* property has an attribute called *RoutedEvent* that indicates which event will trigger the action:

```
<Rectangle.Triggers>
    <EventTrigger
        RoutedEvent="Rectangle.Loaded">
        <BeginStoryboard>
            <Storyboard>
                <ColorAnimation
                    Storyboard.TargetName="brush"
                    Storyboard.TargetProperty="Color"
```

```
                    To="Magenta"
                    Duration="0:0:6"/>
            </Storyboard>
        </BeginStoryboard>
    </EventTrigger>
</Rectangle.Triggers>
```

> **More Info**   See Chapter 5 for more information on resources and styling. See Chapter 9, "Media, Graphics, and Animation," for more information on animation.

The next chapter, "Markup Extensions and Other Features," covers markup extensions that can extend the capabilities of XAML to resolve property values at runtime. It also covers XAML services and security measures in XAML.

Summary

This chapter introduced the new dependency property and routed event systems for XAML and the WPF and Silverlight frameworks.

A dependency property is backed by a regular CLR .NET property and uses the dependency property framework to determine the property value based on various possible sources, including data binding, animation, template resources specified in the XAML, styles, or local values. Dependency properties also provide a value change notification service.

Attached properties are dependency properties that provide dynamic extension of classes without inheritance, and relate child objects to parent objects in a predefined specific context.

Routed events are CLR-type events backed by the *RoutedEvent* class and processed by the WPF event system. You can define a routed event within a XAML file using attribute syntax or implement a routed event in code-behind. Routed events follow one of three possible routing paths: bubble up, tunneling, or direct routing. A routed event can have one object element as the event sender and one or more event receivers (which may include the object that raises the event) that can execute an event handler implemented in code-behind. Like attached dependency properties, attached routed events are a special type of routed event that is specific to XAML and not wrapped by .NET CLR add and remove handler accessors. The attached event is neither owned by event sender nor by event receiver. You can attach an attached routed event arbitrarily to any object element.

CHAPTER 4

Markup Extensions and Other Features

In this chapter:

- Markup Extensions in XAML

- Built-In XAML Extensions

- XAML Markup Extensions in WPF and Silverlight

- Escape Sequences

- Custom Markup Extensions

- Type Converters versus Markup Extensions

- XAML Services

- Security in XAML

- Summary

You'll see a great deal more about data binding in Chapter 8, "Data Binding," including several methods and approaches for binding controls to data, but for now, two key extensions crucial to the implementation of data binding are the *StaticResource* and *Binding* extensions. These extensions, also called *markup extensions*, are placeholders to resolve a property at runtime. Without the use of the *StaticResource* and *Binding* markup extensions, the process of binding would be very cumbersome indeed.

XAML and the WPF and Silverlight implementations of XAML also support several other markup extensions that can be used for tasks besides data binding.

Markup Extensions

XAML, being an XML-based language used to declare objects and the relationships between them, is simple by nature. However, this simplicity comes at a cost—XAML can be quite long-winded at times.

XAML lacks any inherent or built-in knowledge of common artifacts such as arrays, static members of a class, data binding, and so forth. Because XAML can be an integral part of application development, developers need some way to express information about such artifacts in it. Additionally, to be a long-lasting format, XAML had to be extensible.

To provide a solution for all these issues, Microsoft introduced the concept of *markup extensions*. Using markup extensions, you can extend XAML in an elegant way; you can set any property that can be set in XAML using *attribute syntax*. Attribute syntax can provide reference values for a property even if that property does not support an attribute syntax for direct object instantiation.

For example, the following code makes use of attribute syntax to set the value of the *Style* property. The *Style* property takes an instance of the *Style* class, a reference type that typically could not be specified within an attribute syntax string. But here, the attribute references a specific markup extension, *StaticResource*. When that markup extension is processed, it returns a reference to a style which was instantiated earlier as a keyed resource.

```
<UserControl.Resources>
    <SolidColorBrush x:Key="Test" Color="Pink"/>
    <Style TargetType="Border" x:Key="MyBorder">
    <Setter Property="Background" Value="Gray"/>
    </Style>
</UserControl.Resources>
<StackPanel>
    <Border Style="{StaticResource MyBorder}">
    </Border>
</StackPanel>
```

The *System.Windows.Markup* namespace contains the definitions for most of the markup extension classes. These class names end with the suffix *Extension*; however, when you use them in XAML, you can omit the *Extension* suffix. For example, in XAML you represent the *NullExtension* markup class as *x:Null*. Markup extensions may also support parameters, which you specify as a comma-delimited list. Markup extension classes typically have default constructors.

The syntax of a markup extension is an opening brace (*{*), followed by the markup extension name, optionally followed by parameters to the markup extension, and ending with a closing brace (*}*). When the XAML compiler or parser encounters an attribute enclosed in braces, it automatically recognizes it as a markup extension.

Although WPF and Silverlight commonly support various markup extensions, some extensions are supported only by WPF. In contrast, Silverlight-only extensions are rare.

You can also create a custom markup extension by deriving from the *MarkupExtension* class.

Built-In XAML Markup Extensions

Some markup extensions are built in to XAML; that is, they are a part of the native XAML vocabulary. These are not specific to the WPF implementation of XAML; they are features of XAML as a language and are implemented in the *System.Xaml* assembly.

The built-in XAML markup extensions are typically prefixed with *x:* and enclosed within braces, like other markup extensions. However, not all language features that start with *x:* are markup extensions. For instance, the *x:Class* name that you use with an element is an attribute, not a markup extension. Similarly, *x:Key* and *x:Name* are attributes.

 Note There are no built-in markup extensions for string manipulation in XAML.

Some of the built-in XAML markup extensions are described in detail in the following sections.

x:Null

Supported By	
WPF	Yes
Silverlight	Yes

Use this markup extension to specify a null value. This markup extension is supported by both WPF and Silverlight. In some scenarios you may want to assign a null value to an element, style, or similar item. The *x:Null* markup extension proves useful in such scenarios.

Here's an example. Suppose you have defined a style for buttons in a Silverlight application. You now want to prevent a specific button from using that style. To do that, use the markup *<Button Style="{x:Null} " Name=btnOK" ></Button>*. Assigning the *x:Null* markup extension prevents the button from using that style.

```
<Grid x:Name="LayoutRoot" Background="Beige">
     <Grid.Resources>
         <Style TargetType="Button">
             <Setter Property="BorderBrush" Value="Red"></Setter>
             <Setter Property="BorderThickness" Value="4"></Setter>
         </Style>
     </Grid.Resources>
     <Grid.RowDefinitions>
         <RowDefinition Height="Auto"/>
         <RowDefinition Height="Auto"/>
         <RowDefinition Height="Auto"/>
     </Grid.RowDefinitions>
     <Button Grid.Row="0" Name="btnOK" Content="OK" Height="100" Width="200"/>
     <Button Grid.Row="1" Name="btnDone" Content="Done" Height="100" Width="200"/>
     <Button Grid.Row="2" Content="Bye" Style="{x:Null}" Height="100" Width="200"/>
</Grid>
```

As a result of this markup, two buttons will use the predefined *Button* style, but the third button will not have any style, because its style has been assigned the *{x:Null}* markup extension, as shown in bold.

Figure 4-1 shows the outcome of this markup.

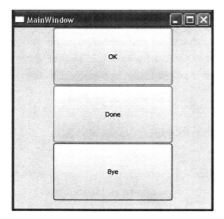

FIGURE 4-1   Using the *X:Null* markup extension.

 Note It's important to remember that setting a value to *null* is not the same as not setting it at all. Dependency properties in WPF obtain their value from a number of sources; therefore, setting a local value takes precedence over values sourced from elsewhere, such as an animation or a style.

Assigning *x:Null* to the background of an element such as *Button* is different from assigning *Transparent* to the background. Consider the following code in a WPF application:

```
<Button Height="200" Width="200" Background="Transparent"
    BorderBrush="Blue" BorderThickness="3" Click="Button_Click"></Button>
```

This code works as expected and renders a transparent button with a blue border. The button is clickable, and when a user clicks the button, you could perform some action.

However, if you change the *Background* to *x:Null,* as shown here, the rendered button will not be clickable.

```
<Button Height="200" Width="200" Background="{x:Null}" BorderBrush="Blue"
    BorderThickness="3" Click="Button_Click"></Button>
```

The reason for this is that in the first case, the background was set to a transparent brush. Even though the brush is transparent, it is still an instance of *SolidColorBrush* with the color *SystemColors. Transparent*. However, in the second case, the brush is set to null, which means there is no brush at all, which renders the button as unclickable.

x:Array

Supported By	
WPF	Yes
Silverlight	No

This markup extension is supported by WPF but is not supported in Silverlight. In XAML 2009, *x:Array* is defined as a language primitive rather than a markup extension.

x:Array lets you to create simple arrays using XAML syntax, as shown here:

```
<x:Array Type="sys:String" xmlns:x="http://schemas.microsoft.com/winfx/2006/xaml"
xmlns:sys="clr-namespace:System;assembly=mscorlib" >
    <sys:String>Orange</sys:String>
    <sys:String>Blue</sys:String>
    <sys:String>Green</sys:String>
    <sys:String>Pink</sys:String>
</x:Array>
```

A typical use of this markup extension would be to provide a list of contents for a *ListBox* or *ComboBox*, as shown here:

```
<ListBox>
    <ListBox.ItemTemplate>
        <DataTemplate>
            <TextBlock Text="{Binding}" Background="PaleGreen"/>
        </DataTemplate>
    </ListBox.ItemTemplate>
    <ListBox.ItemsSource>
        <x:Array Type="sys:String" xmlns:x="http://schemas.microsoft.com/winfx/2006/xaml"
          xmlns:sys="clr-namespace:System;assembly=mscorlib" >
            <sys:String>Orange</sys:String>
            <sys:String>Blue</sys:String>
            <sys:String>Green</sys:String>
            <sys:String>Pink</sys:String>
        </x:Array>
    </ListBox.ItemsSource>
</ListBox>
```

Figure 4-2 shows the outcome of this markup.

FIGURE 4-2 Using *X:Array* with a *ListBox*.

x:Reference

Supported By	
WPF	Yes
Silverlight	No

This markup extension is not supported in Silverlight. In WPF, it is used to reference a previously declared element. Here's an example: A *Label* used to prompt for customer name must set the focus to a text box that will accept the customer name when a user presses a specified access key assigned to the *Label*. In earlier versions of XAML, you could accomplish this explicitly by using *Binding* and *ElementName* to perform the binding.

```
<StackPanel>
    <TextBox Name="customerName" Text="" Height="24" Grid.Row="0" Grid.Column="1"
Margin="20,40,238,40"></TextBox>
    <Label Target='{Binding ElementName=customerName}' Height="27" Width="117" Grid.Row="0"
Grid.Column="0">_Customer Name:</Label>
</StackPanel>
```

The underscore in the *Label* name defines the subsequent character as the access key. In this case, pressing C at runtime will set the focus to the *customerName* text box.

Using the *x:Reference* markup extension, you can now write the same code as the following:

```
<StackPanel>
    <TextBox Name="customerName" Text="" Height="24" Grid.Row="0" Grid.Column="1"
Margin="20,40,238,40">
    </TextBox>
    <Label Target="{x:Reference customerName}" Height="27" Width="117" Grid.Row="0"
Grid.Column="0">_Customer Name:</Label>
</StackPanel>
```

Thus, using *x:Reference*, the code becomes more concise and simpler. Although this example was simple, you can use the *x:Reference* markup extension in more complex scenarios, too.

> **Note** When using *{x:Reference <controlname>}* as the *Target* of a WPF *Label*, the Visual Studio designer throws an *InvalidOperationException* exception with the message "Service provider is missing the *INameResolver* service." The project will compile and execute without any issues, but the Design canvas where the *x:Reference* appears will be disabled because of the exception. As of this book's writing, this is a known issue and should be resolved sometime in the future.

x:Static

Supported By	
WPF	Yes

Silverlight	No

This markup extension produces static values. The values come from value-type code entities that are not directly the type of a target property's value, but can be evaluated to that type. The *x:Static* markup extension is evaluated at runtime when the XAML is actually loaded.

For example, you could use it as shown here:

```
<TextBlock Text="Demo!" >
  <TextBlock.Background>
    <SolidColorBrush Color="{x:Static SystemColors.ControlColor}" />
  </TextBlock.Background>
</TextBlock>
```

The preceding code uses a built-in system type *ControlColor* defined in the *SystemColors* assembly and assigns it to the *Color* property of the brush used to fill the *TextBlock* background.

The following example assigns the *Text* property of a *TextBlock* to the value defined in a custom assembly. This assembly is first referenced in the XAML markup with a prefix; later, that prefix is used to refer to the type:

```
<TextBlock Text="{x:Static Member="local:MyClass.Header}" Grid.Row="0" />
```

In the preceding example, *local* was previously defined as a namespace prefix using this syntax:

```
xmlns:local="clr-namespace:WPFApp"
```

The code-behind class defines a custom type named *MyClass*, which contains a static *readonly* property named *Header*.

```
public class MyClass
{
    public static readonly string Header = "DevCon 2011";
}
```

In this example, specifying *Text="{local:MyClass.Header}"* without using the *x:Static* markup extension would result in a compiler error. The only way you can access the static property defined in the *MyClass* class from markup is by using the *x:Static* markup extension.

This extension can also be useful in scenarios where you want to specify a base style that is defined as a class property:

```
<StackPanel>
  <StackPanel.Resources>
    <ResourceDictionary>
      <Style TargetType="Button" BasedOn="{x:Static local:MyStyle.BaseStyle}" />
    </ResourceDictionary>
  </StackPanel.Resources>
</StackPanel>
```

In the preceding XAML, *MyStyle* is a class that defines a static property named *BaseStyle* of type *Style*.

x:Type

Supported By	
WPF	Yes
Silverlight	No

This markup extension is supported only in WPF, not in Silverlight. It is used to specify the target type for an element—for example, while creating a style. The functionality of this markup extension is identical to *TargetType* in that you can use either interchangeably. The only scenario where using the *x:Type* extension makes more sense is when you're specifying custom objects and want to set the type explicitly.

Here's a simple example of using this extension:

```
<Grid x:Name="LayoutRoot" Background="Beige">
        <Grid.Resources>
            <Style TargetType="{x:Type Button}">
                <Setter Property="BorderBrush" Value="Red"></Setter>
                <Setter Property="BorderThickness"  Value="7"></Setter>
            </Style>
        </Grid.Resources>
        <Grid.RowDefinitions>
            <RowDefinition Height="Auto"/>
            <RowDefinition Height="Auto"/>
            <RowDefinition Height="Auto"/>
        </Grid.RowDefinitions>
        <Button Grid.Row="0" Name="btnOK" Content="OK" Height="100" Width="200"/>
        <Button Grid.Row="1" Name="btnDone" Content="Done" Height="100" Width="200"/>
</Grid>
```

Note that in the preceding code, you could have easily omitted *{x:Type}* in the *TargetType* declaration without making any difference to the output. That is, you could write *TargetType="Button"* in place of *TargetType="{x:Type Button}"*.

XAML Markup Extensions Used in WPF and Silverlight

The following markup extensions are a part of the XAML language and are intrinsic language features:

■ *Binding*   This markup extension binds the values of two properties together. It is most commonly used in data-binding scenarios to bind the value of a *FrameworkElement* instance to a specific piece of data. For example, you can bind a customer name to a text box.

■ *StaticResource*   This markup extension is used to implement a one-time lookup of a resource entry. The resource entry could be defined in the resources section of a container control such as a *Grid*, a *StackPanel*, and so forth.

- *DynamicResource*   This markup extension is used to implement lookup of a resource entry dynamically at runtime.

- *TemplateBinding*   This markup extension is used to bind a property of a control template to a dependency property of the control.

You'll see numerous examples of these extensions discussed in Chapter 8. Apart from specifying property values using markup extensions, you can use two other approaches to assign property values:

- Property assigned a literal string value

- Property assigned a value by a type converter, converted from a literal string

For example, the following markup demonstrates how property element syntax can be used to refer to a *StaticResource* without using markup extensions:

```
<Binding.ValidationRules>
    <StaticResource ResourceKey="IsValidRule"/>
</Binding.ValidationRules>
```

Escape Sequences

In some scenarios you may need to include a pair of braces as a literal in your code as a string text. Typically, XAML processors use an open brace ({) to indicate the start of a markup extension sequence. So when the open brace is encountered, the XAML processor assumes that a markup extension follows. To override this behavior and specify an escape sequence, use a pair of empty braces. The two-brace escape sequence ({}) identifies braces in the subsequent text as literal characters.

For example, the following markup shows an escape sequence for an XML namespace that appears at the start of a XAML attribute value:

```
<StackPanel>
   <TextBlock Text="{}{http://www.contoso.com}" />
</StackPanel>
```

Here, you want to use the namespace *http://www.contoso.com/* and the braces together as a literal, so you specify an escape sequence by using a pair of empty braces. The output produced will include the braces and will display {*http://www.contoso.com*}.

Custom Markup Extensions

Custom markup extensions are useful in scenarios where you need the extension to provide functionality or behavior that is beyond the scope of existing built-in markup extensions.

In earlier versions of Silverlight, you could not create custom markup extensions, but Silverlight 5 added support for them. You create a custom markup extension by extending the *MarkupExtension* class or the *IMarkupExtension* interface.

One of the biggest issues in data binding with Silverlight is that there is no support for an *ObjectDataProvider* class. In some instances, such as when binding to XML data, the lack of support for this class proves to be a huge drawback.

Until Silverlight 5, for example, there was no way to write something like the markup shown here, which binds an XML file and an element within it to a UI element in a Silverlight application declaratively:

```
<ListBox ItemsSource="<some mechanism> Source=Employee.xml, Path=/Manager/FirstName}"
```

You could parse the XML entirely in code in a number of ways—but you had no way to perform a declarative binding in XAML. This is where the custom markup extension feature introduced in Silverlight 5 can come to the rescue.

Use the following steps to create and use such an extension:

1. Create a Silverlight 5 application named **XMLBinderDemo**.

2. Add an XML file named **Employee.xml** to the application that has the following contents:

    ```xml
    <?xml version="1.0" encoding="utf-8" ?>
    <Employee>
      <Manager FirstName="Jonathan" LastName="Foster" />
      <Manager FirstName="Bill" LastName="Malone" />
      <Manager FirstName="Patrick" LastName="Sands" />
      <Engineer FirstName="Weiss" LastName="Charlotte"/>
    </Employee>
    ```

3. Add a reference to the *System.Xml.Linq* assembly.

4. Add a class named *XMLBinderExtension* to the application.

5. Add the following code to the class:

    ```csharp
    namespace XMLBinderDemo
    {
        public class XMLBinderExtension : MarkupExtension
        {
            public string Source { get; set; }
            public string Path { get; set; }
            private static List<string> Parse(string file, string path)
            {
                XDocument xdoc = XDocument.Load(file);
                string[] text = path.Substring(1).Split('/');
                string desc = text[0].ToString();
                string elementname = text[1].ToString();
    ```

```
            List<string> data = new List<string>();
            IEnumerable<XElement> elems = xdoc.Descendants(desc);
            IEnumerable<XElement> elem_list = from elem in elems
                                               select elem;
            foreach (XElement element in elem_list)
            {
                String str0 = element.Attribute(elementname).Value.ToString();
                data.Add(str0);
            }
            return data;
        }


        /// <summary>
        /// Overridden method that returns the source and path to bind to
        /// </summary>
        /// <param name="serviceProvider"></param>
        /// <returns></returns>
        public override object ProvideValue(IServiceProvider serviceProvider)
        {
            if ((Source != null) && (Path != null))
                return Parse(Source, Path);
            else
                throw new InvalidOperationException("Inputs cannot be blank");
        }
    }
}
```

6. Finally, you can write the XAML markup, as shown here:

```
<UserControl x:Class="XMLBinderDemo.MainPage"
    xmlns="http://schemas.microsoft.com/winfx/2006/xaml/presentation"
    xmlns:x="http://schemas.microsoft.com/winfx/2006/xaml"
    xmlns:d="http://schemas.microsoft.com/expression/blend/2008"
    xmlns:mc="http://schemas.openxmlformats.org/markup-compatibility/2006"
    xmlns:local="clr-namespace:XMLBinderDemo"
    mc:Ignorable="d"
    d:DesignHeight="300" d:DesignWidth="400" >
    <Grid x:Name="LayoutRoot" Background="White">
        <ListBox ItemsSource="{local:XMLBinderExtension Source=Employee.xml,
        Path=/Manager/FirstName}" Height="200" Width="200" Background="Beige" />
    </Grid>
</UserControl>
```

The *XMLBinderExtension* class derives from the *MarkupExtension* class defined in the *System.Windows.Markup* assembly. The *MarkupExtension* class provides a base class for XAML markup extension implementations.

The *ProvideValue*() method is typically overridden (or implemented, if inheriting from the interface in the derived class) and returns an object that becomes the value of the target property for this markup extension. In the current example, the *ProvideValue*() method returns an object used as the source for the XML binding.

The general syntax of the *ProvideValue*() method is as follows:

Syntax:

```
public abstract Object ProvideValue(
    IServiceProvider serviceProvider
)
```

 Note In the preceding example, *serviceProvider* indicates a service provider helper that can provide services for the markup extension.

If the service is designed to return a value, the custom markup extension class can throw an exception if the service is unavailable. In addition, if any of the arguments used by the custom markup extension class to provide values are null, or if an argument does not match the expected data type, or if it contains a value that cannot be processed by the custom markup extension, you can throw an exception within the custom markup class. The recommended exception to throw in either or both of these cases is *InvalidOperationException*.

The following XAML markup assigns the CLR namespace *XMLBinderDemo* to the alias *local*. Then it invokes the custom markup extension using this alias and passes the XML file name and path to bind to using the *Source* and *Path* attributes, as shown here:

```
<ListBox ItemsSource="{local:XMLBinderExtension Source=Employee.xml,
    Path=/Manager/FirstName}" Height="200" Width="200" Background="Beige" />
```

This approach makes declarative XML binding possible and much easier to work with.

 Note The *MarkupExtension* type is defined in the *System.Windows.Markup* namespace and not in the System.Xaml namespace. This does not mean that this type is specific to either the WPF or Windows Forms technologies. *MarkupExtension* is in the *System.Xaml* assembly and therefore has no specific framework dependency. This type existed in the CLR namespace for .NET Framework 3.0 and remains in the CLR namespace in .NET Framework 4 to avoid breaking references in existing WPF projects.

Type Converters versus Markup Extensions

Type converters and markup extensions are similar in that they are used by XAML type systems and XAML writers to render object graph components.

Type converters are classes that derive from the *TypeConverter* class in the .NET Framework. The *TypeConverter* class converts a text representation of an object (such as an attribute value or a XAML value node) into an object. You can also use a *TypeConverter* to serialize an object value to a text representation. The *TypeConverter* class was present in the .NET Framework long before the development of XAML. Markup extensions, on the other hand, are classes that derive from the *MarkupExtension* class. Markup extensions are a concept that originated with XAML.

Although type converters and markup extensions have a few characteristics in common, each is represented differently within a XAML node stream. Also, markup extensions return objects in a more elegant manner than type converters. When a type or member includes a type converter implementation, the XAML object writer invokes the type converter.

Type converters are typically associated with types or members, and are invoked when an object graph creation or a serialization method encounters the text representation associated with those entities. Thus, a type converter call is dependent on the type or property definition.

A markup extension is under the control of user code and user-generated markup, and can be called when an application scenario demands it, whereas a type converter is not.

XAML Services

The .NET Framework XAML Services are a set of services and APIs defined in the assembly *System.Xaml*. This is a new assembly introduced with .NET Framework 4, and includes readers, writers, schema classes, and other XAML language features.

The *System.Xaml* assembly also defines types that relate to XAML readers and XAML writers, types for the XAML type system, and other support types related to XAML and .NET Framework XAML Services concepts.

A crucial feature added to XAML Services that was not present in earlier versions of .NET Framework is a type system for XAML.

You can extend the XAML type system functionality of XAML representations into specific features enabled by a framework, an application, and so on that accept and render XAML. The XAML type system provides the APIs required to work with the nodes of a XAML node stream.

Security in XAML

Just as with any other .NET technology, XAML addresses security issues to help ensure that your hard work does not go down the drain because of security loopholes.

Any XAML source that your application did not specifically create or render is categorized as *untrusted XAML*. However, XAML compiled into or stored as a *resx*-type resource within a trusted and signed assembly can be trusted based on the trust level of the assembly. You should typically treat untrusted XAML as if it were untrusted code.

Through XAML, you work with objects, type converters, assemblies in the application domain, and so on. XAML is also popular for rendering UIs in technologies such as WPF and Silverlight. To secure Silverlight-based applications against attacks, Microsoft recommends that you do not pass untrusted XAML strings to the *Load* or *CreateFromXaml* methods.

In addition, you should avoid sharing XAML reader instances, settings for XAML reader/writer classes, or similar such details between trusted and untrusted code.

You must also take care to secure XAML namespace mappings—an untrusted assembly can spoof a trusted assembly's proposed XAML namespace mapping. After the untrusted assembly obtains the XAML namespace mapping, it can grab the object and property information from object sources. Some security measures you can take include using fully qualified assembly names with strong names in XAML namespace mappings, and restricting assembly mapping to a fixed set of reference assemblies.

Summary

- The extensions described in this chapter, also called markup extensions, are placeholders to resolve a property at runtime.

- The *System.Windows.Markup* namespace contains the definitions for most of the markup extension classes.

- *x:Null*, *x:Array*, *x:Reference*, *x:Static*, and *x:Type* are some of the built-in XAML markup extensions.

- *Binding*, *StaticResource*, and *DynamicResource* are some other commonly used markup extensions that form part of the XAML language. See Chapter 8 for more information.

- Custom markup extensions are useful in scenarios where you need the extension to provide functionality or behavior that is beyond the scope of existing built-in markup extensions.

- The .NET Framework XAML Services are a set of services and APIs defined in the assembly *System.Xaml*.

CHAPTER 5

Resources, Styles, and Triggers

In this chapter:

- Resources
- Types of Resources
- Defining Resource Dictionary Files
- Merged Resource Dictionaries
- Scope and Hierarchy of Resources
- Styles
- Triggers
- Troubleshooting Resources, Styles, and Triggers
- Summary

XAML provides some powerful features through resources, styles, and triggers that let you customize the visual appearance and behavior of controls. You can capitalize on these features to transform a dull, ordinary application into an application with a rich, interactive, and striking user interface.

Resources

Resources in Silverlight and WPF provide designers and developers with a way to reuse commonly defined objects. Using resources, you can set the properties of several controls simultaneously. This can help maintain consistency across the application. Defining resources in an application simplifies making changes to the application, because when you modify the resource, all the elements that make use of that resource immediately reflect the change.

Silverlight and WPF provide a *Resources* property for every framework-level element, which you can use to define the resources. This means that you can define specific resources for elements such as *Window*, *UserControl*, *Grid*, *Button*, and so forth. However, the recommended approach is to define the resources at a *Window* or *Page* element level. This is because any resource you define for an element also applies to its child elements. For example, if you define a resource for a *Page* that has a

Grid as a child element, the grid element can also use the page-level resources. However, if you define a resource for the grid element, the resource applies only to the grid element and its child elements; you can't use that resource for the parent *Page*.

For all elements, the *Resources* property is of type *ResourceDictionary*. When you create resources using the *Resources* property, you are actually adding them to a *ResourceDictionary* exposed by the object. Resources can be stored either in resource dictionaries or in a XAML file.

> **Note** You cannot place *UIElement* objects in a resource.

Types of Resources

You can define resources using either XAML or code. The two types of resources are *static* resources and *dynamic* resources.

Static Resources

Supported By	
WPF	Yes
Silverlight	Yes

A static resource is resolved at compile time, after which the XAML processor assigns it to a property while the XAML loads, which occurs before the application runs. The term *StaticResource* references a static resource in XAML and includes the key that uniquely identifies the resource. *StaticResource* is a *markup extension*, which is a placeholder to resolve a property at runtime. Chapter 4, "Markup Extensions and Other Features," covers markup extensions in detail.

After a property obtains a value through a *StaticResource* markup extension, any changes made later to the resource dictionary are ignored. Static resource references must reference only those resources that have been defined *before* the resource reference.

Defining Static Resources Using XAML

You use the *Resources* property of a framework-level element to define resources using XAML. Each resource must have a unique key specified through the *x:Key* attribute.

Suppose that you want to define a *LinearGradientBrush* as a resource on a *Grid* element that you want to apply to several UI elements, including a button. The following XAML markup will help you accomplish this. You can use this markup either in a Silverlight application or a WPF application and therefore, in this case, you declare the resource at the *Grid* level. The *Grid* will contain a button named *btnSubmit* as its child element.

```
<Grid.Resources>
    <LinearGradientBrush x:Key="bgBrush" StartPoint="0.5,0" EndPoint="0.5,1">
        <GradientStop Color="Yellow" Offset="0.0" />
```

```
            <GradientStop Color="Blue" Offset="0.75" />
            <GradientStop Color="Green" Offset="1.0" />
        </LinearGradientBrush>
</Grid.Resources>
```

Here, the markup creates a *LinearGradientBrush* as a resource that is assigned the key *bgBrush*. This unique key is the resource identifier, and you will use it to reference the resource later on.

The *<Grid.Resources></Grid.Resources>* tags enclose the definition of the resource, signifying that this resource has been defined in the *Resources* property of the *Grid* element.

To reference this resource, you will use the *StaticResource* markup extension, as shown in the following markup:

```
<Button x:Name="btnSubmit" Background="{StaticResource bgBrush}" Height="60" Width="120"
    Margin="112,23,168,217"/>
```

In this code shown, the *StaticResource* markup extension uses the key name *bgBrush* to reference the resource. Thus, the background property of the button is resolved to the *LinearGradientBrush* defined earlier.

The complete XAML markup for declaring and using the resource is as follows:

```
<Grid x:Name="LayoutRoot">
    <Grid.Resources>
            <LinearGradientBrush x:Key="bgBrush" StartPoint="0.5,0" EndPoint="0.5,1">
                <GradientStop Color="Yellow" Offset="0.0" />
                <GradientStop Color="Blue" Offset="0.75" />
                <GradientStop Color="Green" Offset="1.0" />
            </LinearGradientBrush>
    </Grid.Resources>
 <Button x:Name="btnSubmit" Background="{StaticResource bgBrush}"
    Height="60" Width="120" Margin="112,23,168,217"/>
</Grid>
```

Because the markup declares *bgBrush* as a resource, you can apply it to several other elements as well. As mentioned earlier, reusing the same object—in this case, *LinearGradientBrush*—as a resource not only promotes consistency, but also eventually makes the code easier to maintain and modify.

Here's another example of defining and using a resource:

```
<UserControl x:Class="SilverlightApp.MainPage"
    xmlns="http://schemas.microsoft.com/winfx/2006/xaml/presentation"
    xmlns:x="http://schemas.microsoft.com/winfx/2006/xaml"
    xmlns:d="http://schemas.microsoft.com/expression/blend/2008"
    xmlns:mc="http://schemas.openxmlformats.org/markup-compatibility/2006"
    mc:Ignorable="d"
    d:DesignHeight="300" d:DesignWidth="400">
    <UserControl.Resources>
        <TextBlock x:Key="copyright"
          Text="Copyright Wingtip Toys 2008"/>
    </UserControl.Resources>
    <ContentControl Content="{StaticResource copyright}"/>
</UserControl>
```

Suppose a Silverlight application has the following code fragment:

```
<Page.Resources>
  <TextBlock x:Key="copyright"
      Text="Copyright Tailspin Toys 2008"/>
</Page.Resources>
<ContentControl Content="{StaticResource copyright}"/>
```

The XAML markup will display the copyright message on the pages of the application.

Note You must always define static resources before referencing them. A *StaticResource* must not attempt to make a forward reference to a resource defined later in the XAML file. Attempting to specify a *StaticResource* to a key that cannot be resolved will result in a XAML parse exception.

You can define strings and other primitives as resources, as shown in the following example:

```
<Grid x:Name="LayoutRoot">
      <Grid.Resources>
          <sys:String x:Key="currencytext">150 dollars</sys:String>
      </Grid.Resources>
      <Button x:Name="btnSubmit" Height="60" Width="120"
       Margin="112,23,168,217" Content="{StaticResource currencytext}"/>
      <TextBlock Text="{StaticResource currencytext }" Margin="12,119,294,156" />
</Grid>
```

Defining Static Resources Programmatically

You use the *ResourceDictionary* class to create a resource programmatically. First, create a new *ResourceDictionary* instance, and then add resources to the dictionary by calling its *ResourceDictionary.Add* method. After creating the resource dictionary, and adding resources to it, you can assign the now-populated *ResourceDictionary* instance to the *Resources* property of any appropriate element.

The following C# code in a Silverlight application shows how to create a resource similar to the one defined in the previous XAML example and assign it to the *Grid* element named *LayoutRoot*.

The code retrieves the resource from the resource dictionary, casts into a *LinearGradientBrush*, and assigns to the *Background* property of the button, *btnSubmit*.

```
ResourceDictionary dict = new ResourceDictionary();
LinearGradientBrush bgBrush = new LinearGradientBrush();
bgBrush.StartPoint = new Point(0.5, 0);
bgBrush.EndPoint = new Point(0.5, 1);
GradientStopCollection stops = new GradientStopCollection();
GradientStop stop1 = new GradientStop();
stop1.Color = Colors.Yellow;
stop1.Offset = 0.0;
stops.Add(stop1);
GradientStop stop2 = new GradientStop();
```

```
stop2.Color = Colors.Blue;
stop2.Offset = 0.75;
stops.Add(stop2);
GradientStop stop3 = new GradientStop();
stop3.Color = Colors.Green;
stop3.Offset = 1.0;
stops.Add(stop3);
bgBrush.GradientStops = stops;
dict.Add("bgBrush", bgBrush);
this.LayoutRoot.Resources = dict;
this.btnSubmit.Background = (LinearGradientBrush)
                            this.LayoutRoot.Resources["bgBrush"];
```

This C# code assumes that you have defined the following XAML markup in the application:

```
<Grid x:Name="LayoutRoot">
    <Button x:Name="btnSubmit" Height="60" Width="120" Margin="112,23,168,217"/>
</Grid>
```

In WPF, you can use the *FindResource()* and *TryFindResource()* methods to look up a particular resource from within the code-behind. Silverlight does not implement these methods.

 Note The XAML processor parses resources and enters them in a resource dictionary in the order in which you specify them.

Dynamic Resources

Supported By	
WPF	Yes
Silverlight	No

A dynamic resource is unresolved at compile time; it is resolved only at runtime. In addition to the *StaticResource* markup extension, WPF also provides the *DynamicResource* markup extension that enables you to reference resources dynamically. In other words, WPF supports both kinds of resources—static resources and dynamic resources—whereas Silverlight supports only static resources and lacks support for dynamic resources. The *DynamicResource* markup extension enables you to defer the resolution of a resource to runtime.

The following example demonstrates the use of *DynamicResource* markup extension. The color of the element changes whenever the Desktop Color changes:

```
<Button>
    <Button.Background>
      <SolidColorBrush Color="{DynamicResource
      {x:Static SystemColors.DesktopColorKey}}" />
    </Button.Background>
  Hello
</Button>
```

When to Use Which Resource

Sometimes you may need to choose between defining a static resource and a dynamic resource. Depending on the requirements, you will need to make a call as to which resource to use.

If your current scenario satisfies one or more of these conditions, you should use a static resource if you are:

- Attempting to set the value of a property that is not on a *DependencyObject* or a *Freezable* element.

- Creating a resource dictionary that will eventually be compiled into a DLL and packaged as part of an application or shared between applications.

- Creating an application design that focuses most of its resources into page- or application-level resource dictionaries.

- Defining a theme for a custom control and resources that are used within the themes.

- Setting an abundance of dependency properties using resources.

On the other hand, if your current scenario satisfies one or more of the following conditions, you should use a dynamic resource when you are:

- Depending on conditions that will be resolved only at runtime to set the values of resources.

- Manipulating the contents of a *ResourceDictionary* during an application lifetime.

- Creating or referencing theme styles for a custom control.

- Designing a complex resource structure that has interdependencies, where a forward reference may be required.

How Static and Dynamic Resources Work

For static resources, the lookup process works as follows:

1. It checks for the requested key in the resource dictionary defined by the element setting the property.

2. It navigates the logical tree upward, to the parent element and its resource dictionary. This upward navigation continues until the lookup process reaches the root element.

3. It concludes by checking application resources.

Resource lookup behavior for a dynamic resource reference is very similar to the lookup behavior in your code that takes place when you call the *FindResource()* or *SetResourceReference()* method in WPF.

The steps taken during resource lookup for a dynamic resource are as follows:

1. The lookup process checks for the requested key in the resource dictionary defined by the element setting the property.

2. The process navigates the logical tree upward, to the parent element and its resource dictionary and continues until it reaches the root element.

3. It checks the application resources.

4. It checks the theme resource dictionary for the currently active theme. If the theme changes at runtime, the lookup process reevaluates the value.

5. Finally, the process checks the system resources.

Defining *ResourceDictionary* Files

If your application is small and needs only a few resources, you can define them in App.xaml. Doing this extends the scope of the resources to the entire application, instead of being constrained to a single element. Most real-world applications, however, require a large number of resources, and you will want to manage these properly. You use a *ResourceDictionary* file to group and organize related resources together. You can later merge multiple resource dictionaries to share them across applications.

Both Silverlight and WPF provide the capability to add a *ResourceDictionary* file through the Project | Add New Item command. The Add New Item dialog box displays a *ResourceDictionary* file as one of the templates.

When you select this template, the dialog box creates a resource dictionary with the default name Dictionary1.xml.

Figure 5-1 shows the Add New Item dialog box displaying the *ResourceDictionary* template.

FIGURE 5-1   Adding a resource dictionary.

The skeleton structure of a default *ResourceDictionary* file is as follows:

```
<ResourceDictionary xmlns="http://schemas.microsoft.com/winfx/2006/xaml/presentation"
                    xmlns:x="http://schemas.microsoft.com/winfx/2006/xaml">
</ResourceDictionary>
```

You can then add resources to this file just as you would define them normally. For example, the following resource dictionary file defines a *LinearGradientBrush* with the key *shadedBrush*:

TestResource.xaml:

```
<ResourceDictionary
    xmlns="http://schemas.microsoft.com/winfx/2006/xaml/presentation"
    xmlns:x="http://schemas.microsoft.com/winfx/2006/xaml" >
    <LinearGradientBrush EndPoint="0.5,1" StartPoint="0.5,0" x:Key="shadedBrush">
        <GradientStop Color="Black" Offset="0"/>
        <GradientStop Color="DarkMagenta" Offset="1"/>
    </LinearGradientBrush>
</ResourceDictionary>
```

You can add the *x:Shared* attribute to a new instance of a resource for each resource request instead of using a shared instance for every request. You can find more on the *x:Shared* attribute at the following link:

http://msdn.microsoft.com/en-us/library/aa970778.aspx

 Note Silverlight XAML does not support the *x:Shared* markup extension.

Merged Resource Dictionaries

Merged dictionaries enable you to share resources across applications by combining multiple resource dictionaries.

Consider an example to understand this concept. This example defines a resource dictionary, DictionaryA.xaml, in one application and then makes use of it in another application that also has a local resource dictionary, DictionaryB.xaml, defined in it.

Create a Merged Resource Dictionary

1. Create a Silverlight Class Library application and add a resource dictionary, DictionaryA.xaml, to it through the Project | Add New Item command.

2. Add the following markup to the resource dictionary:

```
<ResourceDictionary
    xmlns="http://schemas.microsoft.com/winfx/2006/xaml/presentation"
    xmlns:x="http://schemas.microsoft.com/winfx/2006/xaml" >
```

```
        <LinearGradientBrush EndPoint="0.5,1" StartPoint="0.5,0" x:Key="bgBrush">
            <GradientStop Color="Black" Offset="0"/>
            <GradientStop Color="DarkMagenta"  Offset="1"/>
        </LinearGradientBrush>
    </ResourceDictionary>
```

3. Build the application.

4. Create a new Silverlight application. Add a resource dictionary to it named DictionaryB.xaml and insert the following markup into it:

```
<ResourceDictionary
    xmlns="http://schemas.microsoft.com/winfx/2006/xaml/presentation"
    xmlns:x="http://schemas.microsoft.com/winfx/2006/xaml">
    <SolidColorBrush x:Key ="myBrush" Color="DarkGreen"/>
</ResourceDictionary>
```

5. Add a reference to the Silverlight Class Library application. You can then use DictionaryA.xaml as follows:

```
<UserControl x:Class="Dict.MainPage"
     xmlns="http://schemas.microsoft.com/winfx/2006/xaml/presentation"
     xmlns:x="http://schemas.microsoft.com/winfx/2006/xaml">
    <UserControl.Resources>
        <ResourceDictionary>
            <ResourceDictionary.MergedDictionaries>
                <ResourceDictionary Source="DictionaryB.xaml" />
                <ResourceDictionary
                  Source="/SilverlightClassLibrary1;component/ DictionaryA.xaml " />
            </ResourceDictionary.MergedDictionaries>
        </ResourceDictionary>
    </UserControl.Resources>
        <Button Background="{StaticResource shadedBrush}" Content="Resource Dictionaries"
Height="48" Width="148" />
</UserControl>
```

In the markup, the statement *<ResourceDictionary Source="SomeResources.xaml" />* references the locally defined resource dictionary, whereas the statement *<ResourceDictionary Source="/ SilverlightClassLibrary1;component/TestResource.xaml" />* references the resource dictionary defined in the class library. The *MergedDictionaries* property merges these two resource dictionaries.

Scope and Hierarchy of Resources

Resources declared locally within an element—also called *locally defined resources*—override the resources defined for a parent. For example, consider the following code:

```
<UserControl
   xmlns="http://schemas.microsoft.com/winfx/2006/xaml/presentation"
   xmlns:x="http://schemas.microsoft.com/winfx/2006/xaml"
   x:Class="SilverlightApp2.MainPage"
```

```
                Width="640" Height="480">
                 <UserControl.Resources>
                 <RadialGradientBrush GradientOrigin="0.5,0.5" Center="0.5,0.5"
                     RadiusX="0.5" RadiusY="0.5" x:Key="thinBrush">
                     <GradientStop Color="Yellow" Offset="0" />
                     <GradientStop Color="Red" Offset="0.25" />
                     <GradientStop Color="Blue" Offset="0.75" />
                     <GradientStop Color="LimeGreen" Offset="1" />
                 </RadialGradientBrush>
                 </UserControl.Resources>
                 <StackPanel>
                     <Rectangle Fill="{StaticResource thinBrush}" Height="48" Width="148" />
                 </StackPanel>
            </UserControl>
```

Here, when the XAML processor encounters the markup {*StaticResource thinBrush*}, it first looks for the resource definition in the *Rectangle* element, then looks for it under the *StackPanel* element. When it fails to find a resources collection named *thinBrush* in *StackPanel*, the XAML processor checks the *UserControl* and eventually finds the resource collection there. The code creates a radial gradient brush as a resource.

On the other hand, if you declare a resource with the same name under a parent element as well as a child element, the resource defined for the child element overrides the resource declared for the parent element.

The following example illustrates this concept:

```
<UserControl
    xmlns="http://schemas.microsoft.com/winfx/2006/xaml/presentation"
    xmlns:x="http://schemas.microsoft.com/winfx/2006/xaml"
    x:Class="SilverlightApp3.MainPage"
    Width="640" Height="480">
     <UserControl.Resources>
         <RadialGradientBrush GradientOrigin="0.5,0.5" Center="0.5,0.5"
         RadiusX="0.5" RadiusY="0.5" x:Key="radialBrush">
             <GradientStop Color="Yellow" Offset="0.2" />
             <GradientStop Color="Red" Offset="0.5" />
             <GradientStop Color="Blue" Offset="0.75" />
             <GradientStop Color="DarkBlue" Offset="1" />
         </RadialGradientBrush>
     </UserControl.Resources>
     <StackPanel>
         <StackPanel.Resources>
             <RadialGradientBrush GradientOrigin="0.5,0.5" Center="0.5,0.5"
         RadiusX="0.5" RadiusY="0.5" x:Key=" radialBrush ">
                 <GradientStop Color="White" Offset="0.5" />
                 <GradientStop Color="Tomato" Offset="0.75" />
                 <GradientStop Color="DarkBlue" Offset="0.75" />
                 <GradientStop Color="Orange" Offset="0.5" />
             </RadialGradientBrush>
         </StackPanel.Resources>
```

```
            <Button Height="48" Width="148">
                <Button.Resources>
                    <RadialGradientBrush GradientOrigin="0.5,0.5" Center="0.5,0.5"
                        RadiusX="0.5" RadiusY="0.5" x:Key=" radialBrush ">
                        <GradientStop Color="Magenta" Offset="0.75" />
                        <GradientStop Color="Green" Offset="0.25" />
                        <GradientStop Color="White" Offset="0.5" />
                        <GradientStop Color="LimeGreen" Offset="1" />
                    </RadialGradientBrush>
                </Button.Resources>
                <Button.Background>
                    <StaticResource ResourceKey=" radialBrush "/>
                </Button.Background>
            </Button>
        </StackPanel>
</UserControl>
```

Here, the markup declares a resource with the name *radialBrush* on the *UserControl*, the *StackPanel*, and the *Button*, respectively. Then, you the reference the resource for the button background using the *StaticResource* markup extension. In this case, when the XAML processor finds the resource definition in the resources collection of the button, it stops looking any further and applies that resource straight away. Thus, the resources collection of *Button* overrides the collection defined under the parent element.

One of the most common uses of resources is to define styles.

Styles

One of the key advantages of WPF and Silverlight applications is the rich look and feel they offer for user interfaces. Today's applications—whether they are line-of-business (LOB) applications or other types—demand a high level of user experience (UX). This means that your application doesn't just need to have working functionality and performance but must also provide a good (if not awesome) experience for the user.

Using WPF and Silverlight, it's easy to design visually attractive and rich, jazzy user interfaces. However, if your application has many controls (as is normally the case in large real-world applications), it becomes cumbersome to customize the appearance of each and every control.

Here's where styles come to the rescue. Styles let you implement a consistent look and behavior in Silverlight and WPF applications. They provide a way to easily change the visual appearance of a control. You can use styles to apply a set of one or more properties, resources, and even event handlers to one or more elements.

Suppose that you want to create a number puzzle game with a UI consisting of attractive buttons. You want all the buttons to look similar but you want to do this with the least effort possible. Styles can help you achieve this outcome. Figure 5-2 shows an example of using styles to create the UI.

8	2	4
7	6	
3	1	5

FIGURE 5-2 Using styles to implement a consistent look.

Any element that derives from *FrameworkElement* can have a style applied to it.

Figure 5-3 shows another example of a Silverlight Button control using styles.

FIGURE 5-3 Using styles.

Defining Styles

You define styles using the *Style* element. The *Style* element has a *TargetType* attribute that specifies the object to which the style will be applied and a *Key* attribute to uniquely identify the style. You will use this *Key* value later with the *StaticResource* markup extension to apply the style. A *Style* element contains one or more *Setter* elements. A *Setter* element has a *Property* attribute that specifies which property this *Setter* is changing and a *Value* attribute that specifies the property value.

The following XAML snippet shows a simple example of defining a style:

```
<UserControl.Resources>
      <Style x:Key="ButtonStyle" TargetType="Button">
          <Setter Property="FontSize" Value="16" />
      </Style>
</UserControl.Resources>
<StackPanel>
    <Button Content="Submit" Width="150" Height="60"
        Style="{StaticResource ButtonStyle}" x:Name="b1"/>
    <Button Content="OK" Width="150" Height="60"
        Style="{StaticResource ButtonStyle}" x:Name="b2"/>
    <RadioButton Content="Business"></RadioButton>
</StackPanel>
```

The preceding code defines a style resource named *ButtonStyle* that creates a font style that you want to apply to objects of type *Button*. The Style contains only one *Setter* element that sets the *FontSize* property. In the preceding markup, within the *StackPanel*, you create three controls:

```
<StackPanel>
    <Button Content="Submit" Width="150" Height="60"
        Style="{StaticResource ButtonStyle}" x:Name="b1"/>
    <Button Content="OK" Width="150" Height="60"
        Style="{StaticResource ButtonStyle}" x:Name="b2"/>
    <RadioButton Content="Business"></RadioButton>
</StackPanel>
```

However, you apply the style only to the *Button* controls, excluding the *RadioButton* control. This is for two reasons: first, the *TargetType* of the style is set to be *Button*; second, the *Style* property of the *Button* controls is explicitly set to *ButtonStyle*.

Even if you apply the *ButtonStyle* to the *RadioButton* control, it will not succeed; in fact, doing so will result in an exception, because the *TargetType* of the style is *Button*.

 Note You must set the *TargetType* property when you create a style. If you do not, the XAML processor throws an exception.

Instead of using attribute syntax, you can also use property element syntax to define styles. The following XAML snippet shows an example of this:

```xml
<UserControl.Resources>
        <Style x:Key="ButtonStyle" TargetType="Button">
            <Setter Property="Background">
                <Setter.Value>
                    <LinearGradientBrush StartPoint="0,0.5" EndPoint="1,0.5">
                        <GradientStop Color="Black" Offset="0.75"/>
                        <GradientStop Color="Orchid"/>
                    </LinearGradientBrush>
                    </Setter.Value>
                </Setter>
        </Style>
</UserControl.Resources>
<StackPanel>
    <Button Content="Submit" Width="150" Height="60" Style="{StaticResource ButtonStyle}"
x:Name="b1"/>
</StackPanel>
```

This is a more elaborate approach to defining styles. Developers often prefer the more compact approach of using attributes with styles.

You can also define inline styles using XAML, instead of specifying styles through resources. The following XAML, when used in a Silverlight application, applies a style with a custom linear gradient brush to a button:

```xml
<Button Height="90" Width="200">
        <Button.Style>
            <Style TargetType="Button">
                <Setter Property="Button.Background">
                    <Setter.Value>
                        <LinearGradientBrush StartPoint="0,0.5" EndPoint="1,0.5">
                            <GradientStop Color="Black" Offset="0.75"/>
                            <GradientStop Color="Orchid"/>
                        </LinearGradientBrush>
                    </Setter.Value>
                </Setter>
            </Style>
        </Button.Style>
    </Button>
```

If you were to use the preceding style in a WPF application, the only difference would be that you wouldn't have to specify the *TargetType* property—it's considered implicit.

The following XAML snippet creates a *ListBox* in which only one *ListBoxItem* has a large font:

```
<StackPanel>
        <ListBox Width="150" Height="60" x:Name="b1">

            <ListBoxItem Content="B" >
                <ListBoxItem.Style>
                    <Style TargetType="ListBoxItem">
                        <Setter Property="FontSize" Value="24"/>
                    </Style>
                </ListBoxItem.Style>
            </ListBoxItem>
            <ListBoxItem Content="A" />
            <ListBoxItem Content="C" />
            <ListBoxItem />
        </ListBox>
</StackPanel>
```

Figure 5-4 shows the outcome.

FIGURE 5-4 Using inline styles.

A style defined inline instead of in a resource is limited in scope to the containing element. It has no resource key; therefore, you cannot reuse it, even for other elements of the same type.

A style defined in a resource is more adaptable and useful, and is strongly recommended.

It is invalid to specify more than one value in a single *Setter* element. The following XAML snippet will cause the compiler error "Property is set more than once" because a single *Setter* is trying to set both the font and the background:

```
<UserControl.Resources>
        <Style x:Key="ButtonStyle" TargetType="Button">
            <Setter Property="FontSize" Value="16" Property="Background" Value="Orchid"/>
        </Style>
</UserControl.Resources>
<StackPanel>
        <Button Content="Submit" Width="150" Height="60"
            Style="{StaticResource ButtonStyle}" x:Name="b1"/>
        <Button Content="OK" Width="150" Height="60"
             Style="{StaticResource ButtonStyle}" x:Name="b2"/>
        <RadioButton Content="Business"></RadioButton>
</StackPanel>
```

Note It is a recommended that you create styles in the Assets folder. You can also store styles and resources in a separate library that you can reuse across several Silverlight applications.

Implicit Styles

Supported By	
WPF	Yes
Silverlight	Yes

From Silverlight 4 onward, you can set styles implicitly by omitting the *x:Key* attribute in the *Style* definition. When you leave out the *x:Key* attribute, the *TargetType* is used as the *x:Key*, thus making the style implicit for all the objects of that type.

The following XAML snippet illustrates the use of implicit styles:

```
<UserControl.Resources>
      <Style TargetType="Button">
          <Setter Property="FontSize" Value="16" />
      </Style>
</UserControl.Resources>
<StackPanel>
      <Button Content="Submit" Width="150" Height="60"  x:Name="b1"/>
      <Button Content="OK" Width="150" Height="60" x:Name="b2"/>
      <ToggleButton Height="200" Width="200" Content="text"></ToggleButton>
</StackPanel>
```

Here, no *x:Key* was specified for the style; therefore, it will be applied to all buttons—even if they omit the *StaticResource* markup extension. This is because of the implicit style feature.

In the following XAML snippet, an explicit style overrides the implicit style:

```
<UserControl.Resources>
      <Style TargetType="Button">
          <Setter Property="FontSize" Value="16" />
      </Style>
      <Style x:Key="ButtonStyle" TargetType="Button">
          <Setter Property="FontSize" Value="24" />
      </Style>
</UserControl.Resources>
<StackPanel>
      <Button Content="Submit" Width="150" Height="60"  x:Name="b1"/>
      <Button Content="OK" Width="150" Height="60" x:Name="b2"
          Style="{StaticResource ButtonStyle}"/>
      <ToggleButton Height="200" Width="200" Content="text"></ToggleButton>
</StackPanel>
```

The preceding markup will result in a Submit button that uses font size 16, an OK button with font size 24, and a *ToggleButton* with a default font size. Figure 5-5 shows the outcome.

Note If more than one setter in the *Setter* collection has the same *Property* value, the setter that is declared *last* is used. Similarly, if you set a value for the same property in a style and directly on an element, the value set directly on the element takes precedence.

FIGURE 5-5 Overriding implicit styles with explicit ones.

Inheriting Styles

Supported By	
WPF	Yes
Silverlight	Yes

You can reuse an existing style to create a new style and add additional *Setter* elements if required. The *BasedOn* attribute of a *Style* element enables you to implement this functionality.

For example, you could reuse a style named *ButtonStyle* that sets font size to 16 and add a new *Setter* element to set the background to Orchid as follows:

```
<UserControl.Resources>
        <Style x:Key="ButtonStyle" TargetType="Button">
            <Setter Property="FontSize" Value="24" />
        </Style>
        <Style x:Key="InheritedButtonStyle" TargetType="Button"
          BasedOn="{StaticResource ButtonStyle}">
            <Setter Property="Background" Value="Orchid" />
        </Style>
</UserControl.Resources>
<StackPanel>
        <Button Content="Submit" Width="150" Height="60"  x:Name="b1"
            Style="{StaticResource InheritedButtonStyle}"/>
</StackPanel>
```

Here, *InheritedButtonStyle* is a style that inherits or is based on an earlier style, *ButtonStyle*.

Inherited styles, also called *BasedOn* styles, are a great way to apply multiple styles to a control, because you can't use more than one style key in the *StaticResource* reference.

For example, the following XAML snippet is invalid:

```
<Button Content="Submit" Width="150" Height="60" x:Name="b1"
    Style="{StaticResource  Style1 Style2}"/>
```

However, you can achieve the intended result using the *BasedOn* style feature.

> **Tip** You can find some ready-made downloadable styles at the following links:
>
> - *http://www.xamltemplates.net/*
> - *http://gallery.expression.microsoft.com/site/search*
> - *http://reuxables.com*

The Silverlight Toolkit Styles

You'll find a number of pre-created styles that you can use in your applications immediately at *http://www.silverlight.net/learn/videos/all/silverlight-toolkit-using-themes-in-silverlight/*.

If you have a large Line of Business (LoB) application that needs lots of customizations for probably hundreds of controls, you'd be better off defining themes instead of styles. Nikhil Kothari from the Microsoft Developer Division has created a theme primer that you can find at *http://www.nikhilk.net/Silverlight-Themes.aspx*. (Although written for Silverlight 2, the article applies to later versions of Silverlight as well.)

You can find some ready-made themes at *http://www.microsoft.com/downloads/en/details.aspx?FamilyID=e9da0eb8-f31b-4490-85b8-92c2f807df9e&displaylang=en*.

Styles vs. Control Templates

A control template defines the visual appearance of a control. You can customize a control by modifying its default control template. A style can determine the individual properties of a control, whereas a control template determines how the control will display bound data. With a control template, you can collate several smaller controls into a single control to present different views of the bound data.

More on Styles

Creating a project of type Silverlight Business Application automatically creates styles for a business-like template for your pages.

Styles lack support for multiple *TargetType* objects within a single *Style* definition. Therefore, if you want to reuse a *Style* for more than one *TargetType*, such as a *ListBox* and *ComboBox*, you will need to create a common style with a key and then create separate styles for the individual controls to which you want to apply that style and use *BasedOn,* as shown in the following snippet:

```
<UserControl.Resources>
        <Style x:Key="CommonStyle" TargetType="Control">
            <Setter Property="FontSize" Value="24" />
        </Style>
        <Style BasedOn="{StaticResource CommonStyle}" TargetType="ListBox" />
        <Style BasedOn="{StaticResource CommonStyle}" TargetType="ComboBox" />
</UserControl.Resources>
```

If you want to apply alignment to your text using a style, ensure that you use the *TextAlignment* property instead of *HorizontalContentAlignment*. The following XAML snippet shows the correct way to do this:

```xml
<UserControl.Resources>
    <Style x:Key="MyStyle" TargetType="TextBlock">
        <Setter Property="FontSize" Value="24" />
        <Setter Property="TextAlignment" Value="Right" />
    </Style>
</UserControl.Resources>
<StackPanel>
    <TextBlock Text="Submit" Width="150" Height="60"  x:Name="b1" Style="
{StaticResource MyStyle}"/>
</StackPanel>
```

The following code shows a neat little example of using styles and resources with a *ListBox* to customize the appearance of its items:

```xml
<Grid>
        <Grid.Resources>
            <Style x:Key="lstStyle" TargetType="ListBox">
                <Setter Property="Background" Value="PaleGreen"></Setter>
            </Style>
            <Style TargetType="ListBoxItem" >
                <Setter Property="Background">
                    <Setter.Value>
                        <LinearGradientBrush EndPoint="0.5,1" StartPoint="0.5,0">
                            <GradientStop Color="#FF406DC7" Offset="1"/>
                            <GradientStop Color="#FF002C83"/>
                        </LinearGradientBrush>
                    </Setter.Value>
                </Setter>
                <Setter Property="FontFamily"  Value="Trebuchet MS"></Setter>
                <Setter Property="Foreground" Value="White"></Setter>
            </Style>
        </Grid.Resources>
        <ListBox Height="58" HorizontalAlignment="Left" Margin="228,20,0,0" Name="listBox1"
          VerticalAlignment="Top" Width="141" AllowDrop="True"
          Style="{StaticResource lstStyle}">
            <ListBoxItem Content="Trekking"/>
            <ListBoxItem Content="Swimming" />
            <ListBoxItem Content="Cycling" />
            <ListBoxItem Content="Mountaineering" />
            <ListBoxItem Content="Jogging" />
            <ListBoxItem Content="Road Trips" />
            </ListBox>
        <sdk:Label Content="What's your favorite outdoor activity?" Height="28"
          HorizontalAlignment="Left" Margin="33,0,0,0" Name="label1" VerticalAlignment="Top"/>
    </Grid>
```

The output of the preceding code looks like Figure 5-6.

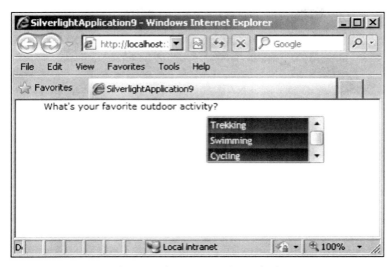

FIGURE 5-6 Using styles to implement a consistent look.

In Chapter 9, "Media, Graphics, and Animation," you will learn about storyboards and animations and can apply them to list boxes and other controls to further enhance their appearance.

The generic.xaml File

A generic.xaml file is typically present in the Themes subfolder of a WPF custom control library or a Silverlight Templated control in a Silverlight Class Library application. This file serves as the default lookup location for any default styles you wish to apply to your controls.

The following XAML snippet shows the contents of a generic.xaml file in a WPF custom control library. The file is located in the Themes subfolder.

```
<ResourceDictionary
    xmlns="http://schemas.microsoft.com/winfx/2006/xaml/presentation"
    xmlns:x="http://schemas.microsoft.com/winfx/2006/xaml"
    xmlns:local="clr-namespace:WpfCustomControlLibrary1">
    <Style TargetType="{x:Type local:CustomControl1}">
        <Setter Property="Template">
            <Setter.Value>
                <ControlTemplate TargetType="{x:Type local:CustomControl1}">
                    <Border Background="{TemplateBinding Background}"
                            BorderBrush="{TemplateBinding BorderBrush}"
                            BorderThickness="{TemplateBinding BorderThickness}">
                    </Border>
                </ControlTemplate>
            </Setter.Value>
        </Setter>
    </Style>
</ResourceDictionary>
```

In generic.xaml only, both *Name* x:*Name* and *x:Key* are optional on Style elements so long as the *TargetType* attribute is specified (the *TargetType* is implicitly used as the key). Another aspect that is unique to generic.xaml is that syntax that references the *{x:Type}* markup extension is supported when you are setting *TargetType* for styles and template resources. This is to support template compatibility and migration with WPF, where the *{x:Type}* markup extension is supported by a backing XAML markup extension. Outside of generic.xaml, the Silverlight XAML parser uses implicit conversion for any property of type *Type*; explicit use of *{x:Type}* is not supported and generates a XAML parse error.

Triggers

Triggers enable you to set or modify attributes of an element based on a specific action. Triggers can either act on single instances of an element or they can affect an entire class of elements.

A simple example of a trigger and its corresponding action is that of a button changing its background color based on a mouse hover or mouse click action.

The *Style*, *ControlTemplate*, and *DataTemplate* elements have a *Triggers* property that contains a set of triggers.

Triggers in WPF are of various types: property triggers, event triggers, data triggers, multi triggers, and multi data triggers.

Property Triggers

Supported By	
WPF	Yes
Silverlight	Yes

Defining a property trigger is simple. You define a *Trigger* element, specify the property change that initiates the trigger, and define the behavior of the trigger.

For example, the following XAML defines a property trigger that changes the font size of the button whenever the mouse hovers over the button:

```
<Window x:Class="WpfApplication.NewMainWindow"
        xmlns="http://schemas.microsoft.com/winfx/2006/xaml/presentation"
        xmlns:x="http://schemas.microsoft.com/winfx/2006/xaml"
        Title="MainWindow" Height="350" Width="525"
        xmlns:sys="clr-namespace:System;assembly=mscorlib"
        xmlns:collections="clr-namespace:System.Collections;assembly=mscorlib"
        xmlns:local="clr-namespace:WpfApplication5"
        >
    <Window.Resources>
        <Style x:Key="ButtonStyle" TargetType="Button">
            <Setter Property="FontSize" Value="16" />
            <Style.Triggers>
                <Trigger Property="IsMouseOver" Value="True">
                    <Setter Property="FontSize" Value="36" />
                </Trigger>
```

```
            </Style.Triggers>
        </Style>
    </Window.Resources>
    <StackPanel>
        <Button Content="Submit" Width="150" Height="60"
            Style="{StaticResource ButtonStyle}" x:Name="b1"/>
    </StackPanel>
</Window>
```

You can also combine two or more properties within a single trigger, as shown in the following example:

```
<Window.Resources>
        <Style x:Key="ButtonStyle" TargetType="Button">
            <Setter Property="FontSize" Value="16" />
            <Style.Triggers>
                <Trigger Property="IsMouseOver" Value="True">
                    <Setter Property="FontSize" Value="36" />
                    <Setter Property="Background" Value="LavenderBlush"/>
                </Trigger>
            </Style.Triggers>
        </Style>
</Window.Resources>
<StackPanel>
    <Button Content="Submit" Width="150" Height="60"
        Style="{StaticResource ButtonStyle}" x:Name="b1"/>
</StackPanel>
```

This markup changes the button's *FontSize* and *Background* properties based on a single property trigger: *IsMouseOver*. Thus, when the user's mouse hovers over the button at runtime, the font size of the *Button* text changes to 36 and its background changes to *LavenderBlush*.

Event Triggers

Supported By	
WPF	Yes
Silverlight	Yes

Event triggers enable you to apply changes to property values in response to events. Event triggers make use of the *Storyboard* element. A *Storyboard* is a collection of one or more *animations*, where an animation is any action such as changing the behavior of elements or transforming their appearances. Chapter 9 covers storyboards and animations in detail.

As an example, the following XAML snippet in a Silverlight application changes the color of a *Rectangle* as it is loaded. The *EventTrigger* property has an attribute called *RoutedEvent* that indicates which event will trigger the action. Silverlight supports only the *Loaded* event in an event trigger:

```
<Rectangle x:Name="rect" Canvas.Top="100"
  Canvas.Left="100" Width="100" Height="100">
        <Rectangle.Fill>
            <SolidColorBrush x:Name="brush" Color="Black"  />
        </Rectangle.Fill>
```

```
            <Rectangle.Triggers>
                <EventTrigger RoutedEvent="Rectangle.Loaded">
                    <BeginStoryboard>
                        <Storyboard>
                            <ColorAnimation Storyboard.TargetName="brush"
                                Storyboard.TargetProperty="Color" To="Magenta"
                                Duration="0:0:6" />
                        </Storyboard>
                    </BeginStoryboard>
                </EventTrigger>
            </Rectangle.Triggers>
        </Rectangle>
```

The following XAML snippet works only in a WPF application. It changes the color of the *ListBox* whenever you select any item in the *ListBox*:

```
<StackPanel x:Name="stackPanel1">
        <ListBox Height="100" Name="listBox1" Width="120">
            <ListBox.Background>
                <SolidColorBrush x:Name="brush" Color="PaleGoldenrod"  />
            </ListBox.Background>
            <ListBoxItem Content="Orange" >
            </ListBoxItem>
            <ListBoxItem Content="Blue" />
            <ListBoxItem Content="Magenta" />
        </ListBox>
        <StackPanel.Triggers>
            <EventTrigger RoutedEvent="ListBox.SelectionChanged" SourceName ="listBox1">
                <EventTrigger.Actions>
                    <BeginStoryboard>
                        <Storyboard>
                            <ColorAnimation Storyboard.TargetName="brush"
                                Storyboard.TargetProperty="Color" To="Tomato"   Duration="0:0:1" />
                        </Storyboard>
                    </BeginStoryboard>
                </EventTrigger.Actions>
            </EventTrigger>
        </StackPanel.Triggers>
    </StackPanel>
```

The preceding code defines a *ListBox* with a *SolidBrush* named *"brush"* that has a background color of *PaleGoldenrod*. It then creates a trigger on the *StackPanel* that targets the brush assigned to the *ListBox* and includes a *Storyboard* that changes the color to blue. This type of trigger is an event trigger, because it fires only when the event takes place.

MultiTriggers

Supported By	
WPF	Yes
Silverlight	No

MultiTriggers let you apply changes to property values based on the state of multiple properties.

The following markup demonstrates an example of a *MultiTrigger*:

```
<Window.Resources>
    <Style TargetType="{x:Type Button}">
        <Style.Triggers>
            <MultiTrigger>
                <MultiTrigger.Conditions>
                    <Condition Property="IsHitTestVisible" Value="True" />
                    <Condition Property="IsCancel" Value="True" />
                </MultiTrigger.Conditions>
                <Setter Property="Background" Value="Yellow" />
            </MultiTrigger>
        </Style.Triggers>
    </Style>
</Window.Resources>
<StackPanel x:Name="stackPanel1">
    <Button Content="" Height=" 60" Width=" 200" IsCancel="True" />
</StackPanel>
```

When the XAML processor encounters a button with *IsHitTestVisible* and *IsCancel* properties set to *true*, the *MultiTrigger* fires and the button background becomes yellow.

DataTrigger

Supported By	
WPF	Yes
Silverlight	No

*DataTrigger*s provide the ability to apply changes to property values in response to changes in data-bound property values.

The following markup in a WPF application demonstrates an example of a *DataTrigger*:

```
<Window.Resources>
        <local:Books x:Key="AuthorsData"/>
        <Style TargetType="DataGridRow">
            <Style.Triggers>
                <DataTrigger Binding="{Binding Path=Author}" Value="Jane Austen">
                    <Setter Property="Background" Value="Yellow" />
                </DataTrigger>
            </Style.Triggers>
        </Style>
        <DataTemplate DataType="{x:Type local:Book}">
            <Canvas Width="160" Height="20">
                <TextBlock FontSize="12"
              Width="130" Canvas.Left="0" Text="{Binding Path=Name}"/>
                <TextBlock FontSize="12" Width="30"
                 Canvas.Left="130" Text="{Binding Path=Author}"/>
            </Canvas>
        </DataTemplate>
    </Window.Resources>
    <StackPanel>
        <DataGrid Width="241" HorizontalAlignment="Center" Background="Beige"
        ItemsSource="{Binding Source={StaticResource AuthorsData}}"/>
    </StackPanel>
```

The markup creates a *DataGrid* where all the rows that contain data where *"author"* is *"Jane Austen"* have a yellow background.

The markup assumes that you have created the following classes in the code-behind:

```
public class Books : ObservableCollection<Book>
    {
        public Books()
            : base()
        {
            Add(new Book("Pride and Prejudice", "Jane Austen"));
            Add(new Book("Far from the Madding Crowd", "Thomas Hardy"));
            Add(new Book("The Day of the Jackal", "Frederick Forsyth"));
            Add(new Book("Blink", "Malcolm Gladwell"));
            Add(new Book("The Color Purple", "Alice Walker"));
            Add(new Book("Emma", "Jane Austen"));
        }
    }
    public class Book
    {
        private string name;
        private string author;
        public Book(string nm, string au)
        {
            this.name = nm;
            this.author = au;
        }
        public string Name
        {
            get { return name; }
            set { name = value; }
        }
        public string Author
        {
            get { return author; }
            set { author = value; }
        }
    }
```

Here, *Books* is an *ObservableCollection* of *Book*, which defines two properties: *Author* and *Name*.

Interaction Triggers

Microsoft Expression Blend also supports a new set of triggers for use with Silverlight called *interaction triggers*. Because Silverlight otherwise supports only event triggers, interaction triggers can be very useful.

Interaction triggers require you to reference the interactivity DLLs provided by Expression Blend.

Thus you will need to have the Microsoft Expression Blend SDK installed on your computer.

By default, when you create a Silverlight (4.0 and later) application using Expression Blend, it does not automatically add references to the interactivity DLLs to your XAML; instead, they're added when you begin an interaction trigger. Here's an example of how you can do that.

Add an Interaction Trigger in Expression Blend

1. Open the *Assets* pane, select *Behaviors,* and then drag the *GoToStateAction* behavior onto the object for which you want to set the interaction trigger.

    Alternatively, you can just add a reference to the System.Windows.Interactivity.dll assembly located in: {Program Files}\Microsoft SDKs\Expression\Blend *XX*\Interactivity\Libraries\ Silverlight, where *XX* is the version of Blend you installed; and then include the respective behavior.

    The following XAML markup demonstrates how you can trigger an interaction between two buttons: clicking one button causes another to behave as though it were also clicked:

```
<UserControl
  xmlns="http://schemas.microsoft.com/winfx/2006/xaml/presentation"
  xmlns:x="http://schemas.microsoft.com/winfx/2006/xaml"
  xmlns:i="http://schemas.microsoft.com/expression/2010/interactivity"
  xmlns:ei="http://schemas.microsoft.com/expression/2010/interactions"
  xmlns:d="http://schemas.microsoft.com/expression/blend/2008"
  xmlns:mc="http://schemas.openxmlformats.org/markup-compatibility/2006"
  mc:Ignorable="d"
  x:Class="SilverlightApplication11.MainPage"
  Width="640" Height="480">
  <Grid>
    <VisualStateManager.VisualStateGroups>
      <VisualStateGroup x:Name="VisualStateGroup"/>
    </VisualStateManager.VisualStateGroups>
    <Button x:Name="btn1" Height="45" Margin="260,123,260,0" VerticalAlignment="Top"
      Width="120" Content="Click Here" d:LayoutOverrides="HorizontalAlignment">
      <i:Interaction.Triggers>
        <i:EventTrigger EventName="Click">
          <ei:GoToStateAction TargetName="btn2" StateName="Pressed"/>
        </i:EventTrigger>
      </i:Interaction.Triggers>
    </Button>
    <Button x:Name="btn2" Height="45" Width="120" Content="OK" Background="Brown"/>
  </Grid>
</UserControl>
```

    Clicking the first button, Click Here, causes the second button to appear in a pressed state.

You can read more about interaction triggers and behaviors at the following links: *http://www. silverlightshow.net/items/Behaviors-and-Triggers-in-Silverlight-3.aspx* and *http://msdn.microsoft.com/ en-us/library/ff726403%28v=Expression.40%29.aspx.*

Troubleshooting Resources, Styles, and Triggers

If you reference a style in a *StaticResource* extension and the style is not defined at all in your application, you will get an *XamlParseException*. However, a *XamlParseException* can occur in several other scenarios as well. For example, if you define a style twice in your application with the same key identifier, you will get a *XamlParseException*. The following code shows an example of such a scenario:

```
<Grid.Resources>
    <Style x:Key="lstStyle" TargetType="ListBox">
      <Setter Property="BorderBrush" Value="Blue"></Setter>
    </Style>
    <Style x:Key="lstStyle" TargetType="ListBox">
      <Setter Property="Background" Value="PaleGreen"></Setter>
    </Style>
<Grid.Resources>
```

To identify why exactly the exception occurred and determine the cause for it, you should view the inner exception of the *XamlParseException* and check its *Message* property. For example, in this case, the message will be "The dictionary key 'lstStyle' is already used. Key attributes are used as keys when inserting objects into a dictionary and must be unique."

The parse exception occurs because both styles have the same key: *lstStyle*.

If the inner exception message says "Cannot find a Resource with the Name/Key", it means that you have specified an invalid or missing resource name or key.

A good approach to debugging a *XamlParseException* is to set the debugger to break on exceptions and then view the call stack.

You can find a few helpful resources on this topic at:

- *http://markegilbert.wordpress.com/2008/03/15/debugging-xaml/*

- *http://joshsmithonwpf.wordpress.com/2007/03/29/tips-on-how-to-debug-and-learn-about-wpf/*

- *http://msdn.microsoft.com/en-us/library/system.windows.markup.xamlparseexception.aspx*

Summary

This chapter introduced the concept of resources, styles, and triggers, all of which are essential components in XAML-based applications targeted at either WPF or Silverlight. By using a combination of resources and styles, you can reuse control styles and properties and also promote consistency throughout your application. Your application will be better organized, easy to maintain, and capable of achieving complex functionality through declarative syntax alone. Understanding how to use resources, styles, and triggers will go a long way toward making you a proficient developer.

PART 3

XAML User Interface Controls

CHAPTER 6

Layout and Positioning System

In this chapter:

- WPF and Silverlight Layout System

- XAML Layout and Positioning Controls

- Common Sizing and Positioning Dependency Properties

- Summary

Usability is a measure of how well, how comfortably, and how fast users can achieve, perform, or successfully execute the functionality of an application—and how satisfied users are at the end of their interaction with the application in terms of achieving their goals.

An efficient, interactive, rich, and usable user interface is a key feature for any successful application. The user interface layout and the sizing and positioning of controls play a vital role in improving the usability of the application service. Generally you would consider the following factors when defining the user interface:

- **Scope of the application**   Some applications must support different types of devices—such as laptops, desktops, mobile phones, and tablets. Each device is likely to have a different screen size and each may have a different screen resolution.

- **Runtime changes**   Depending on the device and the operating system, the application's window size may change at runtime. (The user might resize a window.)

- **Globalization**   Many applications must be able to support different languages, which may include character sets (single- and multi-byte versions) and language direction (left to right and right to left languages).

- **Mode changes**   Rich Internet Applications (RIAs) can work in different modes—such as in-browser mode and out-of-browser mode (OOB)—that you can implement using the Silverlight platform.

This chapter covers the WPF and Silverlight layout system as well as various XAML layout and positioning controls and attributes in details.

The Layout System

Supported By	
WPF	Yes
Silverlight	Yes

Every time the screen is loaded for the first time or refreshed, the window size changes, or a child element is updated (such as change in the display condition of the control or an added or removed child control through code-behind), the WPF and Silverlight layout system calculates the relative sizing and position for each control within the given window, page, or plug-in at runtime. It then renders and arranges the controls to build the dynamic user interface. The layout process includes two distinctive steps:

- **The Measuring Step** In this step the layout system will query each child element of each parent to calculate the desired size, and returns the required values back to the parent *Panel* or other container object. This is a recursive process in which each parent asks its child elements to calculate their desired sizes and return the values back to that parent.

- **The Arranging Step** After obtaining the desired sizes from each child element, the parent container object element determines the best possible size and the bounding box for each child control. It then positions the child control within the bounding box. This process repeats for each child element. When child layout is complete, execution returns back to the container object's parent element. This process repeats to build the user interface dynamically.

The bounding box—the layout slot for a child element—is a rectangle. You can obtain the dimensions of the bounding box rectangle for any *FrameworkElement* control by calling the *LayoutInformation.GetLayoutSlot* method from code-behind. As shown here, the layout slot for a child element can be of the same size as the child element or greater than the child element's size—or the child element size may actually be larger than the layout slot, in which case the child element gets clipped and will be only partially visible.

> **More Info** See the MSDN page at *http://msdn.microsoft.com/en-us/library/ms745058.aspx* for more information about the WPF Layout System. See *http://msdn.microsoft.com/en-us/library/cc645025.aspx* for more information about the Silverlight Layout System.

To demonstrate the WPF and Silverlight layout system, create a WPF application project and name it **DemonstratingLayoutSystem**. Create a new folder named **res** under the project and add three images named **1.jpg**, **2.jpg**, and **Buddy.png** as resource files. Now open the XAML code for the *MainWindow.xaml* file and update it as shown here (changes in bold text):

```
<Window x:Class="DemonstratingLayoutSystem.MainWindow"
        xmlns="http://schemas.microsoft.com/winfx/2006/xaml/presentation"
        xmlns:x="http://schemas.microsoft.com/winfx/2006/xaml"
```

```
        Title="DemonstratingLayoutSystem" Height="700" Width="525">
    <StackPanel>
        <TextBlock
            Text="WPF Layout System Demonstration"
            FontSize="20"
            TextAlignment="Center"
            TextWrapping="Wrap"
            Margin="5"/>
        <WrapPanel Orientation="Horizontal">
            <Image Width="150" Height="100" Margin="2" Source="res/1.jpg"/>
            <Image Width="150" Height="100" Margin="2" Source="res/2.jpg"/>
        </WrapPanel>
        <Image Source="res/Buddy.png" Margin="2"/>
    </StackPanel>
</Window>
```

Layout Slot Size > Child Element Size

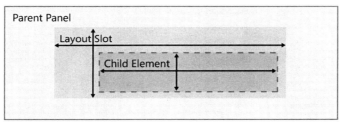

Layout Slot Size = Child Element Size

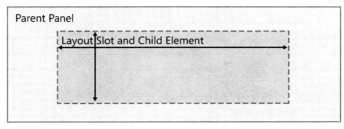

Layout Slot Size < Child Element Size
The Chid Element Is Partially Clipped

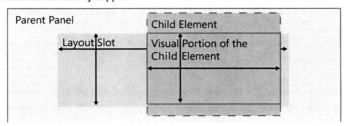

The preceding code changed the main window *Height* and *Width* properties to accommodate all added controls. It also added a *StackPanel* layout and positioning control as the root layout control, and added a *WrapPanel* layout and positioning control as its child to hold the image collection.

Note You can use the same XAML code to create a Silverlight application. The only difference is that the *WrapPanel* control is part of the default WPF user controls library. For Silverlight, it is available in the Silverlight toolkit (*http://silverlight.codeplex.com/*). For Silverlight, you need to add a reference to the Silverlight toolkit to insert the *WrapPanel* control.

Now when you save, compile, and run the project, to render the user interface dynamically the WPF layout system will first perform the measuring step, as shown in Figure 6-1.

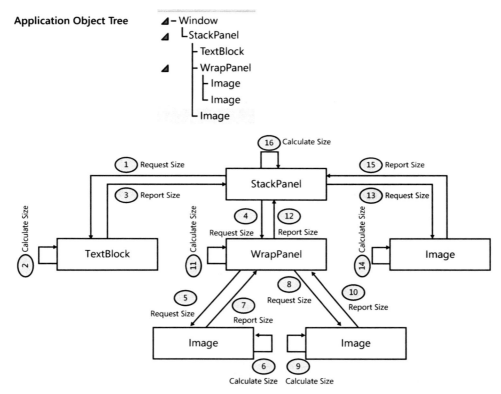

FIGURE 6-1 Understanding the measuring step of the WPF/Silverlight layout system to determine the size and position of each element control.

Figure 6-1 demonstrates how the recursive measuring step of the WPF/Silverlight layout system, following the object tree, reaches out to each child element control to calculate the desired size of each element and report back to its corresponding parent control.

When calculating the desired size of each child control, the layout system measuring process follows two steps to set the *UIElement.DesiredSize* property:

- The child element first considers the core sizing properties such as *Visibility* and *Clip*.

- The child element then measures the defined set *FrameworkElement* properties such as *Height*, *Width*, *MinHeight*, *MinWeight*, *Margin*, and *Style*.

Next, the layout system considers defined child control alignment properties such as *Orientation* and *Dock*.

After this the parent *Panel* determines the best possible size for each child control and the bounding box for each child control. It positions the child control within the bounding box and returns back to its parent element. The output of this example is shown in Figure 6-2.

FIGURE 6-2   The layout system with the default defined window size.

Now resize the window. As you resize the application window, the layout system will rearrange each child control based on the size of the window and the defined sizing properties for each control. In Figure 6-3 you will notice that upon resizing the window, the following occurs:

- The *TextBlock* content gets wrapped to multiple lines because the *TextWrapping* property is set to *Wrap*; it is center-aligned because the *TextAlignment* property is set to *Center*.

- The *WrapPanel* layout and positioning control arranges the child controls horizontally because the *Orientation* property is set to *Horizontal*.

- The child *Image* controls within *WrapPanel* arrange automatically based on the size of the application window. (Compare Figures 6-2 and 6-3.) The second image is shifted to the second row (Figure 6-3). You will also notice that the position and location of both images are rearranged. However, their height and width stays the same, because each Image control's *Height* and *Width* properties are set explicitly.

- The final *Image* control added in the *StackPanel* does not explicitly define its *Height* and *Width* properties, so its size is adjusted based on the window's size.

FIGURE 6-3　Resizing and rearrangement of controls based on the window's resize.

Caution　By now you probably have noticed that the layout system processes the measuring and calculation and arranging steps at runtime when application user interface needs rendering and redrawing. This capability makes the application more flexible and usable, but at the same time the overall computing and rendering process can slow down the application performance. For example, the *Canvas* layout and positioning control is simpler and more straightforward compared to the complex *Grid* layout and positioning control—which naturally takes comparatively more time to render. To achieve maximum application user interface rending performance, use the most appropriate set of layout and positioning controls and define the overall user interface layout with the minimum possible number of controls.

XAML Layout and Positioning Controls

As discussed in Chapter 2, "Object Elements and Attributes," the *System.Windows.Controls.Panel* is a base class of layout containers and provides a set of layout and positioning controls that range from very basic to advanced. These controls act as a main or subcontainer for group of user controls so that you can arrange them in specific positions and in a particular order to build a meaningful user interface.

> **Note** The WPF *Panel* class provides the full set of layout and positioning controls. However, the Silverlight *Panel* class includes all the key layout and positioning controls as part of the default library; remaining controls such as *WrapPanel* are part of the Silverlight toolkit (*http://silverlight.codeplex.com/*). To use these latter controls, you need to add a reference to the Silverlight toolkit. The following sections specify whether the layout and positioning control being discussed is part of the default Silverlight platform (specified as *Default Control*) or is available with the Silverlight toolkit (*Toolkit Control*).

Canvas

Supported By	
WPF	Yes
Silverlight	Yes (Default Control)

The *System.Windows.Controls.Canvas* layout and positioning control is the simplest control. It provides Window Forms such as layout capabilities, letting you place controls using absolute positioning, defined with *x* and *y* coordinates. The coordinates are relative to the parent *Canvas* control.

> **Caution** If you do not explicitly define coordinates for *Canvas* controls or if you define the same coordinate for multiple controls, they will overlap. The *ZIndex* property defines the overlapping behavior (which control appears on top) when controls overlap. You'll see more about this topic later in this section.

The WPF version of the *Canvas* class provides four attached properties: The *Left* and *Right* attached properties control the *x* coordinate; the *Top* and *Bottom* attached properties control the *y* coordinate.

- **Canvas.Top**   This property can be set in XAML and is read/write through code-behind. It determines the position of the top edge of an element relative to the top edge of its parent *Canvas* element. This attached property is available for both WPF and Silverlight.

- **Canvas.Bottom**   This property can be set in XAML and is read/write through code-behind. It determines the position of the bottom edge of an element relative to the bottom edge of its parent canvas element. This attached property is available only in WPF.

- **Canvas.Left**   This property can be set in XAML and is read/write through code-behind. It determines the position of the left edge of an element relative to the left side of its parent *Canvas* element. This attached property is available for both WPF and Silverlight.

- **Canvas.Right**   This property can be set in XAML and is read/write through code-behind. It determines the position of the right edge of an element relative to the right side of its parent *Canvas* element. This attached property is available only in WPF.

Figure 6-4 illustrates positioning a child element using these four *Canvas* attached properties.

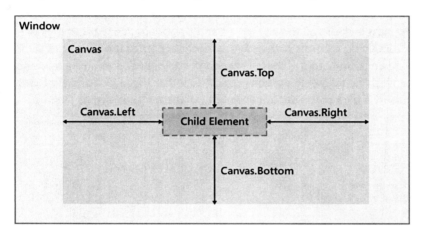

FIGURE 6-4   *Top, Bottom, Left,* and *Right* attached properties of the *Canvas* control to position a child element.

The following WPF application XAML code snippet demonstrates the use of these attached properties (see bold font) for several *Button* controls to place them in absolute positions relative to their parent *Canvas* element:

```
<Window x:Class="LayoutControlsExample.MainWindow"
        xmlns="http://schemas.microsoft.com/winfx/2006/xaml/presentation"
        xmlns:x="http://schemas.microsoft.com/winfx/2006/xaml"
        Title="MainWindow" Height="350" Width="525">
    <Canvas Background="LightBlue" Height="300" Width="500">
        <Button
            Canvas.Top="0"
            Canvas.Left="0"
            Content="Top=0 and Left=0"/>
        <Button
            Canvas.Top="50"
            Canvas.Left="100"
            Canvas.Bottom="0"
            Canvas.Right="0"
            Content="Top=50 and Left=100 and Bottom=0 and Right=0"/>
        <Button
            Canvas.Top="150"
            Canvas.Left="250"
            Content="Top=150 and Left=250"/>
        <Button
            Canvas.Bottom="0"
```

```
        Canvas.Right="0"
        Content="Bottom=0 and Right=0"/>
    </Canvas>
</Window>
```

If you create, compile, and run the project, you will see the output shown in Figure 6-5.

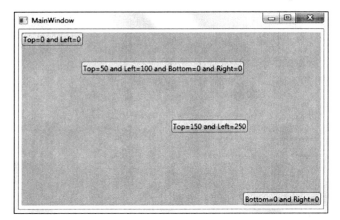

FIGURE 6-5 Demonstrating *Top, Bottom, Left,* and *Right* attached properties of the *Canvas* control.

Note Notice that in the preceding code snippet, the button with the content *"Top=50 and Left=100 and Bottom=0 and Right=0"* defines all four attached properties. However, as shown in the output in Figure 6-5, when both *Top* and *Bottom* attached properties are defined for a child control, the *Top* property takes priority and will be considered instead of the *Bottom* property. Similarly when both *Left* and *Right* attached properties are defined for a child control, the *Left* property takes priority, and it will be considered instead of the *Right* property.

Absolute positions for child controls are relative to the immediate parent *Canvas* control. To demonstrate this, let's add an additional *Canvas* control with white background as a child control to the existing *Canvas* and move the last two buttons into the child *Canvas* control, as shown here in bold:

```
<Window x:Class="LayoutControlsExample.MainWindow"
        xmlns="http://schemas.microsoft.com/winfx/2006/xaml/presentation"
        xmlns:x="http://schemas.microsoft.com/winfx/2006/xaml"
        Title="MainWindow" Height="350" Width="525">
    <Canvas Background="LightBlue" Height="300" Width="500">
        <Button
            Canvas.Top="0"
            Canvas.Left="0"
            Content="Top=0 and Left=0"/>
        <Button
            Canvas.Top="50"
            Canvas.Left="100"
            Canvas.Bottom="0"
```

```
                    Canvas.Right="0"
                    Content="Top=50 and Left=100 and Bottom=0 and Right=0"/>
            <Canvas Background="White" Top="80" Left="50" Height="200" Width="400">
                <Button
                    Canvas.Top="150"
                    Canvas.Left="250"
                    Content="Top=150 and Left=250"/>
                <Button
                    Canvas.Bottom="0"
                    Canvas.Right="0"
                    Content="Bottom=0 and Right=0"/>
            </Canvas>
        </Canvas>
    </Window>
```

Compile and run the project. You will get the output shown in Figure 6-6.

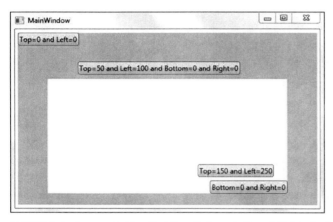

FIGURE 6-6 Demonstrating that *Top, Bottom, Left,* and *Right* attached properties relate to the immediate parent *Canvas* control.

The *Canvas* layout and positioning control facilitates absolute positioning of its child controls—it does not provide other layout control features such as the following:

- Positioning child elements relative to other layout controls such as *StackPanel* or *Grid*.

- Automatic resizing and positioning of child controls when a user resizes the application window. As shown in Figure 6-7, when you use the *Canvas* control, child controls will not resize or adjust to the resized window. Instead, the child controls will maintain their original size. Depending on the resize results, child controls may become partially or completely invisible.

Sometimes two or more controls may overlap each other. In that case for WPF applications, you can use the *Panel.ZIndex* attached property value to determine which overlapping control will appear in the foreground and which one will appear in the background. Higher *ZIndex* values mean that the control will appear closer to the foreground; lower *ZIndex* values place the control further toward the background. To demonstrate this, change the *Button* controls within the child *Canvas* control as shown here (in bold text) so that they overlap. The *ZIndex* values will now determine which button appears in the foreground.

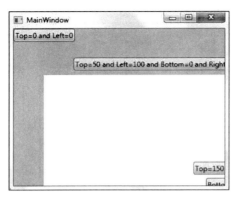

FIGURE 6-7 Absolutely positioned child controls within the *Canvas* control.

```
......
        <Canvas Background="White" Top="80" Left="50" Height="200" Width="400">
            <Button
                Canvas.Top="50"
                Canvas.Left="50"
                Content="Button One"
                Panel.ZIndex="50"/>
            <Button
                Canvas.Top="40"
                Canvas.Left="70"
                Content="Button Two"
                Panel.ZIndex="40"/>
        </Canvas>
......
```

The preceding code defines one *Button* control with a *ZIndex* value of *50* and another with a *ZIndex* of *40*. If you compile and run the project now, the button with the *ZIndex* value of *50* appears in the foreground, while the button with the *ZIndex* value *40* appears below it. As a result, the latter button is only partially visible, as shown in Figure 6-8.

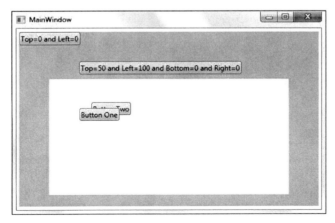

FIGURE 6-8 The *Panel.ZIndex* attached property of the WPF platform controls which child element appears in the foreground and which one appears in the background.

Caution The *Panel.ZIndex* attached property is available only for the WPF platform. It's not available to the Silverlight platform.

StackPanel

Supported By	
WPF	Yes
Silverlight	Yes (Default Control)

WPF and Silverlight provide a series of layout and positioning controls, of which the *System. Windows.Controls.StackPanel* is probably the simplest. It provides relative positioning based on the Window, Page, or UserControl's window size.

As illustrated in Figure 6-9, you can use the *StackPanel* control to stack a collection of child controls vertically (the default) or horizontally using the *StackPanel.Orientation* property. The collection of child controls can also include one or more layout and positioning controls.

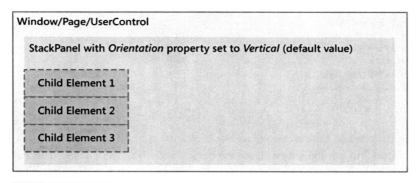

FIGURE 6-9 The *StackPanel.Orientation* property determines the direction to stack children control vertically or horizontally.

To test it, let's replace the *Canvas* layout and positioning controls (both the parent and child *Canvas* controls) from the previous example and adjust the *Button* control properties appropriately. In the following code snippet, the changes are highlighted in bold text.

```
<Window x:Class="LayoutControlsExample.MainWindow"
        xmlns="http://schemas.microsoft.com/winfx/2006/xaml/presentation"
        xmlns:x="http://schemas.microsoft.com/winfx/2006/xaml"
        Title="MainWindow" Height="350" Width="525">
    <StackPanel Background="LightBlue" Height="300" Width="500">
        <Button Content="Button 1" Margin="2"/>
        <Button Content="Button 2" Margin="2"/>
        <StackPanel
            Background="White"
            Height="200"
            Orientation="Vertical">
            <Button Content="Button 3" Margin="2"/>
            <Button Content="Button 4" Margin="2"/>
        </StackPanel>
    </StackPanel>
</Window>
```

The preceding code snippet defines two nested stack panels. The *Orientation* property is not set for the root stack panel but for the child stack panel—it's set to *Vertical*. However, the controls should appear stacked vertically because vertical is the default setting. If you compile and run the project, you will find the result as expected, shown in Figure 6-10.

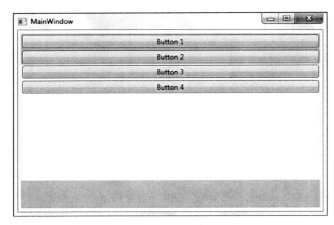

FIGURE 6-10 *StackPanel* layout and positioning controls stacking all child elements vertically.

Now change the *Orientation* property of the child *StackPanel* control from *Vertical* to *Horizontal* (as shown here in bold).

```
<Window x:Class="LayoutControlsExample.MainWindow"
        xmlns="http://schemas.microsoft.com/winfx/2006/xaml/presentation"
        xmlns:x="http://schemas.microsoft.com/winfx/2006/xaml"
        Title="MainWindow" Height="350" Width="525">
```

```
<StackPanel Background="LightBlue" Height="300" Width="500">
    <Button Content="Button 1" Margin="2"/>
    <Button Content="Button 2" Margin="2"/>
    <StackPanel
        Background="White"
        Height="200"
        Orientation="Horizontal">
        <Button Content="Button 3" Margin="2"/>
        <Button Content="Button 4" Margin="2"/>
    </StackPanel>
</StackPanel>
</Window>
```

As shown in Figure 6-11, the change causes Button 3 and Button 4 to be stacked horizontally.

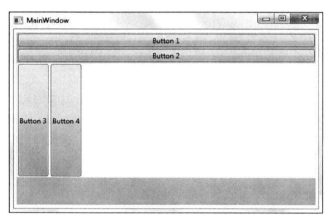

FIGURE 6-11   Setting the child *StackPanel Orientation* to *Horizontal* to stack its child elements horizontally.

You probably have noticed two things from Figures 6-10 and 6-11:

- Collections of child elements are positioned according to the properties set for the *immediate parent element*. The nested *StackPanel* has its *Orientation* property set to *Horizontal*. Even though its parent *StackPanel* has the default vertical orientation, it stacks its child controls horizontally.

- The default value of the *HorizontalAlignment* and *VerticalAlignment* of child controls under the *StackPanel* control is set to *Stretch*. Because the example defined no specific *Height* and *Width* properties for the buttons, the layout engine adjusts the button *Width* and *Height* to cover the entire available area.

Note If you resize your sample application window, then some of the button controls will not be visible (depending on the resized window size). *StackPanel* implements the *IScrollInfo* interface so that you can wrap the host *StackPanel* control in a *ScrollViewer* control to implement horizontal and/or vertical scroll bars. For more information on the *ScrollViewer* control, see Chapter 7, "Forms and Functional Controls."

Along with the *StackPanel.Orientation* property of the *StackPanel* control, you can also use the *FrameworkElement.FlowDirection* property to set the direction of child controls (in the context of the parent element) to *LeftToRight* (default setting) or *RightToLeft*.

> **Note** The *FrameworkElement.FlowDirection* property is not specific to the *StackPanel* control; it is applicable to all controls that inherit from the *FrameworkElement* class. Also, it is important to note that you can only set the direction to either left to right or right to left. Top-to-bottom or bottom-to-top settings are not available.

To demonstrate the *FlowDirection* property, update the nested child *StackPanel* control in the preceding sample application to set the *FlowDirection* property to *RightToLeft,* as shown here in bold font.

```
<StackPanel
    Background="White"
    Height="200"
    Orientation="Horizontal"
    FlowDirection="RightToLeft">
    <Button Content="Button 3" Margin="2"/>
    <Button Content="Button 4" Margin="2"/>
</StackPanel>
```

When you compile and run the project, Button 3 and Button 4 are now arranged in the right-to-left direction, as shown in Figure 6-12.

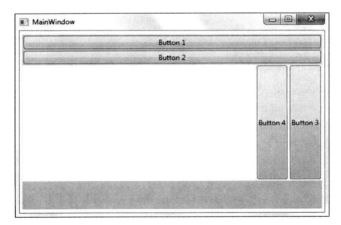

FIGURE 6-12   The *FrameworkElement.FlowDirection* property.

Grid

Supported By	
WPF	Yes
Silverlight	Yes (Default Control)

The *Grid* is a relatively complex layout and positioning control that has more sophisticated capabilities for arranging child controls in a tabular matrix format. You do that by adding the child controls to specific rows and columns of the *Grid* control. Figure 6-13 illustrates the row and column definitions of a *Grid* control.

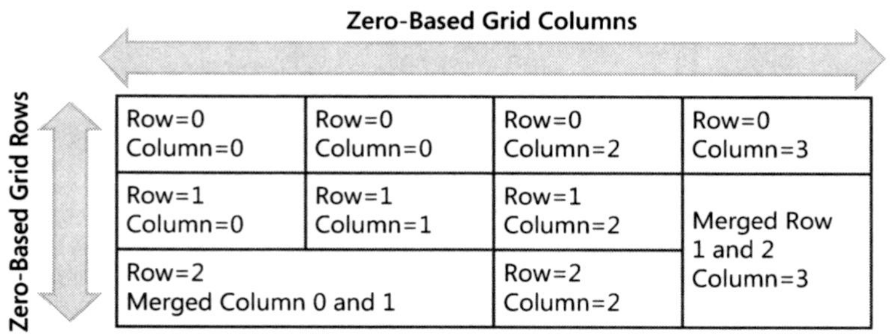

FIGURE 6-13 Defining *Grid* layout container.

From Figure 6-13, you can determine the following:

- A *Grid* can contain a number of rows and columns. By default, a *Grid* contains one row and one column when no specific number of rows and/or columns have been defined.

- The rows and columns of the *Grid* control are indexed starting from 0; in other words, you would specify the first row and column have index values of 0.

- You can merge adjacent rows and column cells (see the highlighted cells in Figure 6-13) to create a more complex layout to support application requirements.

- You can make the border of a *Grid* control visible or not visible (the default setting).

Each *Grid* cell can contain one child element. That child element can be a form and functional control such as a *TextBox* or *Button,* or it can be a layout and positioning control container, such as a *StackPanel* or a *Canvas* that itself may contain a collection of child controls.

Defining the Grid

You use the *Grid.RowDefinitions* and *Grid.ColumnDefinitions* properties to define the collection of rows and columns and their appropriate properties. *Grid.RowDefinitions* contains one or more *RowDefinition* elements, where each element represents one row of the grid. *Grid.ColumnDefinitions* contains one or more *ColumnDefinition* elements, where each element represents one column of the *Grid* control. Again, one row and one column are the default if you don't specify the number of rows and/or columns explicitly.

The following XAML code snippet represents a *Grid* with three rows and three columns:

```
<Window x:Class="LayoutControlsExample.MainWindow"
        xmlns="http://schemas.microsoft.com/winfx/2006/xaml/presentation"
        xmlns:x="http://schemas.microsoft.com/winfx/2006/xaml"
        Title="MainWindow" Height="300" Width="300">
```

```
<Grid Background="LightBlue">
    <Grid.RowDefinitions>
        <RowDefinition></RowDefinition>
        <RowDefinition></RowDefinition>
        <RowDefinition></RowDefinition>
    </Grid.RowDefinitions>
    <Grid.ColumnDefinitions>
        <ColumnDefinition></ColumnDefinition>
        <ColumnDefinition></ColumnDefinition>
        <ColumnDefinition></ColumnDefinition>
    </Grid.ColumnDefinitions>
</Grid>
</Window>
```

Figure 6-14 shows the resulting *Grid* in the Visual Studio designer, with three columns and three rows.

FIGURE 6-14   *Grid* layout with three columns and three rows.

Sizing Grid Columns and Rows

You use the *Width* property of the *ColumnDefinition* element and the *Height* property of the *RowDefinition* element to define the width of each column and the height of each row. The *Grid* control supports proportional sizing (the default setting), also known as *star sizing*, and absolute or automatic sizing of the rows and columns.

Proportional sizing   Revisit Figure 6-14 and you will notice that the width of the columns and height of the rows are determined proportionally. Each cell receives 1 times width and height of the available space. If you look closely at Figure 6-14, you will notice that *1** appears on the top and left sides of the grid, showing the equal proportional sizing of each cell. Thus you use an asterisk (*) to define the proportional sizing of row and column. Now make the first column and first row 2 times proportional to the available space and other two columns and two rows 1 time proportional to the available space. The following is the updated XAML code snippet (updated portion in bold font), and the resultant proportional spacing *Grid* layout is shown in Figure 6-15.

```
<Grid Background="LightBlue">
    <Grid.RowDefinitions>
        <RowDefinition Height="2*"></RowDefinition>
        <RowDefinition></RowDefinition>
        <RowDefinition></RowDefinition>
    </Grid.RowDefinitions>
    <Grid.ColumnDefinitions>
        <ColumnDefinition Width="2*"></ColumnDefinition>
        <ColumnDefinition></ColumnDefinition>
        <ColumnDefinition></ColumnDefinition>
    </Grid.ColumnDefinitions>
</Grid>
```

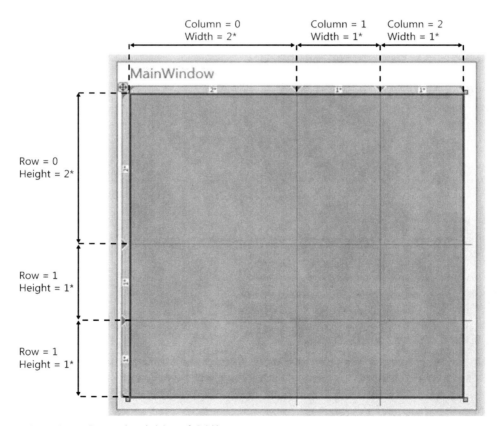

FIGURE 6-15 Proportional sizing of *Grid* layout.

Absolute sizing You can also assign an absolute size to individual rows and columns by providing specific values for the *Height* and *Width* properties in the *RowDefinition* and *ColumnDefinition* elements, respectively. The following code updates the example to set the second-row height and the second-column width to 50 pixels and the third-row height and third-column width to 75 pixels.

The first row and first column will fill up all the remaining space because the first row height and first column width are set to asterisk (*). The resulting *Grid* layout is shown in Figure 6-16.

```
<Grid Background="LightBlue">
    <Grid.RowDefinitions>
        <RowDefinition Height="*"></RowDefinition>
        <RowDefinition Height="50"></RowDefinition>
        <RowDefinition Height="75"></RowDefinition>
    </Grid.RowDefinitions>
    <Grid.ColumnDefinitions>
        <ColumnDefinition Width="*"></ColumnDefinition>
        <ColumnDefinition Width="50"></ColumnDefinition>
        <ColumnDefinition Width="75"></ColumnDefinition>
    </Grid.ColumnDefinitions>
</Grid>
```

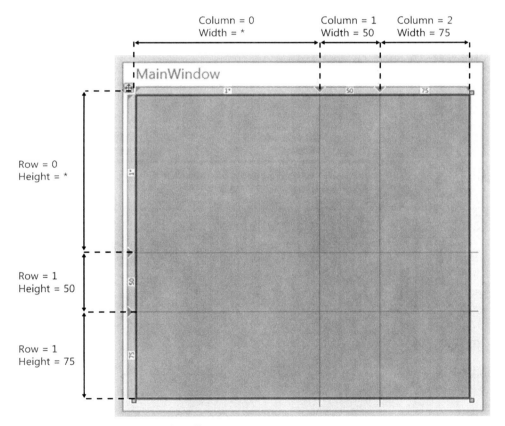

FIGURE 6-16 Absolute sizing of *Grid* layout.

Automatic sizing At times you need to resize a *Grid* column and row automatically to fit its contents. Automatic sizing supports this feature. You can enable automatic sizing for any row and column by setting the *Height* and *Width* properties to *Auto* in the related *RowDefinition* and *ColumnDefinition* elements.

The following XAML code snippet is updated (the updated portion is in bold font) to set the second-row height and column width to automatic.

```
<Grid Background="LightBlue">
    <Grid.RowDefinitions>
        <RowDefinition Height="*"></RowDefinition>
        <RowDefinition Height="Auto"></RowDefinition>
        <RowDefinition Height="75"></RowDefinition>
    </Grid.RowDefinitions>
    <Grid.ColumnDefinitions>
        <ColumnDefinition Width="*"></ColumnDefinition>
        <ColumnDefinition Width="50"></ColumnDefinition>
        <ColumnDefinition Width="75"></ColumnDefinition>
    </Grid.ColumnDefinitions>
</Grid>
```

The resulting *Grid* layout is shown in Figure 6-17. Notice that the *Grid* does not yet have any added content. The second-row height and second-column width are both set to *Auto*, so they render with a size of 0—the second row and column are not visible. The third column and row maintain their size because they were assigned an absolute size; the first row and column enlarge to take up the remaining space.

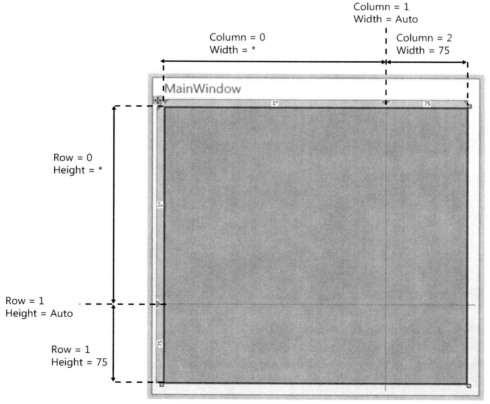

FIGURE 6-17 Column 0 and Row 0 set to Proportional sizing, Column 1 and Row 1 set to Automatic sizing, and Column 2 and Row 2 set to Absolute sizing.

Adding Content to Grid

Each Grid cell can contain only one child element. That child element can be one of the form and functional controls such as *TextBox* or *Button* or can contain a layout and positioning control container such as *StackPanel* or *Canvas*. You can also merge adjacent rows and column cells to create a more complex layout.

The *Grid* control provides *Grid.Row* and *Grid.Column* attached properties so that you can add a child element to a specific row and column:

- The *Grid.Row* attached property defines the row of the grid into which content is placed. The first row is index 0. The default value is 0.

- The *Grid.Column* attached property defines the column of the grid into which content is placed. The first column is index 0. The default value is 0.

The *Grid* control also provides *Grid.RowSpan* and *Grid.ColumnSpan* attached properties. You use these to merge adjacent rows and column cells, and place content in the combined area:

- The *Grid.RowSpan* attached property defines the number of rows the content will occupy. The default value is 1.

- The *Grid.ColumnSpan* attached property defines the number of columns the added content will occupy. The default value is 1.

Let's extend the example and add a few *Button* controls to demonstrate how different types of *Grid* sizing (proportional, absolute, and automatic) affect the sizing of the content. Here's the updated XAML:

```
<Window x:Class="LayoutControlsExample.MainWindow"
        xmlns="http://schemas.microsoft.com/winfx/2006/xaml/presentation"
        xmlns:x="http://schemas.microsoft.com/winfx/2006/xaml"
        Title="MainWindow" Height="300" Width="300">
    <Grid Background="LightBlue" ShowGridLines="True">
        <Grid.RowDefinitions>
            <RowDefinition Height="*"></RowDefinition>
            <RowDefinition Height="Auto"></RowDefinition>
            <RowDefinition Height="75"></RowDefinition>
        </Grid.RowDefinitions>
        <Grid.ColumnDefinitions>
            <ColumnDefinition Width="*"></ColumnDefinition>
            <ColumnDefinition Width="Auto"></ColumnDefinition>
            <ColumnDefinition Width="75"></ColumnDefinition>
        </Grid.ColumnDefinitions>
        <Button
            Grid.Row="0"
            Grid.Column="0"
            Content="Button 1"
            Background="LightGray"/>
        <Button
            Grid.Row="0"
            Grid.Column="1"
            Content="Button 2"
            Background="LemonChiffon"/>
```

```
    <Button
        Grid.Row="0"
        Grid.Column="2"
        Grid.RowSpan="2"
        Content="Button 3"
        Background="LightGray"/>
    <Button
        Grid.Row="1"
        Grid.Column="0"
        Content="Button 4"
        Background="LemonChiffon"/>
    <Button
        Grid.Row="1"
        Grid.Column="1"
        Content="Button 5"
        Background="LightGray"/>
    <Button
        Grid.Row="2"
        Grid.Column="0"
        Grid.ColumnSpan="2"
        Content="Button 6"
        Background="LightGray"/>
    <Button
        Grid.Row="2"
        Grid.Column="2"
        Content="Button 7"
        Background="LemonChiffon"/>
    </Grid>
</Window>
```

This version contains seven buttons in a 3x3 *Grid*. Each *Button* control contains *Grid.Row* and *Grid.Column* attached properties to specify the row and cell into which the button will be placed at runtime. Button 3 also has a *Grid.RowSpan* attached property so that it will span rows 0 and 1. Similarly, Button 6 defines a *Grid.ColumnSpan* attached property, so it will span columns 0 and 1. Also note that at *Grid* control level, the *ShowGridLine* property of *Grid* is set to *True*, which makes the grid lines visible at runtime (to help show you how the buttons span two rows and two columns clearly).

If you compile and run the project now, you will get the output shown in Figure 6-18.

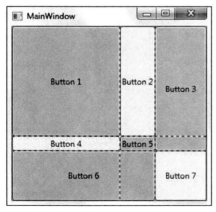

FIGURE 6-18 Adding content that spans multiple rows and columns.

From Figure 6-18, you can see the following:

- The third row (row index 2) and third column (column index 2) have absolute height and width settings of 75 pixels; the buttons located in the second row and second column are sized accordingly.

- The second row (row index 1) and second column (column index 1) are set to have automatic sizing. As a result, the second column width and second row height are set to the size of the buttons placed in them.

- The first row (row index 0) and first column (column index 0) are set to have proportional sizing. As a result, the first column width and first column height get calculated at runtime so that they fill up the remaining space in the window. Buttons placed in the first row and first column will be sized accordingly.

If you resize the window now, you will notice that the absolute and automatic positioned columns (columns 1 and 2) and rows (rows 1 and 2) and the content (in this example, buttons) will not be resized, whereas the proportionally sized column and row will resize automatically. If the window size becomes too small, that row and/or column may become completely invisible.

Like *StackPanel*, the *Grid* control also implements the *IScrollInfo* interface so that you can wrap the *Grid* control in a *ScrollViewer* control to implement horizontal and/or vertical scroll bars. For more information on the *ScrollViewer* control, see Chapter 7.

UniformGrid

Supported By	
WPF	Yes
Silverlight	No

The *System.Windows.Controls.Primitives.UniformGrid* control is a simplified version of the *Grid* control that arranges child elements—one element per cell—in a tabular matrix format where each cell is the same size.

Like the *Grid* control, the *UniformGrid* control can contain *n* number of rows and *m* number of columns. You use the *Rows* and *Columns* dependency properties to define the number of rows and columns within the *UniformGrid* control.

The following XAML code snippet defines a *UniformGrid* with two rows and three columns:

```
<Window x:Class="LayoutControlsExample.MainWindow"
        xmlns="http://schemas.microsoft.com/winfx/2006/xaml/presentation"
        xmlns:x="http://schemas.microsoft.com/winfx/2006/xaml"
        Title="MainWindow" Height="300" Width="300">
    <UniformGrid Rows="2" Columns="3">
    </UniformGrid>
</Window>
```

Unlike the *Grid* control, the size of each cell in a *UniformGrid* control always remains the same. You can control the overall height and width of the *UniformGrid* control by defining the *Height* and *Width* properties; otherwise, it follows the height and width of its parent element.

The preceding example doesn't define *Height* and *Width* explicitly for the *UniformGrid*, so it will adjust its height and width to 300 pixels, which is defined in its parent *Window* element. In contrast, the following code snippet sets the *UniformGrid* control *Height* and *Width* properties to 200 pixels.

```
<UniformGrid Rows="2" Columns="3" Height="200" Width="200">
</UniformGrid>
```

Like the *Grid* control, each *UniformGrid* cell can contain one child element, either a form and functional control such as *TextBox* or *Button*, or a layout and positioning control container such as *StackPanel* or *Canvas*. Unlike the *Grid*, you cannot merge adjacent rows and column cells.

Also unlike the *Grid* control, the *UniformGrid* control does not provide attached properties such as *Grid.Row* and *Grid.Column*. Instead, child controls of the *UniformGrid* are added in the order in which you define them in the XAML file.

The following example defines a *UniformGrid* control with two rows and three columns containing five buttons, which are added to *UniformGrid* in definition order (see Figure 6-19):

```
<Window x:Class="LayoutControlsExample.MainWindow"
        xmlns="http://schemas.microsoft.com/winfx/2006/xaml/presentation"
        xmlns:x="http://schemas.microsoft.com/winfx/2006/xaml"
        Title="MainWindow" Height="300" Width="300">
    <UniformGrid Rows="2" Columns="3" Background="LightBlue">
        <Button Content="Button 1" Background="LightGray"/>
        <Button Content="Button 2" Background="LemonChiffon"/>
        <Button Content="Button 3" Background="LightGray"/>
        <Button Content="Button 4" Background="LemonChiffon"/>
        <Button Content="Button 5" Background="LightGray"/>
    </UniformGrid>
</Window>
```

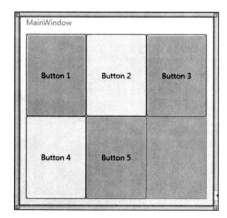

FIGURE 6-19 Content added in the *UniformGrid* control.

As Figure 6-19 shows, all five *Button* controls have the same size. Notice that the last cell is empty, because only five buttons were added.

The *UniformGrid* control has a *FirstColumn* dependency property, which defines the number of leading blank cells in the first row of the *UniformGrid*. If you write *FirstColumn="1"* in the XAML for the preceding example, as shown in Figure 6-20, the first cell in the first row will be blank:

```
<UniformGrid Rows="2" Columns="3" FirstColumn="1" Background="LightBlue">
   ...
</UniformGrid>
```

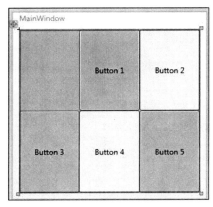

FIGURE 6-20 Setting the *FirstColumn* dependency property of the *UniformGrid* control to 1 causes the first cell to be left empty when the *UniformGrid* adds its child controls.

WrapPanel

Supported By	
WPF	Yes
Silverlight	Yes (Toolkit Control)

The *System.Windows.Controls.WrapPanel* layout and positioning control is similar to the *StackPanel* control in that:

- It arranges child controls in the horizontal or vertical direction based on the value (*Horizontal* or *Vertical*) you set for the *Orientation* dependency property. The default value is *Horizontal*. Note that the default value for *StackPanel* is *Vertical*. Revisit Figure 6-9 to clarify the orientation behavior.

- You can also use the *FrameworkElement.FlowDirection* property to set the direction of child controls (in the context of the parent element): either *LeftToRight* (the default setting), or *RightToLeft*.

The key difference between the *StackPanel* and the *WrapPanel* controls is that when the child elements are positioning themselves, the remaining child elements automatically wrap to a new row when they reach the edge of the *WrapPanel*.

Previous examples in this chapter used a *WrapPanel* control to demonstrate the layout system. Revisit the *DemonstratingLayoutSystem* project and Figures 6-2 and 6-3, and you'll notice that based on the application window size, the *WrapPanel* child *Image* control wraps to a new row. (See Figure 6-3.)

The *WrapPanel* control also provides two additional dependency properties—*ItemHeight* and *ItemWidth*—that you can use to set a specific height and width for all child items contained within the *WrapPanel*. This feature lets you place child elements uniformly within the *WrapPanel*. If you do not set these properties, the size of the child element is the determining factor.

When the *Height* property of one or more child elements is defined along with the *ItemHeight* property, the *ItemHeight* property value takes precedence over the child element's *Height* property value. The same behavior is also applicable for the *ItemWidth* property of the *WrapPanel* control and the *Width* property of children elements.

> **Note** The *WrapPanel* control is a part of the default WPF user controls library; for Silverlight, it is available in the Silverlight toolkit (*http://silverlight.codeplex.com/*). For Silverlight you need to add a reference to the Silverlight toolkit to insert the *WrapPanel* control.

DockPanel

Supported By	
WPF	Yes
Silverlight	Yes (Toolkit Control)

The *System.Windows.Controls.DockPanel* layout and positioning control places content around the edges of the panel: top, bottom, left, and right. To facilitate this feature, the *DockPanel* control has a *DockPanel.Dock* attached property that a child element uses to determine its position within a parent *DockPanel*. The possible values are *Left*, *Right*, *Top*, and *Bottom*. The default value is *Left*.

The following XAML code snippet adds five buttons that are docked by default to the left edge of the panel. (The *DockPanel.Dock* attached property is not defined explicitly within each child *Button* control.)

```
<Window x:Class="LayoutControlsExample.MainWindow"
        xmlns="http://schemas.microsoft.com/winfx/2006/xaml/presentation"
        xmlns:x="http://schemas.microsoft.com/winfx/2006/xaml"
        Title="MainWindow" Height="300" Width="300">
    <DockPanel Background="LightBlue">
        <Button Content="Button 1" Background="LightGray"/>
        <Button Content="Button 2" Background="LemonChiffon"/>
        <Button Content="Button 3" Background="LightGray"/>
        <Button Content="Button 4" Background="LemonChiffon"/>
        <Button Content="Button 5" Background="LightGray"/>
    </DockPanel>
</Window>
```

Figure 6-21 illustrates the default behavior of child controls added to a *DockPanel*.

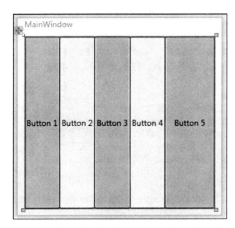

FIGURE 6-21 Default behavior of the *DockPanel* control.

Here each added *Button* control is placed using the default *DockPanel.Dock="Left"* value. Note that the first four buttons are equally sized horizontally, whereas *Button 5* is stretched to fill the remaining space of the *DockPanel*. This is because the default behavior of *DockPanel* is to resize the last added element to fill any remaining space. You can control this behavior by using the *DockPanel. LastChildFill* dependency property. The default value is *True*, which is why you get the result shown in Figure 6-21. If you change the *LastChildFill* dependency property to *False*, as shown in the following code snippet, you will see the result shown in Figure 6-22:

```
<DockPanel LastChildFill="False" Background="LightBlue">

    ...

</DockPanel>
```

FIGURE 6-22 *DockPanel.Dock="Left"* and *DockPanel.LastChildFill="False"*.

With that change, all five buttons are now equally sized, and some remaining space (the light blue background on the right side of the *DockPanel*) has been left unfilled because the *DockPanel* no longer stretches the fifth button to fill the remaining space.

Next, let's define different possible values of the *DockPanel.Dock* attached property to demonstrate them. This example keeps the *LastChildFill* property to its default value, *True*:

```
<DockPanel LastChildFill="True" Background="LightBlue">
    <Button DockPanel.Dock="Top" Content="Top Button" Background="LemonChiffon"/>
    <Button DockPanel.Dock="Bottom" Content="Bottom Button" Background="LemonChiffon"/>
    <Button DockPanel.Dock="Left" Content="Left Button" Background="LemonChiffon"/>
    <Button DockPanel.Dock="Right" Content="Right Button" Background="LemonChiffon"/>
    <Button DockPanel.Dock="Left" Content="Last Child" Background="LightGray"/>
</DockPanel>
```

This example also changes the *Content* and *Background* property values to make the output a bit more user-friendly.

Figure 6-23 shows the outcome of running the preceding XAML code snippet. Here the buttons are added in the sequence *Top*, *Bottom*, *Left*, *Right* by setting the appropriate value for their *DockPanel.Dock* attached properties, and the last button is again stretched to fill the remaining space.

FIGURE 6-23 Child *Button* controls added with *DockPanel.Dock* set in the sequence *Top, Bottom, Left, Right,* and *Left* (for the last child) and *LastChildFill* is set to *True*.

If you now change the *DockPanel.Dock* property value for each button to add them in a different order—*Left, Top, Right, Bottom*—and leave the last button stretched to fill the remaining space, you will get a different outcome, as shown in Figure 6-24. The related XAML code snippet is shown here:

```
<DockPanel LastChildFill="True" Background="LightBlue">
    <Button DockPanel.Dock="Left" Content="Left Button" Background="LemonChiffon"/>
    <Button DockPanel.Dock="Top" Content="Top Button" Background="LemonChiffon"/>
    <Button DockPanel.Dock="Right" Content="Right Button" Background="LemonChiffon"/>
    <Button DockPanel.Dock="Bottom" Content="Bottom Button" Background="LemonChiffon"/>
    <Button DockPanel.Dock="Left" Content="Last Child" Background="LightGray"/>
</DockPanel>
```

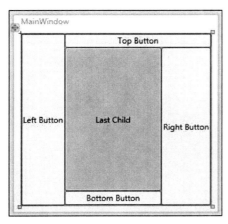

FIGURE 6-24 Child *Button* controls added with *DockPanel.Dock* set in the order of *Left, Top, Right, Bottom,* and *Left* (for the last child) and *LastChildFill* set to *True*.

> **Note** Like the *WrapPanel* control, the *DockPanel* control is part of the default WPF user controls library, whereas for Silverlight it is available in the Silverlight toolkit (*http://silverlight. codeplex.com/*). For Silverlight you need to add a reference to the Silverlight toolkit to insert the *DockPanel* control.

TabPanel

Supported By	
WPF	Yes
Silverlight	Yes

The *System.Windows.Controls.Primitives.TabPanel* layout and positioning control hosts *TabItem* objects on a *TabControl,* handles its layout, and defines the logic for multiple rows of *TabItem* objects.

The *TabControl* object can contain multiple *TabItem* objects that share the same screen space. You can have only one *TabItem* object visible at a time. You have to select each *TabItem* to make its related element(s) visible.

Each *TabItem* can contain one child element, but as usual, in addition to UI controls, that element can be another layout and positioning control, including *Canvas, StackPanel,* or *Grid,* which can contain multiple child elements. The *TabItem.Header* property defines the name of the *TabItem.*

The following example demonstrates two tabs: *Tab #1* and *Tab #2*. Each tab contains a *Canvas* control with a different background color—*Red* for the first tab and *Green* for the second:

```
<Window x:Class="LayoutControlsExample.MainWindow"
        xmlns="http://schemas.microsoft.com/winfx/2006/xaml/presentation"
        xmlns:x="http://schemas.microsoft.com/winfx/2006/xaml"
        Title="MainWindow" Height="300" Width="300">
```

```xaml
<TabPanel Background="LightBlue">
    <TabControl Height="200" Width="200">
        <TabItem Header="Tab #1">
            <Canvas Background="Red"/>
        </TabItem>
        <TabItem Header="Tab #2">
            <Canvas Background="Green"/>
        </TabItem>
    </TabControl>
</TabPanel>
</Window>
```

Figure 6-25 shows the generated output.

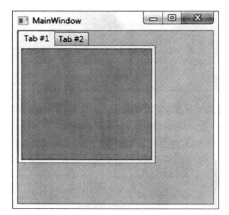 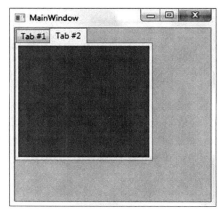

FIGURE 6-25   Two *TabPanel* tabs with different background colors.

In Figure 6-25, the tab headers are aligned to the top relative to the tab content, which is the default behavior. The *TabControl* object contains a *TabStripPlacement* dependency property that controls how tab headers align relative to the tab content. The default value is *Top*. You can also align tab headers to *Left*, *Right*, or *Bottom*. This feature is demonstrated in the following example:

```xaml
<Window x:Class="LayoutControlsExample.MainWindow"
        xmlns="http://schemas.microsoft.com/winfx/2006/xaml/presentation"
        xmlns:x="http://schemas.microsoft.com/winfx/2006/xaml"
        Title="MainWindow" Height="300" Width="300">
    <TabPanel Background="LightBlue">
        <StackPanel>
            <TabControl TabStripPlacement="Top" Height="75" Width="200">
                <TabItem Header="Tab #1">
                    <Canvas Background="Red"/>
                </TabItem>
                <TabItem Header="Tab #2">
                    <Canvas Background="Green"/>
                </TabItem>
            </TabControl>
            <TabControl TabStripPlacement="Bottom" Height="75" Width="200">
                <TabItem Header="Tab #1">
```

```
                    <Canvas Background="Red"/>
                </TabItem>
                <TabItem Header="Tab #2">
                    <Canvas Background="Green"/>
                </TabItem>
            </TabControl>
            <TabControl TabStripPlacement="Left" Height="75" Width="200">
                <TabItem Header="Tab #1">
                    <Canvas Background="Red"/>
                </TabItem>
                <TabItem Header="Tab #2">
                    <Canvas Background="Green"/>
                </TabItem>
            </TabControl>
            <TabControl TabStripPlacement="Right" Height="75" Width="200">
                <TabItem Header="Tab #1">
                    <Canvas Background="Red"/>
                </TabItem>
                <TabItem Header="Tab #2">
                    <Canvas Background="Green"/>
                </TabItem>
            </TabControl>
        </StackPanel>
    </TabPanel>
</Window>
```

Figure 6-26 shows the output of this example.

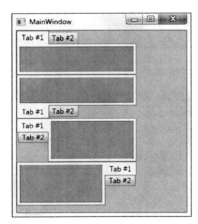

FIGURE 6-26 Demonstrating *TabControl.TabStripPlacement* dependency property.

 Note To use the *TabControl* in a Silverlight application, you need to add a reference to the *System.Windows.Controls* namespace and assembly to the *UserControl* element.

Common Sizing and Positioning Properties

So far in this chapter you've covered the key layout and positioning controls for WPF and Silverlight that derive from the *System.Windows.Controls.Panel* class. The *Panel* class is derived instead from the *System.Windows.FrameworkElement* class, which provides a set of common sizing dependency properties such as *Height* and *Width* and positioning dependency properties such as *VerticalAlignment, HorizontalAlignment,* and *Margin.* You've seen these used in examples already. This section provides a quick overview of that set of common sizing and positioning properties.

Sizing Properties

Supported By	
WPF	Yes
Silverlight	Yes

The *System.Windows.FrameworkElement* class provides the following sizing dependency properties that can control the height and width of the element:

- **Height**   Defines the height of the element

- **Width**   Defines the width of the element

- **MinHeight**   Defines the minimum height constraint of the element

- **MinWidth**   Defines the minimum width constraint of the element

- **MaxHeight**   Defines the maximum height constraint of the element

- **MaxWidth**   Defines the maximum width constraint of the element

By defining *MinHeight* and *MaxHeight* for an element, you can define a range for the possible height for that specific element. Similarly, by defining *MinWidth* and *MaxWidth* for an element, you are defining a range of possible width values for that specific element.

The following example demonstrates how you can use these sizing properties to control the height and width of an element and its behavior when a window gets resized:

```
<Window x:Class="LayoutControlsExample.MainWindow"
        xmlns="http://schemas.microsoft.com/winfx/2006/xaml/presentation"
        xmlns:x="http://schemas.microsoft.com/winfx/2006/xaml"
        Title="MainWindow" Height="300" Width="300">
    <StackPanel Background="LightBlue">
        <Button Content="Default Height and Width"/>
        <Button Height="50" Width="200" Content="Height=50 and Width=200"/>
        <Button MinHeight="20" MaxHeight="100" Content="MinHeight=20 and MaxHeight=100"/>
        <Button MinWidth="200" MaxWidth="250" Content="MinWidth=200 and MaxWidth=250"/>
    </StackPanel>
</Window>
```

Figure 6-27 shows the default output of this example and the impact on the element resizing when the window is resized.

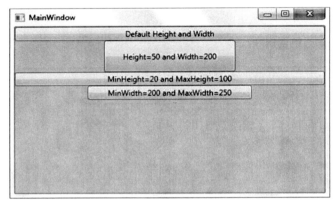

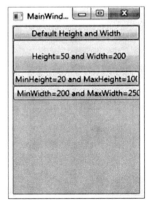

FIGURE 6-27 Demonstrating *MinHeight*, *MaxHeight*, *Height*, *MinWidth*, *MaxWidth*, and *Width* dependency properties.

Alignment Properties

Supported By	
WPF	Yes
Silverlight	Yes

Controls Position Alignment

In addition to the sizing properties, the *System.Windows.FrameworkElement* class provides the following horizontal and vertical alignment dependency properties that can determine the relative position of a control by aligning the control horizontally and vertically in the layout space allocated by the parent control.

- **HorizontalAlignment**   Defines how the control is aligned horizontally in the layout space available within the parent control. The possible values are:

  - **Left**   Left horizontal alignment.

  - **Right**   Right horizontal alignment.

  - **Center**   Horizontally aligned in center.

  - **Stretch**   Stretch the control horizontally to fill up the available space. This is the default value.

- **VerticalAlignment**   Defines how the control is aligned vertically in the layout space available within the parent control. The possible values are:

  - **Top**   Aligned with top of the parent element available space.

  - **Bottom**   Aligned with bottom of the parent element available space.

  - **Center**   Vertically aligned in center.

  - **Stretch**   Stretch the control vertically to fill up the available space. This is the default value.

> **Note** The *Stretch* value of the *HorizontalAlignment* and *VerticalAlignment* dependency properties will be in effect only if the *Height* and *Width* properties are not explicitly defined for that control.

The following example demonstrates how you can apply *HorizontalAlignment* and *VerticalAlignment* dependency properties with different possible values to *Button* controls.

```
<Window x:Class="LayoutControlsExample.MainWindow"
        xmlns="http://schemas.microsoft.com/winfx/2006/xaml/presentation"
        xmlns:x="http://schemas.microsoft.com/winfx/2006/xaml"
        Title="MainWindow" Height="300" Width="300">
    <StackPanel>
        <TextBlock
```

```
        HorizontalAlignment="Center"
        Text="Horizontal Alignment Example"
        FontWeight="Bold"/>
    <StackPanel Height="100" Width="250" Background="LightBlue">
        <Button HorizontalAlignment="Center" Content="Center"/>
        <Button HorizontalAlignment ="Left" Content="Left"/>
        <Button HorizontalAlignment ="Right" Content="Right"/>
        <Button HorizontalAlignment ="Stretch" Content="Stretch (Default)"/>
    </StackPanel>
    <TextBlock
        HorizontalAlignment="Center"
        Text="Vertical Alignment Example"
        FontWeight="Bold"/>
    <StackPanel Height="100" Width="250"
        Background="LightYellow" Orientation="Horizontal">
        <Button VerticalAlignment="Center" Content="Center"/>
        <Button VerticalAlignment ="Top" Content="Top"/>
        <Button VerticalAlignment ="Bottom" Content="Bootom"/>
        <Button VerticalAlignment ="Stretch" Content="Stretch (Defalut)"/>
    </StackPanel>
  </StackPanel>
</Window>
```

Figure 6-28 presents the output application window.

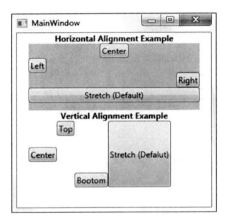

FIGURE 6-28 The *HorizontalAlignment* and *VerticalAlignment* dependency properties.

Caution The *HorizontalAlignment* and *VerticalAlignment* dependency properties are applicable only to the control that can position itself relatively within the allocated space in the layout. If the control requires absolute positioning, such as the *Canvas* layout and positioning control, you cannot apply *HorizontalAlignment* and *VerticalAlignment* properties.

Controls Content Alignment

Similar to the way *System.Windows.FrameworkElement* class provides the horizontal and vertical alignment dependency properties to position elements relatively—either horizontally and/or vertically—the *System.Windows.Controls.Control* class provides horizontal and vertical alignment dependency properties to align control content horizontally and vertically.

- **HorizontalContentAlignment**   Defines how the control content is aligned horizontally. The possible values are:

  - **Left**   Left horizontal alignment. This is the default value.

  - **Right**   Right horizontal alignment.

  - **Center**   Horizontally aligned in center.

  - **Stretch**   Stretch the control horizontally to fill up the available space.

- **VerticalContentAlignment**   Defines how the control content is aligned vertically. The possible values are:

  - **Top**   Aligned with top of the parent element available space. This is the default value.

  - **Bottom**   Aligned with bottom of the parent element available space.

  - **Center**   Vertically aligned in center.

  - **Stretch**   Stretch the control vertically to fill up the available space.

The following example demonstrates how you can apply *HorizontalContentAlignment* and *VerticalContentAlignment* dependency properties with different possible values to the content of the *Button* controls:

```
<Window x:Class="LayoutControlsExample.MainWindow"
        xmlns="http://schemas.microsoft.com/winfx/2006/xaml/presentation"
        xmlns:x="http://schemas.microsoft.com/winfx/2006/xaml"
        Title="MainWindow" Height="300" Width="300">
    <StackPanel>
        <TextBlock
            HorizontalAlignment="Center"
            Text="Horizontal Content Alignment Example"
            FontWeight="Bold"/>
        <StackPanel Height="100" Width="250" Background="LightBlue">
            <Button HorizontalContentAlignment="Center" Content="Center"/>
            <Button HorizontalContentAlignment ="Left" Content="Left  (Default)"/>
            <Button HorizontalContentAlignment ="Right" Content="Right"/>
            <Button HorizontalContentAlignment ="Stretch" Content="Stretch"/>
        </StackPanel>
        <TextBlock
            HorizontalAlignment="Center"
            Text="Vertical Content Alignment Example"
            FontWeight="Bold"/>
        <StackPanel Height="100" Width="250"
            Background="LightYellow" Orientation="Horizontal">
```

```
                <Button VerticalContentAlignment="Center" Content="Center"/>
                <Button VerticalContentAlignment ="Top" Content="Top (Defalut)"/>
                <Button VerticalContentAlignment ="Bottom" Content="Bootom"/>
                <Button VerticalContentAlignment ="Stretch" Content="Stretch"/>
            </StackPanel>
        </StackPanel>
</Window>
```

Figure 6-29 presents the output application window.

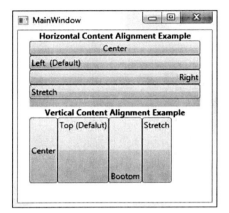

FIGURE 6-29   Effects of the *HorizontalContentAlignment* and *VerticalContentAlignment* dependency properties.

Margin Property

Supported By	
WPF	Yes
Silverlight	Yes

To structure the user interface, it is critical to provide proper spacing between two controls. The *System.Windows.FrameworkElement.Margin* dependency property defines the outer spacing (in pixels) for an element.

You can define the outer margin (space) for all four sides using the *Margin* property:

- To provide a uniform margin on all four sides of the element, you need to specify only a single value (*0* or greater) for the *Margin* property. For example, by defining *Margin="10"* for the element, the outer spacing for all four sides will be set to 10 pixels.

- To define one outer spacing value for the left and right sides and another outer spacing value for the top and bottom sides, you define two comma-separated values (*0* or greater) to the *Margin* property. The first value sets the left and right margins; the second value sets the top and bottom margins. For example, by defining *Margin="10,20"* for an element, the outer spacing for the left and right sides of the element will be 10 pixels and the outer spacing for the top and bottom sides will be 20 pixels.

- To define a specific outer spacing for each side, you define four comma-separated values (of *0* or greater) for the *Margin* property. The values apply to the element in clockwise fashion: the first value sets the left margin, the second value sets the top margin, the third value sets the right margin, and the fourth and last value sets the bottom margin. For example, defining *Margin="10,20,30,40"* for an element sets the left margin to 10 pixels while the top, right, and bottom margins are 20, 30, and 50 pixels, respectively.

The following example demonstrates how you can apply *FrameworkElement.Margin* to *Button* controls. This example uses a *Border* control to demonstrate allocated margin spacing clearly for different *Button* controls:

```
<Window x:Class="LayoutControlsExample.MainWindow"
        xmlns="http://schemas.microsoft.com/winfx/2006/xaml/presentation"
        xmlns:x="http://schemas.microsoft.com/winfx/2006/xaml"
        Title="MainWindow" Height="300" Width="300">
    <StackPanel>
        <Border BorderBrush="Black" BorderThickness="2">
            <Button Margin="10" Content="AllSides=10"/>
        </Border>
        <Border BorderBrush="Black" BorderThickness="2">
            <Button Margin="10,20" Content="Left,Right=10 Top,Bottom=20"/>
        </Border>
        <Border BorderBrush="Black" BorderThickness="2">
            <Button Margin="10,20,30,40" Content="Left=10, Top=20, Right=30, Bottom=40"/>
        </Border>
    </StackPanel>
</Window>
```

Figure 6-30 presents the output application window.

FIGURE 6-30 The *Margin* dependency property.

Padding Property

Supported By	
WPF	Yes
Silverlight	Yes

As you just saw, the *Margin* dependency property defines the outer spacing of an element. In contrast, the *Padding* dependency property defines the inner spacing (in pixels) on all four sides between the element's border and its contents.

Like the *Margin* dependency property, you can also set the *Padding* property in three ways that define how much inner spacing to render between the left, right, top, and bottom sides of the element border and that element's contents:

- To provide a uniform margin for all four sides of the element, specify a single value (0 or greater) for the *Padding* property.

- To define the same inner spacing value for the left and right sides and a different inner spacing value for the top and bottom sides, you use two comma-separated values (0 or greater) for the *Padding* property; the first value sets the left and right side margins while the second value sets the top and bottom margins.

- To define specific inner spacing for each side, use four comma-separated values (0 or greater) for the *Padding* property. Again, the values get applied in clockwise fashion, starting with the left side. For example, by defining *Padding="10,20,30,40"* for the element, inner spacing for the left side is set to 10 pixels, and the top, right, and bottom sides are set to 20, 30, and 40 pixels, respectively.

Extend the earlier example that demonstrates the *Margin* property by adding *Padding* to the *Button* controls:

```
<Window x:Class="LayoutControlsExample.MainWindow"
    xmlns="http://schemas.microsoft.com/winfx/2006/xaml/presentation"
    xmlns:x="http://schemas.microsoft.com/winfx/2006/xaml"
    Title="MainWindow" Height="400" Width="300">
  <StackPanel>
      <Border BorderBrush="Black" BorderThickness="2">
          <Button Margin="10"
              Padding="10" Content="AllSides=10"/>
      </Border>
      <Border BorderBrush="Black" BorderThickness="2">
          <Button Margin="10,20"
              Padding="10,20" Content="Left,Right=10 Top,Bottom=20"/>
      </Border>
      <Border BorderBrush="Black" BorderThickness="2">
          <Button Margin="10,20,30,40"
              Padding="10,20,30,40" Content="Left=10, Top=20, Right=30, Bottom=40"/>
      </Border>
  </StackPanel>
</Window>
```

Figure 6-31 presents the output application window.

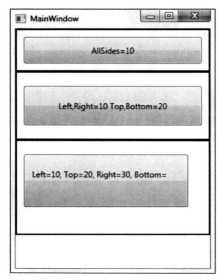

FIGURE 6-31 The *Padding* dependency property.

Visibility Property

Supported By	
WPF	Yes
Silverlight	Yes

By default, all WPF and Silverlight elements are visible. However, you will find many use cases where you want to control element visibility at design and runtime. Based on the specific business logic, you will have to make one or more elements visible or not visible. This change in control visibility can impact the layout and positioning of other elements.

The WPF *UIElement.Visibility* dependency property controls the visibility of user interface elements. The *Visibility* property has three possible state values:

- **Visible**   This state makes the element visible at runtime. This is the default state for all user interface elements.

- **Hidden**   This state makes the element invisible at run\time, but the hidden elements still consume their allocated space in the layout.

- **Collapsed**   This state makes the element invisible at run\time. Collapsed elements do not consume any space.

Note The WPF version of the *UIElement.Visibility* dependency property can take any of the preceding values: *Visible*, *Hidden*, or *Collapsed*. However, the Silverlight version of the *UIElement.Visibility* dependency property supports only two state values—*Visible* and *Collapsed*. For the Silverlight version of UI elements, there is no *Hidden* state.

Invisible controls do not process any events or input commands, and do not participate in the tab sequence. Many use cases require checking the visibility state of UI element(s) in the code-behind when performing specific business logic at runtime. The *UIElement.IsVisible* dependency property returns the visibility state of the UI element so that you can identify invisible controls and enable them to implement business logic.

Note The default value of the *IsVisible* dependency property is *false*, which indicates that the *Visibility* state of that specific UI element is *Visible*. When *IsVisible* is *true*, the *Visibility* state of the corresponding UI element is either *Hidden* or *Collapsed* for WPF UI elements, and *Collapsed* for Silverlight UI elements.

The following WPF application example demonstrates how you can apply the *UIElement.Visibility* dependency property to *Button* controls, and shows the impact of the *Hidden* and *Collapsed* states on the layout. As mentioned earlier, if you use a similar example and run it as a Silverlight application, you will not be able to use the *Hidden* state:

```
<Window x:Class="LayoutControlsExample.MainWindow"
        xmlns="http://schemas.microsoft.com/winfx/2006/xaml/presentation"
        xmlns:x="http://schemas.microsoft.com/winfx/2006/xaml"
        Title="MainWindow" Height="300" Width="300">
    <StackPanel>
    <StackPanel>
        <StackPanel>
            <TextBlock Text="All Buttons Visible"
                HorizontalAlignment="Center" FontWeight="Bold"/>
            <Button Visibility="Visible" Content="Button1"/>
            <Button Visibility="Visible" Content="Button2"/>
            <Button Visibility="Visible" Content="Button3"/>
        </StackPanel>
        <StackPanel>
            <TextBlock Text="Button2 is Hidden"
                HorizontalAlignment="Center" FontWeight="Bold"/>
            <Button Visibility="Visible" Content="Button1"/>
            <Button Visibility="Hidden" Content="Button2"/>
            <Button Visibility="Visible" Content="Button3"/>
        </StackPanel>
        <StackPanel>
            <TextBlock Text="Button2 is Collapsed"
                HorizontalAlignment="Center" FontWeight="Bold"/>
            <Button Visibility="Visible" Content="Button1"/>
            <Button Visibility="Collapsed" Content="Button2"/>
```

```
                    <Button Visibility="Visible" Content="Button3"/>
                </StackPanel>
            </StackPanel>
        </Window>
```

Figure 6-32 shows the running application window. As you can see, when the Button2 *Visibility* property is set to *Hidden*, the layout retains the required area for the Button2 element. In contrast, when the Button2 *Visibility* property is set to *Collapsed*, the layout does not maintain that area; Button3 shifts upward, so it's positioned immediately below Button1.

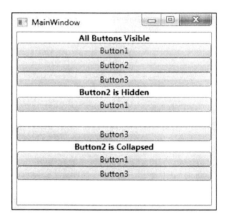

FIGURE 6-32   Setting the *UIElement.Visibility* dependency property.

Summary

WPF introduced a flexible layout system that supports rendering XAML elements that have been defined with relative sizing and positioning, creating a fluid user interface that can adapt to changing conditions at run time.

This chapter covered the WPF and Silverlight layout systems as well as various XAML layout and positioning controls and their attributes.

The *System.Windows.Controls.Panel* is a base class for layout containers. It provides a set of layout and positioning controls that range from very basic, such as *Canvas* and *StackPanel,* to more advanced controls such as *Grid*. These controls can act as either a main or a subcontainer for a group of user controls, letting you arrange controls in specific positions and in a particular order to build a meaningful user interface.

Common sizing dependency properties such as *Height* and *Width* and positioning dependency properties such as *VerticalAlignment, HorizontalAlignement, Margin,* and *Padding* help to align the control and its content, define specific heights and widths for elements, and define outer and inner spacing between controls and their content. The *Visibility* property lets you control the element visibility dynamically so that you can implement key use cases.

Chapter 7 provides a more in-depth exploration of different form and functional XAML controls and their basic features.

Form and Functional Controls

In this chapter

- Action Controls
- Text Editing Controls
- Functional Controls to Improve Usability
- Functional Controls to Control and Monitor Behavior
- Summary

Chapter 6, "Layout and Positioning System," gave you a detailed overview of the key XAML layout and positioning controls, and of sizing and positioning dependency properties. With that information in hand, you are ready to start building user interfaces (UIs) with XAML.

The form and functional XAML controls are core, critical controls for building rich and interactive user interfaces. You usually add them to a UI as child controls of one of the layout and positioning controls in the XAML file at design time, or create them using code-behind to implement a specific use case at runtime.

Form controls enable and process different types of user input. The Microsoft WPF and Silverlight platform provide a rich set of form controls, including:

- **Action controls**   Controls such as *Button*, *CheckBox*, *RadioButton*, and *RepeatButton* can accept user input in terms of mouse or stylus pen click, key press (such as pressing the Enter key), or selection/pressing with a finger to perform a particular action.

- **Text editing**   Controls such as *TextBox*, *PasswordBox*, *RichTextBox*, *Calendar*, and *DatePicker*, which can accept simple and/or rich text entry through keyboard, mouse, stylus, or your fingers that can be processed using data binding within XAML or using the code-behind at runtime.

Functional controls provide a different set of features that make your user interfaces cleaner and more usable, let you control and monitor application behavior, and provide support for interacting with file systems and printers through generic dialogs:

- **Controls to improve usability**   Functional controls such as *Label*, *TextBlock*, *Border*, *Popup*, *ToolTip*, *ToolBarPanel*, *Menu*, and *ContextMenu* help you organize and categorize information and actions, and provide useful visual guidance for people using your applications.

- **Controls to control and monitor application and content behavior** Functional controls such as *ScrollBar*, *ScrollViewer*, *StatusBar*, *ProgressBar*, and *Thumb* controls enable developers to control the visible areas of the application and provide various types of status information, such as a status or progress bar.

 More Info This chapter provides a high-level overview of only commonly used form and functional controls. See the MSDN page at *http://msdn.microsoft.com/en-us/library/ms752324.aspx* for a more complete overview of available WPF XAML controls. See *http://msdn.microsoft.com/en-us/library/cc645072.aspx* for a more complete overview of available Silverlight XAML controls.

The majority of form and functional control classes inherit from the *System.Windows.Controls. Control* class and thus can use *ControlTemplate* to define and customize the appearance of the control. The *Control* class provides basic properties for setting the background and foreground of a control, configuring the appearance of text within the control, and enabling control templating.

Action Controls

Action controls are mainly *Button* type controls such as *Button*, *HyperlinkButton*, *CheckBox*, *Radio-Button*, and *RepeatButton* controls that you use to execute specific actions upon clicking or selecting them.

The *ButtonBase* Class

System.Windows.Controls.Premitives.ButtonBase is a base class for a set of *Button* type controls available for WPF and Silverlight platforms. This class also provides a common set of properties and events that are available to derived *Button* type controls:

- *ClickMode* This dependency property defines when to raise the *Click* event:
  - Upon mouse hover by setting value to *Hover*.
  - Upon mouse click, or by pressing the Enter key.
  - When the button has focus, pressing the spacebar by setting the value to *Press*.
  - Upon mouse button release by setting the value to *Release*. The default value is *ClickMode. Release*.

- *Command* This dependency property defines the command (*ApplicationCommands*, *NavigationCommands*, or custom command) to execute when the button is pressed. The default value is *null*. You usually use this property when you want to execute some predefined commands, such as *Close*, *Copy*, *PrintPreview*, *Save*, *Zoom*, *FirstPage*, *LastPage*, and *NextPage*.

More Info See the MSDN page at *http://msdn.microsoft.com/en-us/library/ system.windows.input.navigationcommands.aspx* for more details about the *NavigationCommands* class. See *http://msdn.microsoft.com/en-us/library/system. windows.input.applicationcommands.aspx* for more information about the *ApplicationCommands* class.

■ **IsPressed** This dependency property returns *true* when the button state is pressed; otherwise, it returns *false*. The default value is *false*.

ButtonBase also provides a *Click* event that is raised whenever the *Button* control is clicked. Remember that exactly when the *Click* event occurs depends on the setting of the *ClickMode* property, as discussed earlier in this section.

The *ButtonBase* class derives from the *System.Windows.Controls.ContentControl* class, which allows any button-type XAML control to contain any type of an object, including a string, image, or *UIElement*. It also allows you to create a custom appearance (including animation and graphics) for the button types that use *ControlTemplate*. You can control appearance based on different visual states of the control, such as *Normal*, *MouseOver*, *Pressed*, *Disabled*, *Focused*, and *Unfocused*.

The following subsections provide an overview of various *Button* type controls inherited from the *ButtonBase* class and available for both the WPF and Silverlight platforms.

Button

Supported By	
WPF	Yes
Silverlight	Yes

A regular basic button has a rectangular shape and uses simple text as its content. The following XAML code snippet defines a basic button with the control identifier name *x:Name* set to *Button1*, and the *Content* set to the string *"Button Text."* Its *Click* event fires the method *Button1_Click* defined in code-behind:

```
<Button
    x:Name="Button1"
    Content="Button Text"
    Click="Button1_Click"/>
```

The code-behind implementation of the *Click* event for the *Button1* named button control is shown here:

```
private void Button1_Click(object sender, RoutedEventArgs e)
{
    //Code goes here…
}
```

You could change the button's content to any single *UIElement* control, which could be a layout and positioning control containing a collection of children controls. The following XAML code snippet defines a button with its *Content* set to a *StackPanel* control containing an *Image* and a *TextBlock* control containing the string "*Button Text*," text and its *Click* event set to the *Button2_Click* code-behind method:

```
<Button
    x:Name="Button2"
    Click="Button2_Click">
    <StackPanel>
        <Image Source="buttonimage.jpg"/>
        <TextBlock Text="Button Text"/>
    </StackPanel>
</Button>
```

The ability to change content lets you customize buttons to some degree, but you can go far beyond that. For example, you can change the button's appearance to make it non-rectangular. This next example makes the button take on a star shape!

To do this, you define a *ControlTemplate* with its *TargetType* set to *Button*. Then when you add a *Button* control, you set its *Style* property to the appropriate *ControlTemplate* to apply the custom visual appearance that the *ControlTemplate* defines (in this case, a star-shaped button). The following code defines the *ControlTemplate* as a local *Window* resource and then applies that style to a *Button*:

```
<Window
    xmlns="http://schemas.microsoft.com/winfx/2006/xaml/presentation"
    xmlns:x="http://schemas.microsoft.com/winfx/2006/xaml"
    xmlns:ed="http://schemas.microsoft.com/expression/2010/drawing"
    x:Class=" FormsFunctionalControls.MainWindow"
    Width="640" Height="480">
    <Window.Resources>
        <Style x:Key="StartButton" TargetType="Button">
            <Setter Property="Template">
                <Setter.Value>
                    <ControlTemplate TargetType="Button">
                        <Grid>
                            <ed:RegularPolygon
                                Fill="#FF21238F"
                                InnerRadius="0.47211"
                                PointCount="5"
                                Stretch="Fill"
                                UseLayoutRounding="False"/>
                            <ContentPresenter
                                HorizontalAlignment=
                                    "{TemplateBinding HorizontalContentAlignment}"
                                VerticalAlignment=
                                    "{TemplateBinding VerticalContentAlignment}"/>
                        </Grid>
                    </ControlTemplate>
                </Setter.Value>
            </Setter>
        </Style>
    </Window.Resources>
```

```
<StackPanel>
    <Button
        x:Name="StarButton"
        Content="Star Button"
        Foreground="White"
        Height="144"
        Margin="152,80,240,0"
        Style="{StaticResource StartButton}"
        VerticalAlignment="Top"
        Click="StarButton_Click"/>
    </StackPanel>
</Window>
```

The preceding XAML code may look quite complex, but don't worry—you don't typically write such code manually; instead, a Microsoft development and design tool named Microsoft Expression Blend handles the creation of this complex XAML.

Using Microsoft Expression Blend, you create a star shape by selecting the *Star* shape from the available *Shape* types, and then customizing the *Star* shape on the design surface. When you're satisfied with its appearance, you can right-click the star shape and select the *Make Into Control* option, selecting the *Button* control type from the controls collection and providing an identifier. You set the scope to the same document—Window:Window. Doing that defines a *ControlTemplate* targeted to the *Button* type control. If you look at the XAML definition of the newly created control, you will find more code than is shown in the preceding example. The additional code manages the visual states of the *Button* control. If you're following along, you can delete the extra code for this example, and just keep the code to create the star-shaped button.

> **Note** To use a star shape drawn using Expression Blend, you need to add the namespace *xmlns:ed="http://schemas.microsoft.com/expression/2010/drawing"*, as shown in the preceding code example. You also have to add a reference to the *Microsoft.Expression. Drawing* assembly to the application project.

Figure 7-1 shows the three buttons—a regular basic button, a button with the image and text, and the star-shaped button—as an output of the project.

FIGURE 7-1 Demonstrating the *Button* control.

HyperlinkButton

Supported By	
WPF	No
Silverlight	Yes

The *System.Windows.Controls.HyperlinkButton* class provides a *HyperlinkButton* XAML control for only the Silverlight platform that lets you create a button that navigates to a defined link.

The key properties of the *HyperlinkButton* class are:

- **NavigateUri**   This dependency property defines an absolute or application-relative URI to which to navigate when the *HyperlinkButton* control is clicked.

> **Caution**   You must set the *EnableNavigation* parameter to *all* at Silverlight plug-in object level to enable navigation to absolute URIs. If the *EnableNavigation* parameter is set to *none*, you can enable only application-relative URIs through the *HyperlinkButton*, and the application will throw a *SecurityException* if you try to navigate the absolute URI. See *http://msdn.microsoft.com/en-us/library/dd833071. aspx* for more information on the *EnableNavigation* parameter.

- **TargetName**   This dependency property defines how the defined targeted web page should be opened: in a new window or in the current active window. If the value is set to *_blank*, *_media*, or *_search*, the targeted page will open in a new window. If the value is set to *_parent*, *_self*, *_top*, or blank (""), the targeted page will open in the current active window.

The following XAML code snippet creates a hyperlink button with its *Content* set to *Visit TechnologyOpinion.com*, an absolute URI set to *http://www.technologyopinion.com*, and *TargetName* set to *_blank*. When a user clicks the text, the application will open the *technologyopinion* website in a new window. The output of the Silverlight application is shown in Figure 7-2.

```
<HyperlinkButton
    Content="Visit TechnologyOpinion.com"
    FontSize="18" Margin="30"
    NavigateUri="http://www.technologyopinion.com"
    TargetName="_blank"/>
```

FIGURE 7-2   Demonstrating the *HyperlinkButton* control.

RepeatButton

Supported By	
WPF	Yes
Silverlight	Yes

While you are developing Windows or web-based applications, you certainly will come across cases in which you need to implement continuous operation—from the point at which you click a control to the point at which you release that control. This will reduce the number of clicks to just one click that the user has to click to achieve a specific functionality. Some examples are continuous increasing/decreasing volume and continuous zoom-in/zoom-out of a window/image.

For WPF and Silverlight platform, the *System.Windows.Controls.RepeatButton* class provides a *RepeatButton* XAML control, which enables the *Click* events repeatedly when you press the *Repeat-Button* until you release it. The *Delay and Interval* dependency properties control the behavior of the repeating *Click* event:

- **Delay** This dependency property defines the delay in milliseconds for the *Click* event to raise after the *RepeatButton* is pressed. The default value is the value of *SystemParameters.KeyboardDelay*, which varies from 250 milliseconds to 1 second.

- **Interval** This dependency property defines the interval between two repeating *Click* events. The default value is the value of *SystemParameters.KeyboardDelay*, which varies from 250 milliseconds to 1 second.

The following example contains two *RepeatButton* controls with the *Delay* set to 250 milliseconds and *Interval* set to 100 milliseconds. The *Increase Size* repeat button will repeatedly increase the size of the *Image* control to 10 pixels until the height of the image reaches 500 pixels. The *Decrease Size* repeat button will repeatedly decrease the size of the *Image* control to 10 pixels until the height of the image reduces to 50 pixels. It also defines the *Click* event code-behind method name so that you can implement required business to increase/decrease the size of the image through managed code-behind:

```
<Window x:Class="FormsFunctionalControls.MainWindow"
        xmlns="http://schemas.microsoft.com/winfx/2006/xaml/presentation"
        xmlns:x="http://schemas.microsoft.com/winfx/2006/xaml"
        Title="MainWindow" Height="350" Width="525">
    <StackPanel>
    <StackPanel HorizontalAlignment="Center" Orientation="Horizontal">
        <RepeatButton
            Content="Increase Size"
            Interval="100"
            Delay="250"
            Height="25" Width="100"
            Margin="10"
            Click="RepeatButton_Click" />
        <RepeatButton
            Content="Decrease Size"
            Interval="100"
            Delay="250"
            Height="25" Width="100"
```

```
                Margin="10"
                Click="RepeatButton_Click_1" />
        </StackPanel>
            <TextBlock x:Name="currentstatus"
                Text="Increasing/Decreasing Image Size"
                FontSize="12" HorizontalAlignment="Center"/>
            <Image
                x:Name="image"
                Height="50" Width="50"
                MinHeight="50" MinWidth="50" Margin="10"
                Source="Resources/Tulips.jpg"/>
        </StackPanel>
</Window>
```

The code-behind implementation of both *RepeatButton* controls' *Click* events are shown in the following code. The code changes the *TextBlock* control *Text* property to show that it's either increasing or decreasing the image size, and implements the logic to increase/decrease the image size by 10 pixels for each key press until the image reaches predefined upper or lower size thresholds:

```
private void RepeatButton_Click(object sender, RoutedEventArgs e)
{
    currentstatus.Text = "Increasing Image Size";
    if (image.Height < 500)
    {
        image.Height += 10;
        image.Width += 10;
    }
}
private void RepeatButton_Click_1(object sender, RoutedEventArgs e)
{
    currentstatus.Text = "Decreasing Image Size";
    if (image.Height > 50)
    {
        image.Height -= 10;
        image.Width -= 10;
    }
}
```

Figure 7-3 shows the output of this sample application. When you click and hold the *RepeatButton*, the image size will continuously increase or decrease until it reaches the threshold size.

ToggleButton

So far, you've seen *Button* type controls that perform some action when clicked. In certain practical scenarios you want to let users select one or more options from a group. For example, you might select one or more choices to indicate your skill level with various Microsoft platform technologies, or select a gender (male or female) while filling out a form. The familiar Windows forms platform has the *CheckBox* control (for selecting one or more choices) and the *RadioButton* control (to select one option from a group of options) so you can implement such use cases. The WPF and Silverlight platforms supply similar—but enhanced—controls.

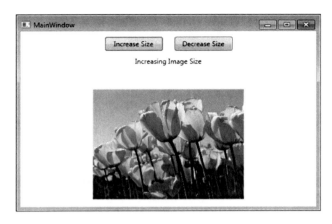

FIGURE 7-3 The *RepeatButton* control in action.

The *System.Windows.Controls.Primitives.ToggleButton* class is a base class for *System.Windows. Controls.CheckBox* and *System.Windows.Controls.RadioButton* XAML controls, by which you manage selection states. The *ToggleButton* class provides the following key properties to define possible states and retrieve the current state information:

- **IsThreeState** This dependency Boolean property, when *true*, defines three states for a *CheckBox* or *RadioButton* control: *Checked*, *UnChecked*, and *Intermediate*. When *false*, the control has only two states: *Checked* and *UnChecked*. The default value is *false*.

- **IsChecked** This dependency property returns *true* when the control is checked or selected, or *false* otherwise. If the *IsThreeState* property is set to *true*, *IsChecked* can contain a third *Intermediate* state representation, which you can define by setting it to *null*.

The *ToggleButton* class also introduces three state-specific events to capture state changes and let you implement code-behind for state-specific logic:

- **Checked** This routed event occurs when a *ToggleButton* is checked.

- **UnChecked**   This routed event occurs when a *ToggleButton* is unchecked.

- **Intermediate**   This routed event occurs when a *ToggleButton* state becomes *Intermediate*. This event can occur only when the *IsThreeState* property is set to *true*.

CheckBox

Supported By	
WPF	Yes
Silverlight	Yes

The *System.Windows.Controls.CheckBox* control allows users to select (by checking) or unselect/ clear (by clearing) the control. If the *IsThreeState* dependency property is set to *true*, the control can also be in an intermediate state (neither selected nor cleared).

RadioButton

Supported By	
WPF	Yes
Silverlight	Yes

The *System.Windows.Controls.RadioButton* control allows users to choose one option from a group of radio buttons. Developers can check the *IsChecked* property to determine whether any particular radio button is checked. Unlike the *CheckBox* control, a user cannot clear a *RadioButton* control; however, you can clear the selection through code-behind by setting the *IsChecked* property of the specific *RadioButton* to *false*.

The *RadioButton* control introduces a new *GroupName* dependency property with which you define a group that can contain one or more *RadioButton* controls. At any given time, only one *RadioButton* control can be selected within any one group.

An Example   The following example defines three *CheckBox* controls with which users can select their skills from among various Microsoft technologies. By default, the example selects the Silverlight skill using the *IsChecked* property. The Silverlight and WCF skills *CheckBox* controls can have an *Intermediate* state because their *IsThreeState* property is set to *true*. The example also includes two *RadioButton* controls with their *GroupName* property set to *genderselection*, which enables users to select their gender. By default, the example application selects the *Male* related *RadioButton* control by setting its *IsChecked* property to *true*. For demonstration purposes the *CheckBox* control named *checkbox1* fires all three possible events—*Checked*, *UnChecked*, and *Intermediate*. It also sets the *Checked* and *UnChecked* states for the *RadioButton* control named *radiobutton1*. Here's the XAML code:

```
<Window x:Class="FormsFunctionalControls.MainWindow"
        xmlns="http://schemas.microsoft.com/winfx/2006/xaml/presentation"
        xmlns:x="http://schemas.microsoft.com/winfx/2006/xaml"
        Title="MainWindow" Height="350" Width="525">
    <StackPanel>
        <StackPanel Margin="10">
            <TextBlock
```

```
                  Text="Select technical skills on Microsoft platform"
                  Margin="5" FontWeight="Bold"/>
            <CheckBox
                  x:Name="checkbox1"
                  IsThreeState="True"
                  IsChecked="True"
                  Content="Silverlight"
                  Checked="checkbox1_Checked"
                  Unchecked="checkbox1_Unchecked"
                  Indeterminate="checkbox1_Indeterminate"/>
            <CheckBox
                  x:Name="checkbox2"
                  IsThreeState="True"
                  Content="WCF"/>
            <CheckBox
                  x:Name="checkbox3"
                  Content="SQL Server"/>
        </StackPanel>
        <StackPanel Margin="10">
            <TextBlock Text="Select your gender" Margin="5" FontWeight="Bold"/>
            <RadioButton
                  x:Name="radiobutton1"
                  GroupName="genderselection"
                  IsChecked="True"
                  Content="Male"
                  Checked="radiobutton1_Checked"
                  Unchecked="radiobutton1_Unchecked"/>
            <RadioButton
                  x:Name="radiobutton2"
                  GroupName="genderselection"
                  Content="Female"/>
        </StackPanel>
    </StackPanel>
</Window>
```

The following code snippet shows the related code-behind event handler implementations for the *checkbox1* and *radiobutton1* controls defined in the preceding XAML:

```
private void checkbox1_Checked(object sender, RoutedEventArgs e)
{
}
private void checkbox1_Unchecked(object sender, RoutedEventArgs e)
{
}
private void checkbox1_Indeterminate(object sender, RoutedEventArgs e)
{
}
private void checkbox2_Checked(object sender, RoutedEventArgs e)
{
}
private void radiobutton1_Checked(object sender, RoutedEventArgs e)
{
}
private void radiobutton1_Unchecked(object sender, RoutedEventArgs e)
{
}
```

Figure 7-4 shows this example at runtime. Note that the Silverlight check box is selected, the WCF check box is in the *Intermediate* state, and the SQL server check box is not selected.

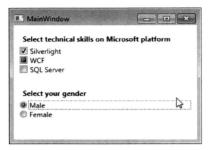

FIGURE 7-4 The *CheckBox* and *RadioButton* controls in action.

Text Editing Controls

Text editing controls such as *TextBox*, *RichTextBox*, *AutoCompleteBox*, and *PasswordBox* allow users to input single- and multiple-line simple and rich text.

The *TextBoxBase* Class

In WPF the *TextBox* and *RichTextBox* (covered in the next section) controls derive from the *System. Windows.Controls.Primitives.TextBoxBase* abstract base class, which provides basic text editing functionality. In Silverlight the *TextBox* and *RichTextBox* controls are derived directly from the *System. Windows.Controls.Control* class.

TextBoxBase provides a common set of properties and events for *TextBox* and *RichTextBox* controls, including:

- **AcceptsReturn**   A dependency property that defines the behavior of the *TextBox* and *RichTextBox* controls when users press the Enter key. If set to *true*, the *TextBox* and *RichTextBox* controls insert a new line at the cursor position upon an Enter key press. When set to *false* they ignore the Enter key. The default value is *false* for the *TextBox* control and *true* for the *RichTextBox* control.

- **AcceptsTab**   This dependency property defines the behavior of the *TextBox* and *RichTextBox* controls when users press the Tab key. When set to *true* the controls insert a tab character at the cursor position upon a Tab key press. When set to *false*, focus moves to the next user control when users press Tab. The default value is *false* for both the *TextBox* and *RichTextBox* controls.

- **IsUndoEnabled**   This dependency property defines whether undo-action support is enabled for both the *TextBox* and *RichTextBox* controls. When set to *false* at runtime through code-behind, the undo stack will be cleared. The default value is *true* for both the *TextBox* and *RichTextBox* controls.

- **UndoLimit**   This dependency property defines the number of eligible undo-action items stored in a queue in the undo stack. If you set this property at run time through code-behind, the undo stack will be cleared and redefined based on the new value. If you set the property value to *0, the* undo feature is disabled. The default value is *-1*, which means there's no pre-defined limit to the undo queue; instead, the limit is dependent on the amount of memory available at any given time.

- **CanUndo**   This dependency property defines whether the most recent action can be undone. This feature is very common while you are entering some information. The property returns *true* if the greatest recent action can be undone; otherwise it returns *false*. This property has no default value.

- **CanRedo**   This dependency property defines whether the most recent undo action can be re-created—a common task when users are entering information. The property returns *true* if the most recent undo action can be redone; otherwise, it returns *false*. This property has no default value.

- **HorizontalScrollBarVisibility**   This dependency property defines whether a horizontal scrollbar is hidden or how it is shown. The four possible values (in the *ScrollBarVisibility* enumeration) are *Disabled*, *Auto*, *Hidden*, and *Visible*. The default value is *Hidden* for both the *TextBox* and *RichTextBox* controls.

- **VerticalScrollBarVisibility**   This dependency property defines whether a vertical scrollbar is hidden or how it is shown. The four possible values (defined in the *ScrollBarVisibility* enumeration) are *Disabled*, *Auto*, *Hidden*, and *Visible*. The default value is *Hidden* for both the *TextBox* and *RichTextBox* controls.

TextBoxBase also provides two key events that help users implement code-behind logic when text in the controls changes or when the text selection has been changed, either by users or through code-behind:

- **TextChanged**   When this event is set, the event occurs every time the content within the control changes, whether through user action or through code-behind. For the *TextBox* control, content is always simple text; for the *RichTextBox* control, content can include text, images, and table objects.

- **SelectionChanged**   When this event is set, the event occurs every time the content selection within the control changes, whether changed by the user or through code-behind. For the *TextBox* control, the selected content is always simple text, whereas for *RichTextBox* control, content can include text, images, and table objects.

TextBox

Supported By	
WPF	Yes
Silverlight	Yes

The *Textbox* control is one of the most basic user input controls—it lets users input simple (no images, bullet lists, tables, and so on) unformatted text. A *Textbox* can contain one or more lines of text. WPF and Silverlight platforms both provide this basic control; however, the implementations differ slightly.

The following are some of the key properties of the *TextBox* control:

- **Text**   This dependency property defines the content of the *TextBox*. The default value is an empty string (""). Setting the *Text* property from code-behind replaces the existing content with the new defined string value.

- **TextAlignment**   This dependency property defines the text alignment, which can be left-aligned (*Left*), right-aligned (*Right*), center-aligned (*Center*), or justified (*Justify*). The default value is *Left*.

- **TextWrapping**   This dependency property controls whether text wraps to a new line when it reaches the edge of the *TextBox* control. The value can be *WrapWithOverflow*, *NoWrap* (the default value), or *Wrap*.

- **MaxLength**   This dependency property defines the number of characters that users can enter manually. The default value is zero (*0*), which indicates no limit. This setting does not apply a limit to text set programmatically.

- **MaxLines**   This dependency property controls the size of the *TextBox* control—how many lines of text it will display. Although this property controls how many lines will be visible at any given time, it has no impact on the actual text value; in other words, the number of lines of text may exceed the number of lines set by this property. If you set the *Height* property of the *TextBox* control, the *MaxLines* property will be ignored. The default value is *Int32.MaxValue*, which is equal to 2,147,483,647.

- **MinLines**   This dependency property controls the size of the *TextBox* control—its value is the minimum number of lines the control will display. The control will resize if necessary to display the minimum number of lines set by this property. If you set the *Height* property of the *TextBox* control, the *MinLines* property will be ignored. The default value is *1*.

- **SelectedText**   This property returns a copy of the text selected in the *TextBox* control. Setting this value replaces the currently selected text with the new value.

- **SelectionLength**   This property defines the number of characters currently selected in the *TextBox* control. If you set this value through code-behind, it automatically adjusts the selection end point. During the adjustment process the control ensures that the end selection point is valid. For example, it won't end the selection at an invalid character position such as a carriage return or tab character. The default value is *zero (0)*.

- **SelectionStart**   This property defines the character index of the character at the beginning of the current selection.

RichTextBox

Supported By	
WPF	Yes
Silverlight	Yes

The *System.Windows.Controls.RichTextBox* control provides a wealth of editing capabilities. The *RichTextBox* control can host formatted text paragraphs, hyperlinks, UIElements, bulleted and numbered lists, images, and tables. This control can also host *FlowDocument* objects to provide rich editing capabilities.

The WPF and Silverlight platforms introduced the *System.Windows.Documents.FlowDocument* class, which is derived from the *System.Windows.FrameworkContentElement* class. This class can host and format a flow of content, and offers advanced document features such as pagination and columns. The *FlowDocument* class provides developers with endless opportunities to develop rich content for both Windows and web applications. The flow document can contain a group of one or more of the following child content elements derived from the abstracted *System.Windows.Documents. Block* class:

- **System.Windows.Documents.BlockUIContainer**   This class lets you embed XAML *UIElement* controls (such as *Button*, *Image*, and *Shape* controls) as flow content.

- **System.Windows.Documents.List**   This class enables the insertion of a collection of bulleted or numbered list items as flow content.

- **System.Windows.Documents.Paragraph**   This class supports plain text insertion as well as a group of *Inline* flow content elements such as *Bold*, *Figure*, *Floater*, *Hyperlink*, *InlineUIContainer*, *Italic*, *LineBreak*, *Run*, *Span*, and *Underline* that provide text-formatting capabilities.

- **System.Windows.Documents.Section**   This class enables you to insert a group of other content elements—*BlockUIContainer*, *List*, *Paragraph*, *Section*, and *Table*—derived from the *Block* class as child elements of the *Section* element.

- **System.Windows.Documents.Table**   This class enables the insertion of content in a matrix grid format (in rows and columns). The *Table* element can contain *FlowDocument*, *TableCell*, *ListBoxItem*, *ListViewItem*, *Section*, *Floater*, and *Figure* elements.

The *RichTextBox* control introduces the following two properties:

- **IsDocumentEnabled**   This property determines whether the user can interact with the *UIElement* and *ContentElement* objects inserted within the *RichTextBox* control. If the property is set to *true*, the user can interact with these objects; when set to *false*, the objects become read-only.

- **Selection**   This property returns a *System.Windows.Documents.TextSelection* object that contains the current selection in the *RichTextBox*. The default *TextSelection* object returned has a read-only *IsEmpty* property value set to *true*. To select the content within the *RichTextBox* control from code-behind you need to call the *System.Windows.Documents.TextRange.Select* method.

TextBox and *RichTextBox* Example

You have seen examples that use the *TextBox* control in earlier chapters of this book. This example demonstrates some additional attributes of the *TextBox* control, and the use of the *RichTextBox* control.

The following XAML code snippet performs the following actions:

- Sets key attributes of the *TextBox* control   Allows multiple lines by setting *AcceptsReturn* to *true*. Initiates text wrapping automatically by setting *TextWrapping* to *Wrap*. Horizontal and vertical scroll bars will be automatically visible. A maximum of 15 lines and minimum of 3 lines will be visible.

- Defines events of the *TextBox* control   The *TextChanged* event fires the *textbox_TextChanged* method in code-behind, and the *SelectionChanged* event fires the *textbox_SelectionChanged* method in code-behind.

- Inserts multiple *Paragraph, Section,* and *List* elements   These have various attributes, including a right-aligned paragraph with a variety of fonts and formatting (bold, underlined, and italic), an inline *Image*, an inline *Grid UIElement* control, and bullet list items.

```
<StackPanel>
    <StackPanel>
        <TextBlock Margin="5" FontWeight="Bold">
            Multi-line and Text Wrapping Enabled TextBox Control Example
        </TextBlock>
        <TextBox
            x:Name="textbox"
            Text="Default Text"
            TextWrapping="Wrap"
            AcceptsReturn="True"
            TextAlignment="Left"
            HorizontalScrollBarVisibility="Auto"
            VerticalScrollBarVisibility="Auto"
            MaxLines="15"
            MinLines="3"
            TextChanged="textbox_TextChanged"
            SelectionChanged="textbox_SelectionChanged"/>
    </StackPanel>
<StackPanel>
    <TextBlock Margin="5" FontWeight="Bold">RichTextBox Control Example</TextBlock>
        <RichTextBox>
            <FlowDocument>
                <Paragraph
                    FontSize="16"
                    TextAlignment="Right"
                    FontFamily="Courier New">
                    <Underline>
                        Right aligned formatted paragraph with
                        <Bold>
                            bold font
                        </Bold>
                        <LineBreak/>
                        <Italic>
                            Second formatted line with Italic font
                        </Italic>
```

```
            </Underline>
    </Paragraph>
    <Section>
        <Paragraph>
            This is inline image..
            <InlineUIContainer>
                <Image
                    Source="Resources/Tulips.jpg"
                    Height="150" Width="200"
                    Stretch="UniformToFill"/>
            </InlineUIContainer>
        </Paragraph>
        <List>
            <ListItem>
                <Paragraph>
                    List Item 1
                </Paragraph>
            </ListItem>
            <ListItem>
                <Paragraph>
                    List Item 2
                </Paragraph>
            </ListItem>
        </List>
    </Section>
    <Paragraph>
        <LineBreak/>
        Inserting Grid Panel to the RichTextBox
        <LineBreak/>
        <InlineUIContainer>
            <Grid>
                <Grid.ColumnDefinitions>
                    <ColumnDefinition/>
                    <ColumnDefinition/>
                </Grid.ColumnDefinitions>
                <Grid.RowDefinitions>
                    <RowDefinition/>
                    <RowDefinition/>
                </Grid.RowDefinitions>
                <Border Grid.Row="0" Grid.Column="0" Background="Beige">
                    <TextBlock HorizontalAlignment="Center"
                        VerticalAlignment="Center"
                        Text="Row = 0, Column = 0"/>
                </Border>
                <Border Grid.Row="0" Grid.Column="1"
                    Background="BurlyWood">
                    <TextBlock HorizontalAlignment="Center"
                        VerticalAlignment="Center"
                        Text="Row = 0, Column = 1"/>
                </Border>
                <Border Grid.Row="1" Grid.Column="0"
                    Grid.ColumnSpan="2"
                    Background="DarkKhaki"
                    BorderThickness="2"
BorderBrush="Black">
                    <StackPanel HorizontalAlignment="Center"
                        VerticalAlignment="Center" >
```

```
                                    <TextBlock Text="Row = 0, Column = 1"/>
                                    <TextBlock
                                        HorizontalAlignment="Center"
                                        Text="ColumnSpan = 2"/>
                            </StackPanel>
                        </Border>
                    </Grid>
                </InlineUIContainer>
            </Paragraph>
        </FlowDocument>
    </RichTextBox>
    </StackPanel>
</StackPanel>
```

The following code snippet shows the code-behind events implementation for *TextBox* controls:

```
private void textbox_TextChanged(object sender, TextChangedEventArgs e)
{
}
private void textbox_SelectionChanged(object sender, RoutedEventArgs e)
{
}
```

If you run the project now, you will see that the height of the *TextBox* control is automatically sized to display three lines, displaying *Default Text* in the first line. The *RichTextBox* displays the populated content at the design time. Figure 7-5 shows the output of this example. I have entered 16 lines of text in the *TextBox* control; line 3 is wrapped to two lines and displays a maximum of 15 lines with the horizontal scroll bar.

FIGURE 7-5 *TextBox, RichTextBox,* and *Border* controls example.

PasswordBox

Supported By	
WPF	Yes
Silverlight	Yes

You often need to build a user interface where users can enter sensitive information, such as a password, social security number, or PIN code. In such cases, you want to mask the user entry with some predefined character rather than displaying the actual entry text. The *System.Windows.Controls. PasswordBox* control is designed to facilitate such entries. It provides the ability to enter a single line of non-wrapping content so that a user can enter sensitive information. Each entered character gets displayed as a specified password character based on the *PasswordChar* property value.

The key properties of the *PasswordBox* control are:

- **PasswordChar**   This dependency property defines the masking character that will be displayed, replacing each input character entered by the user. The default value is a bullet character (●).

- **MaxLength**   This property defines the maximum number of characters allowed in the *PasswordBox*. The default value is zero (*0*), which represents no limit.

- **Password**   This property defines the current password value of the *PasswordTextBox*. It retrieves the entered password value as plain text stored in memory.

- **SecurePassword**   This property defines the current password value as a *SecureString*. The returned text is encrypted and will be deleted from the computer memory. This approach prevents the potential security risk of keeping the password string in plain text in memory as with the *Password* property.

> **Note** See the MSDN page at *http://msdn.microsoft.com/en-us/library/system.security .securestring.aspx* for more detail about the *System.Security.SecureString* class.

The *PasswordBox* control introduces *PasswordChanged* routed event, which occurs number of times the *Password* property changes.

The following example demonstrates the *PasswordBox* control with the *PasswordChar* set to an asterisk (*). It allows a maximum 10-character password by setting *MaxLength* to 10, and also fires the *PasswordChanged* event to display the entered password in plain text back to the user. Note that displaying the entered password is implemented only for demonstration purposes; for security reasons, you would never implement this feature in real-world applications:

```
<StackPanel>
    <TextBlock Margin="5" FontWeight="Bold">Enter Password</TextBlock>
    <PasswordBox
        x:Name="passwordbox"
        PasswordChar="*"
        MaxLength="10"
```

```
                    PasswordChanged="passwordbox_PasswordChanged"/>
         <TextBlock Margin="5" FontWeight="Bold">Display Entered Password</TextBlock>
         <TextBlock x:Name="displaypassword"/>
</StackPanel>
```

Here's the *PasswordChanged* event handler code:

```
private void passwordbox_PasswordChanged(object sender, RoutedEventArgs e)
{
    displaypassword.Text = passwordbox.Password;
}
```

Figure 7-6 shows the running application after entering the password *mypassword*.

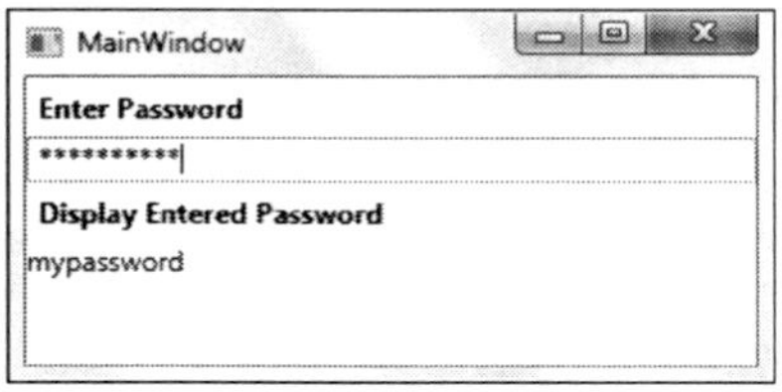

FIGURE 7-6 The *PasswordBox* control example.

StickyNoteControl

Supported By	
WPF	Yes
Silverlight	No

Annotation features are extremely useful when performing various text-centric processes such as reading, reviews, and sign-offs. Annotation has been a popular feature in Microsoft Office and Adobe products because they can help replace or reduce paper-based processes. With the help of the WPF platform, Microsoft is providing capabilities to build annotation features into your Windows applications. WPF document viewing controls such as *DocumentViewer*, *FlowDocumentPageViewer*, *FlowDocumentReader*, and *FlowDocumentScrollViewer* support annotation features. Note that the annotation feature is not yet available for the Silverlight platform.

The sticky note is a handy annotation tool in day-to-day life. You either use a handwritten note or an electronically typed, text-edited note. The *System.Windows.Controls.StickyNoteControl* class provides a *StickyNoteControl* control, which lets users add either inked (handwritten) or typed text notes. By default, a *StickyNoteControl* is a resizable rectangle that overlays the original content. Based on the type of sticky note you create, it contains either a *RichTextBox* control, which supports typed text, or an *InkCanvas* control, which enables handwritten note entry.

The control provides dependency properties such as *Author*, which provides the name of the author who created the sticky note. You can also determine the type of the sticky note (*Text* or *Ink*) through the *StickyNoteType* property. In addition, it provides properties such as *CaptionFontFamily*, *CaptionFontStyle*, and *CaptionFontSize* that define the appearance of the sticky note's caption. For full details on all of this control's properties, see *http://msdn.microsoft.com/en-us/library/system.windows.controls.stickynotecontrol.aspx.*

To demonstrate the sticky note feature, the following XAML code snippet creates two shortcut menu items to create *Text-* and *Ink*-type sticky notes on an XPS document displayed using a *DocumentViewer* control:

```
<Window x:Class="FormsFunctionalControls.MainWindow"
        xmlns="http://schemas.microsoft.com/winfx/2006/xaml/presentation"
        xmlns:x="http://schemas.microsoft.com/winfx/2006/xaml"
        xmlns:ann="clr-namespace:System.Windows.Annotations;assembly=PresentationFramework"
        Title="MainWindow" Height="600" Width="525">
    <Grid>
        <DocumentViewer x:Name="documentview" Loaded="documentview_Loaded">
            <DocumentViewer.ContextMenu>
                <ContextMenu>
                    <MenuItem
                        Command="ann:AnnotationService.CreateTextStickyNoteCommand"
                        Header="Add Text Note" />
                    <MenuItem
                        Command="ann:AnnotationService.CreateInkStickyNoteCommand"
                        Header="Add Ink Note" />
                </ContextMenu>
            </DocumentViewer.ContextMenu>
        </DocumentViewer>
    </Grid>
</Window>
```

Note that the XAML root node contains a reference to the *System.Windows.Annotation* namespace. This reference defines the *CreateTextStickyNoteCommand* and *CreateInkStickyNoteCommand* methods of the *AnnotationService* class, which create text or ink type sticky notes on the selected area. The code also defines the *Loaded* event for the *DocumentViewer* control, which will call the *documentview_Loaded* event handler in the code-behind. That code opens the specified XPS file and enables the annotation services.

To enable annotation services and read XPS-type documents, you need to add *UIAnnotationtype* and *ReachFramework.dll* assemblies to the project. You'll need to add the following references to the code-behind class:

```
using System.Windows.Annotations;
using System.Windows.Annotations.Storage;
using System.Windows.Xps;
using System.Windows.Xps.Packaging;
using System.IO;
```

Next, implement the *documentview_Loaded* method to load and open a predefined XPS document in the *DocumentViewer* control, and then start the annotations service by calling the *StartAnnotation* method. Here's the code-behind:

```
private void documentview_Loaded(object sender, RoutedEventArgs e)
{
    XpsDocument xpsdocument = new
        XpsDocument
            ("C:/Users/aghoda/Documents/Books/XAML/Projects/Chapter7/XPSSample.xps",
                FileAccess.Read);
    FixedDocumentSequence fds = xpsdocument.GetFixedDocumentSequence();
    documentview.Document = fds;
    StartAnnotations();
    documentview.Focus();
}
```

Next, define the *StartAnnotations()* method as shown here, which creates an annotation store and then starts the annotation services:

```
private AnnotationService _annotService = null;
private FileStream _annotStream = null;
private XmlStreamStore _annotStore = null;
private readonly string _annotStorePath = @"annotations.xml";
private void StartAnnotations()
{
    // If there is no AnnotationService yet, create one.
    if (_annotService == null)
        // docViewer is a document viewing control named in Window1.xaml.
        _annotService = new AnnotationService(documentview);
    // If the AnnotationService is currently enabled, disable it.
    if (_annotService.IsEnabled == true)
        _annotService.Disable();
    // Open a stream to the file for storing annotations.
    _annotStream = new FileStream(
        _annotStorePath, FileMode.OpenOrCreate, FileAccess.ReadWrite);
    // Create an AnnotationStore using the file stream.
    _annotStore = new XmlStreamStore(_annotStream);
    // Enable the AnnotationService using the new store.
    _annotService.Enable(_annotStore);
}
```

Note The preceding code example was taken directly from MSDN (*http://msdn.microsoft. com/en-us/library/ms748864.aspx*).

Run the project, and the *XPSSample.xps* file opens. Select a portion of the XPS text area and right-click to get the shortcut menu (Figure 7-7), from which you can choose to add either a text or ink sticky note.

Note You can find a complete example that demonstrates all the possible annotation services at *http://msdn.microsoft.com/en-us/library/ms771648.aspx*.

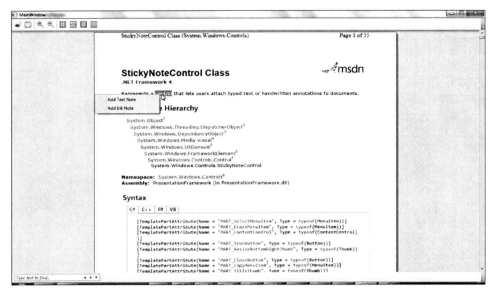

FIGURE 7-7 Adding a text or ink sticky note.

You can add multiple text and ink-type sticky notes, as shown in Figure 7-8.

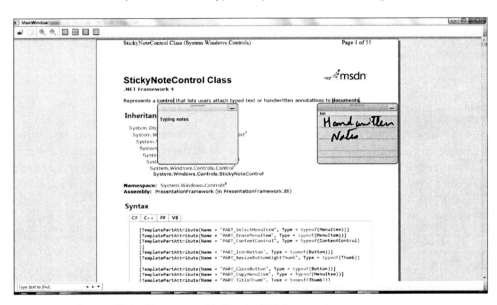

FIGURE 7-8 Text and ink sticky notes added to the XPS document.

Functional Controls to Improve Usability

Functional controls such as *Label*, *TextBlock*, *Border*, *ToolTip*, *Menu*, and *ContextMenu* help to organize and categorize information and different actions and provide useful visual guidance while you are working on the application.

Label

Supported By	
WPF	Yes
Silverlight	Yes (SDK)

The *System.Windows.Controls.Label* control provides user interface information with support for a shortcut access key. Unlike traditional Windows Forms label controls, the XAML *Label* control can not only display simple text but can also contain any *UIElement* because the *Label* class inherits from the *System.Windows.Controls.ContentControl* class.

The *Label* control provides a *Target* dependency property that defines which element should gain the focus when a user presses the Alt key along with the label's defined access key.

The following XAML code snippet defines a label for the *TextBox* control with the shortcut access key set to Alt + U (or ALT + u):

```
<StackPanel Orientation="Horizontal">
    <Label
        Content="_User ID:"
        Target="{Binding ElementName=userid}"
        Width="50" Height="25" FontSize="12"/>
    <TextBox Name="userid" Width="100" Height="25" FontSize="12" />
</StackPanel>
```

Be sure to note the format the *Target* property uses to bind the targeted element. You will use the regular binding format with the attribute *ElementName* set to the targeted element's *Name* property, which must be unique within the given scope in XAML. Also, in the *Content* property, you need to add an underscore (_) before the character you want to set as the label's access key. In this case we want to use U as the access key, so add an underscore before the U character, so it becomes *_User ID*.

Figure 7-9 shows the output of this example. The figure shows the *U* with an underline character in the label, which indicates that U is the shortcut access key.

FIGURE 7-9   Label control with access key.

Note You can use the same XAML code to create a Silverlight application. The only difference is that the *Label* control is part of the default WPF user controls library; for Silverlight it's available in the Silverlight SDK (*http://www.microsoft.com/download/en/details.aspx?id=7335*). For Silverlight you need add a reference to the Silverlight SDK to insert the *Label* control.

TextBlock

Supported By	
WPF	Yes
Silverlight	Yes

The *System.Windows.Controls.TextBlock* control provides an alternative to the *Label* control that adds unique features. The *TextBlock* control can contain not only single or multiple lines of plain text, but may also contain *Inline* flow content elements such as *LineBreak*, *Bold*, *Italic*, *Hyperlink*, and *InlineUIContainer* to format the content.

Some of the key properties of the *TextBlock* control are:

- **Text**   This dependency property contains the plain text for the *TextBlock* control. The default value is an empty string ("").

- **TextAlignment**   This dependency property defines the horizontal text alignment: left-aligned (*Left*), right-aligned (*Right*), center-aligned (*Center*), or justified (*Justify*). The default value is left-aligned.

- **TextWrapping**   This dependency property defines whether text wraps to a new line when it reaches the edge of the *TextBox* control. It can contain *WrapWithOverflow*, *NoWrap* (the default value), or *Wrap*.

- **TextEffects**   A dependency property used to apply one or more text effects based on the *TextEffect* objects collection. The default value is *null*.

- **TextDecorations**   A dependency property for visually decorating (altering the appearance) the text. The four possibilities are *Underline*, *Strikethrough*, *Baseline*, and *Overline*. The default value is *null*.

- **TextTrimming**   This dependency property determines how text will trim when it overflows the edge of the *TextBlock* control. You can set this value to *None* (no text trimming), *CharacterEllipsis* (trim text at character boundary and add an ellipsis (...) in place of the remaining text), and *WordEllipsis* (trim text at word boundary and add ellipsis in place of the remaining text). The default value is *None*.

- **InLines**   This dependency property defines an *InlineCollection* containing *Inline* elements such as *Bold*, *Hyperlink*, *Italic*, *Underline*, and *Span* as part of the *TextBlock* content.

- **FontFamily, FontSize, FontStretch, FontStyle, and FontWeight** These dependency properties define different font characteristics.

- **Background** A dependency property that defines a *Brush* to fill the background of the *TextBlock* control content area.

The following code snippet shows an example of a *TextBlock* control that contains simple text, a *Button* control as an *InlineUIContainer*, and formatted text. Figure 7-10 shows the output of this sample:

```
<StackPanel>
    <TextBlock
        Text="Simple Text in TextBlock Control"
        Height="20" Width="200"
        Margin="5"
        Background="Gray"
        HorizontalAlignment="Right"/>
    <TextBlock>
        <InlineUIContainer>
            <Button Content="Button"/>
        </InlineUIContainer>
        TextBlock Control with Inline
        <Italic>Button</Italic>
        Control and Text with
        <Bold>Bold font</Bold>
    </TextBlock>
</StackPanel>
```

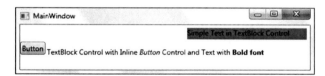

FIGURE 7-10 Demonstrating the *TextBlock* control.

Border

Supported By	
WPF	Yes
Silverlight	Yes

The *System.Windows.Controls.Border* control enables drawing of a border and/or background around a control. This control enables you to create a separation between two controls by creating a border with required thickness and also allows you to define the background. You can have only one element as child to the *Border* control. However, if you place one of the layout and positioning controls derived from the *Panel* class as a child element of the *Border*, the *Panel* control can contain one or more child elements.

Some of the key properties of the *Border* control are:

- **Background**   This dependency property defines a *Brush* to fill the background of the area defined by the border. It does not have any default value.

- **BorderBrush**   This dependency property defines a *Brush* to draw the outer border color. It does not have any default value.

- **BorderThickness**   This dependency property defines relative width (thickness) of the boundaries of the border. It has no default value.

- **CornerRadius**   This dependency property defines the degree to which corners of the border boundaries are rounded. It does not have any default value.

- **Padding**   This dependency property defines the *Thickness* value, which controls the space between the *Border* and its child element. It has no default value.

Revisit the earlier section of this chapter, "*TextBox* and *RichTextBox* Examples," to see an example that uses a *Border* control within a *Grid* element.

ToolTip

Supported By	
WPF	Yes
Silverlight	Yes

Tooltip is a common, functional UI element that you use mainly to provide a small amount of guidance text at runtime for any element or for any process. A *Tooltip* is a pop-up window that typically appears when you hover the mouse pointer over an element.

Both WPF and Silverlight provide support for displaying tooltips for any element both within XAML and through code-behind. The *System.Windows.Controls.ToolTipService* class provides a set of attached properties and static methods that enable a tooltip for an element; the *System.Windows. Controls.ToolTip* class creates a pop-up window that displays the tooltip information for an element.

The key attached properties of the *ToolTipService* class are:

- **Placement**   This attached property defines where the tooltip pop-up window appears in relation to the user interface element to which the tooltip applies. This property holds *PlacementMode* enumeration values. The possible values are *Bottom*, *Top*, *Right*, *Left*, and *Mouse*. The first four place the tooltip at the corresponding side of the target element, while *Mouse* causes the tooltip to appear at the mouse pointer position. The *Placement* property of the *ToolTipService* class takes precedence over the *Placement* property of the *ToolTip* class.

- **PlacementTarget**   This attached property defines the target element relative to which the tooltip will appear. You can set the *Tooltip* property for a parent element and then target a child visual element by using the property. When this property is not defined the tooltip always targets the visible parent element. When this property is not defined and the parent element is not visible, the tooltip appears at the upper-left corner of the current screen window. The *PlacementTarget* property of the *ToolTipService* class takes precedence over the *PlacementTarget* property of the *ToolTip* class.

- **ToolTip** This attached property defines tooltip content (simple text or element objects).

The *ToolTipService* class also provides *Get* and *Set* methods to get or set the value of the preceding attached properties.

The key attached properties of the *ToolTip* class are:

- **IsOpen** This property defines whether the tooltip window is visible (*true*) or not visible (*false*). The default value is *false*.

 Caution Use the *IsOpen* property only from code-behind. If used in XAML, the application will not function properly.

- **Placement** This attached property defines the placement of the tooltip pop-up window in the context of the user interface element for which you are setting the tooltip-using values from the *PlacementMode* enumerations. The four values—*Bottom*, *Top*, *Right*, and *Left*—cause the tooltip to appear at the bottom, top, right, or left of the target element; the value *Mouse* places the tooltip at the current mouse pointer position. The *Placement* property of the *ToolTipService* class takes precedence over the *Placement* property of the *ToolTip* class.

- **PlacementTarget** This attached property specifies a target element that controls the position where the tooltip appears. You can set the *Tooltip* property for a parent element and then target a child visual element using this property. When this property is not defined, the tooltip target is the visible parent element. When this property is not defined and the parent element is not visible, the tooltip will appear in the upper-left corner of the current screen window. The *PlacementTarget* property of the *ToolTipService* class takes precedence over the *PlacementTarget* property of the *ToolTip* class.

- **HorizontalOffset and VerticalOffset** These dependency properties define the horizontal and vertical distance (respectively) between the target element and the tooltip pop-up window alignment point. The default value is *0*.

The *ToolTip* class also provides two events. The *Opened* event occurs when a *ToolTip* becomes visible and the *Closed* event occurs when a *ToolTip* pop-up windows is closed and is no longer visible.

The *ToolTipService* class also provides *Get* and *Set* methods to get or set the value of the preceding attached properties.

In WPF, you can use the attached *ToolTip* property for an element or the *ToolTip* property from the *System.Windows.Controls.ToolTipService* class. In the following code snippet, the first *Button* control uses the *ToolTipService* class with its *ToolTip* property set to create a tooltip containing some simple text with a *Border* element. The second *Button* control uses the *ToolTip* attached property to create a similar tooltip.

```
<StackPanel>
    <Button Content="Submit">
        <ToolTipService.ToolTip>
            <Border BorderBrush="Black" BorderThickness="2" Background="Beige" Padding="5">
                <TextBlock Text="Click to Submit your changes"/>
            </Border>
        </ToolTipService.ToolTip>
    </Button>
    <Button Content="Cancel">
        <Button.ToolTip>
            <Border BorderBrush="Black" BorderThickness="2" Background="Beige" Padding="5">
                <TextBlock Text="Click to Cancel your changes"/>
            </Border>
        </Button.ToolTip>
    </Button>
</StackPanel>
```

Figure 7-11 shows the output of this example.

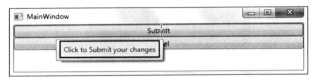

FIGURE 7-11   Demonstrating the *TextBlock* control.

 Note In Silverlight, only the *ToolTipService* class with its *ToolTip* property is available.

Menu

Supported By	
WPF	Yes
Silverlight	No

The majority of Window applications contain a menu bar. The menu bar can hold one or more menu items arranged in hierarchical fashion to create menus and submenus. You can associate each menu item with some action to be performed by attaching an event or executing a command.

The *System.Windows.Controls.Menu* class provides a *Menu* control for WPF that can contain one or more *MenuItem* controls—each of which can itself contain one or more actionable child elements.

The *Menu* class has an *IsMainMenu* dependency property that determines whether the *Menu* control receives a main menu activation notification when a user presses the ALT or F10 key. The default value is *true*.

The *System.Windows.Controls.MenuItem* class, which derives from the *System.Windows.Controls. HeaderedItemsControl*, can contain a header and collection of *MenuItem* objects that function as a submenu. A *MenuItem* can function in one of the following ways:

- As a header (top-level) menu item containing submenu items

- As a selectable menu item that can execute a command or raise an event

- As a menu item that can be checked or cleared

- As a menu item separator

The key properties of the *MenuItem* class are:

- **Command**   This dependency property defines the command to execute when a user selects the menu item. The command fires immediately after the *Click* event. The command is raised on the element in a specific order of priority:

  - When the *CommandTarget* property is set on the *MenuItem*, the element specified by *CommandTarget* is used.

  - The *PlacementTarget* of a *ContextMenu* that contains the *MenuItem*.

  - The focus target of the main window that contains the *Menu*.

  - The *MenuItem* that was clicked.

- **CommandParameter**   This dependency property defines a parameter to pass to the *Command* property of the *MenuItem*.

- **CommandTarget**   This dependency property defines the target element on which to raise the *Command* of the *MenuItem*. The default value is *null*. If this property is not set, the element with the keyboard focus receives the command.

- **Icon**   This dependency property defines the icon that appears with the *MenuItem*. The default value is *null*.

- **InputGestureText**   This dependency property defines an input gesture (a shortcut) that fires the command for the specified *MenuItem*. The default value is an empty string ("").

- **IsCheckable**   This dependency property defines whether the *MenuItem* can be checked (*true*) or not (*false*). The default value is *false*.

- **IsChecked**   This dependency property defines whether the *MenuItem* is currently checked (*true*) or not (*false*). The default value is *false*.

- **IsPressed**   This dependency property defines whether the *MenuItem* is currently pressed (*true*) or not (*false*). The default value is *false*.

- **Role**   This dependency property defines the role of the *MenuItem*. Possible values are:

- *TopLevelItem*   A top-level menu item that can invoke commands

- *TopLevelHeader*   A header for top-level menus

- *SubMenuItem*   A submenu item that can invoke command

- *SubMenuHearder*   A header for a submenu

- **StaysOpenOnClick**   This dependency property defines whether an opened submenu remains open after clicking a *MenuItem* within that submenu. The default value is *false*.

The key events of the *MenuItem* class are:

- **Checked**   Occurs when a *MenuItem* is checked

- **UnChecked**   Occurs when a *MenuItem* is cleared

- **Click**   Occurs when a *MenuItem* is clicked

- **SubmenuOpened**   Occurs when the *IsSubmenuOpen* property changes to *true*

- **SubmenuClosed**   Occurs when the *IsSubmenuOpen* property changes to *false*

Here's a brief example. The following code snippet creates a menu with various characteristics:

```
<StackPanel>
    <Menu>
        <MenuItem Header="_Menu">
            <MenuItem Header="_Copy" Command="Copy"/>
            <MenuItem
                Header="Menu Item _1"
                IsCheckable="True"
                Checked="MenuItem1_Checked"
                Unchecked="MenuItem1_Unchecked"/>
            <Separator/>
            <MenuItem
                Header="Menu Item 2"
                InputGestureText="Ctrl+2"
                Click="MenuItem2_Click"/>
        </MenuItem>
    </Menu>
</StackPanel>
```

Figure 7-12 shows the output of this example.

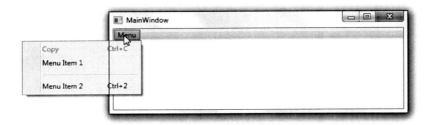

FIGURE 7-12   Demonstrating the *Menu* control.

ContextMenu

Supported By	
WPF	Yes
Silverlight	Yes (through code-behind)

Like the menu bar, the majority of content-driven Window applications also support context menus. Context menus are usually implemented as a right mouse click pop-up menu tied to the context of a specific element. The context menu can contain one or more menu items in hierarchical and non-hierarchical format to create menu and submenu. You can associate each menu item with some action to be performed by attaching an event or executing a command.

ContextMenu for WPF Platform

The *System.Windows.Controls.ContextMenu* class provides a Windows pop-up menu control for WPF that can contain one or more *MenuItem* controls, each of which can contain one or more actionable child elements.

The key properties of the *MenuItem* class are:

- **Placement** This dependency property defines the placement of the *ContextMenu* pop-up window in relation to the user interface element to which the context menu applies. This property can contain the following values from the *PlacementMode* enumeration: *Absolute*, *Relative*, *Bottom*, *Center*, *Right*, *AbsolutePoint*, *RelativePoint*, *Mouse*, *MousePoint*, *Left*, *Top*, and *Custom*.

> **More Info** The *PlacementMode* enumeration values are well named, but if you need more information, see *http://msdn.microsoft.com/en-us/library/system.windows.controls.primitives.placementmode.aspx.*

- **PlacementTarget** This dependency property defines the target element for the *Context-Menu*. When this property is not defined, the *ContextMenu* will target the parent element. The default value is *null*. You use the *PlacementTarget* property of the *ContextMenuService* class to target a different UI element than the parent.

- **PlacementRectangle** This dependency property defines the rectangle area where the *ContenxMenu* appears. The default value is *Empty*.

- **HorizontalOffset and VerticalOffset** These dependency properties define the horizontal and vertical distance (respectively) between the target element and the *ContextMenu* pop-up window alignment point. The default value is *0*.

- **IsOpen** This property defines whether the *ContextMenu* pop-up window is visible (*true*) or not visible (*false*). The default value is *false*.

- **StaysOpen** This dependency property controls whether the *ContextMenu* pop-up window stays open until the *IsOpen* property changes to *false* or whether it closes automatically (*false*). The default value is *false*.

Much like the *ToolTip* class, the *ContextMenu* class also provides two events. The *Opened* event occurs when the *ContextMenu* opens and the *Closed* event occurs when the *ContextMenu* pop-up window closes.

Revisit the preceding section on the *StickyNoteControl* in this chapter to see an example that uses the *ContextMenu* control.

ContextMenu for Silverlight

With Silverlight 4, you can enable a right mouse click pop-up context menu with the help of two newly introduced events: *MouseRightButtonDown* and *MouseRightButtonUp*. You can define these in both XAML and code-behind, using a three-step approach:

1. Set *MouseRightButtonDown* and *MouseRightButtonUp* events for the control you want to display in the right mouse click context menu in the XAML file.

2. Set *MouseButtonEventArgs.Handled* to *true*, and then use the *MouseRightButtonDown* event to remove the default Silverlight context menu that occurs on a right mouse click and substitute your custom right mouse click menu.

3. Create a custom right mouse click context menu using the *PopUp* class.

The following XAML code snippet demonstrates step 1. It defines *MouseRightButtonDown* and *MouseRightButtonUp* events for a *TextBox* control to enable a right mouse click custom context menu.

```
<UserControl x:Class="ContextMenu_Silverlight.MainPage"
    xmlns="http://schemas.microsoft.com/winfx/2006/xaml/presentation"
    xmlns:x="http://schemas.microsoft.com/winfx/2006/xaml"
    xmlns:d="http://schemas.microsoft.com/expression/blend/2008"
    xmlns:mc="http://schemas.openxmlformats.org/markup-compatibility/2006"
    mc:Ignorable="d"
    d:DesignHeight="300" d:DesignWidth="400">
    <StackPanel>
        <TextBlock>Demonstrating Context Menu in Silverlight</TextBlock>
        <TextBox x:Name="contextmenutextbox"
                MouseRightButtonDown="contextmenutextbox_MouseRightButtonDown"
                MouseRightButtonUp="contextmenutextbox_MouseRightButtonUp"/>
    </StackPanel>
</UserControl>
```

The following code-behind demonstrates step 2, which disables the default Silverlight context menu:

```
private void contextmenutextbox_MouseRightButtonDown
    (object sender, MouseButtonEventArgs e)
{
    e.Handled = true;
}
```

For the first part of step 3:

- Add a reference to the *System.Windows.Controls.Primitives* so that you can use the *Popup* class to create an instance of the custom pop-up window:

```
using System.Windows.Controls.Primitives;
```

- Now define a *Popup* instance at the class level:

```
Popup contextMenu = new Popup();
```

- Next, implement the *MouseRightButtonUp* event to define the pop-up context menu. This example creates two *Button* controls within a *StackPanel* and displays the *Popup* by setting the *IsOpen* dependency property to *true*:

```
private void contextmenutextbox_MouseRightButtonUp
    (object sender, MouseButtonEventArgs e)
{
    StackPanel panel1 = new StackPanel();
    panel1.Background = new SolidColorBrush(Colors.LightGray);
    //Menu Item 1
    Button menuitem1 = new Button();
    menuitem1.Content = "Menu Item 1";
    menuitem1.Width = 100;
    menuitem1.Margin = new Thickness(3);
    //Click event to provide Menu Item 1 functionality
    menuitem1.Click += new
    RoutedEventHandler(menuitem1_Click);

    //Menu Item 2
    Button menuitem2 = new Button();
    menuitem2.Content = "Menu Item 2";
    menuitem2.Width = 100;
    menuitem2.Margin = new Thickness(3);
    //Click event to provide Menu Item 2 functionality
    menuitem2.Click += new
    RoutedEventHandler(menuitem2_Click);

    panel1.Children.Add(menuitem1);
    panel1.Children.Add(menuitem2);

    contextMenu.Child = panel1;
    //set display location to current cursor
    contextMenu.VerticalOffset = e.GetPosition(null).Y;
    contextMenu.HorizontalOffset = e.GetPosition(null).X;
    //show the context menu
    contextMenu.IsOpen = true;
}
```

- Finally, implement the *Click* events for both the *Button* controls defined for the context menu:

```
private void menuitem1_Click(object sender, RoutedEventArgs e)
{
    MessageBox.Show("Menu Item 1 Related Code..");
    contextMenu.IsOpen = false;
```

```
    }
    private void menuitem2_Click(object sender, RoutedEventArgs e)
    {
        MessageBox.Show("Menu Item 2 Related Code..");
        contextMenu.IsOpen = false;
    }
```

When you run this project and right-click within the *TextBox* control, instead of the Silverlight default context menu, you will see the custom context menu displayed based on your current mouse pointer position, as shown in Figure 7-13.

FIGURE 7-13   A custom *ContextMenu* in a Silverlight application.

Functional Controls to Control and Monitor Behavior

Functional controls such as *ScrollBar*, *ScrollViewer*, *Slider*, and *ProgressBar* help to control and monitor both application and content behavior and visibility. The following sections describe these controls.

The *RangeBase* Class

The *System.Windows.Controls.Primitives.RangeBase* class provides behavior to handle a range of values and a selected value within that range. It is the base class for the *ScrollBar*, *Slider*, and *ProgressBar* controls. The *RangeBase* class uses *value coercion* to ensure that the current value is within the range. (In other words, the value remains between or equal to the minimum and maximum defined values.) The system raises an *ArgumentException* if any of the properties defining the end points of the range are set to a value that does not make sense, such as setting *Minimum* to *NaN* or *SmallChange* (the minimum change amount) to a value less than zero.

Key properties provided by the *RangeBase* class are:

- **Value**   This dependency property holds the current value of the range control. The default value is *0*. If the *Value* property is set to less than the *Minimum* property value, it automatically resets to the value of the *Minimum* property.

- **LargeChange**   This dependency property specifies the amount by which the *Value* increases or decreases when the user changes the value by a large amount. The default value is *1*. (Note that the *ProgressBar* control inherited from this class does not use this property.)

- **SmallChange**   This dependency property defines the amount by which the *Value* increases or decreases when the user changes the value by a small amount. The default value is *0.1*. (Note that the *ProgressBar* control inherited from this class does not use this property.)

- **Maximum**   This dependency property defines the highest possible *Value* of the range element. The default value is *1*, which is applicable to the *ScrollBar* control. The *Slider* control overrides this default property and sets it to *10* by default, whereas the *ProgressBar* control overrides and sets it to *100* by default.

- **Minimum**   This dependency property defines the smallest possible *Value* of the range element. The default value is *0*.

The *RangeBase* class provides a *ValueChanged* event that gets raised whenever the value of the range control changes.

ScrollBar

Supported By	
WPF	Yes
Silverlight	Yes

The *System.Windows.Controls.Primitives.ScrollBar* class is visually represented by two *RepeatButton* controls and a *Thumb* control that corresponds positionally to the currently selected value within the defined range.

Key properties provided by the *ScrollBar* class are:

- **Orientation**   This dependency property controls whether the *ScrollBar* displays vertically or horizontally:

  - For WPF, the *ScrollBar* control's default *Orientation* value is *Vertical*.

  - For Silverlight, the *ScrollBar* control's default *Orientation* value is *Horizontal*.

- **ViewportSize**   This dependency property specifies the amount of content currently visible according to the position of the thumb within the scrollbar. The default value is *0*.

- **Track**   This property defines the *System.Windows.Controls.Primitives.Track* for a *ScrollBar* control. The *Track* handles positioning and sizing the *Thumb* control and two *RepeatButton* controls used to set the *Value*. This property is available for the WPF version of the *ScrollBar* control only.

The *ScrollBar* control also provides a *Scroll* event that occurs multiple times when a user drags the *Thumb* control of the *ScrollBar* to change its position (and the *Value*).

The following XAML code snippet demonstrates horizontal and vertical scrollbars, as shown in Figure 7-14:

```
<StackPanel>
    <TextBlock Text="Horizontal Scroll Bar"/>
    <ScrollBar Orientation="Horizontal" Width="200"
```

```
          Minimum="0" Maximum="100"
          SmallChange="1" LargeChange="10" Value="50"/>
     <TextBlock Text="Vertical Scroll Bar"/>
     <ScrollBar Orientation="Vertical" Width="20" Height="150"/>
</StackPanel>
```

FIGURE 7-14   Horizontal and vertical *ScrollBar* controls.

Slider

Supported By	
WPF	Yes
Silverlight	Yes

The *System.Windows.Controls.Slider* control is similar to the *ScrollBar* control, but additionally provides the capability to select a particular value from within a range.

The key properties provided by the *Slider* class are:

■ **Orientation**   This dependency property controls whether the slider displays vertically or horizontally:

  • For WPF, the default is *Vertical*.

  • For Silverlight, the default is *Horizontal*.

■ **IsDirectionReversed**   This dependency property defines the direction of increasing value of a *Slider* control. The default value is *false*, which means that values increase as the thumb moves up for vertical sliders or right for horizontal sliders. When *true,* the direction of increasing values reverses: down for vertical sliders and left for horizontal sliders.

■ **IsFocused**   This dependency property determines whether the *Slider* control has focus (*true*) or not (*false*). The default value is *false*.

The following XAML code snippet demonstrates horizontal and vertical sliders, as shown in Figure 7-15:

```
<StackPanel>
    <TextBlock Text="Horizontal Slider"/>
    <Slider Orientation="Horizontal" Width="200"
```

```
            Minimum="0" Maximum="100"
            SmallChange="1" LargeChange="10"/>
    <TextBlock Text="Vertical Slider"/>
    <Slider Orientation="Vertical" Width="20" Height="150"
            IsDirectionReversed="True"/>
</StackPanel>
```

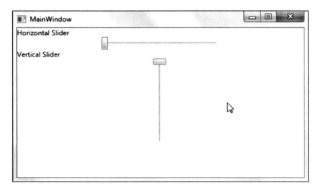

FIGURE 7-15 Two *Slider* controls in their initial default positions.

Note that for the vertical slider, the *IsDirectionReversed* property is set to *true*, which is why the default position of the vertical slider is at the topmost position.

ProgressBar

Supported By	
WPF	Yes
Silverlight	Yes

The *System.Windows.Controls.ProgressBar* control is intended to show users the progress of some operation. You can define the following two visual styles for the *ProgressBar* control using the *IsIndeterminate* property:

■ For a *ProgressBar* with a repeating pattern, set the *IsIndeterminate* property to *true*.

■ For a *ProgressBar* that gets filled progressively based on a value, set the *IsIndeterminate* property to *false*, and then define the range by setting the *Minimum* and *Maximum* properties and the value using the *Value* property.

The following XAML code snippet demonstrates both repeating and filling progress bars, as shown in Figure 7-16:

```
<StackPanel>
    <TextBlock Text="Repeating Pattern Progress Bar"/>
    <ProgressBar Height="20" Width="200" IsIndeterminate="True"/>
    <TextBlock Text="Filling Progress Bar"/>
    <ProgressBar Height="20" Width="200" IsIndeterminate="False"
        Minimum="0" Maximum="100" Value="30"/>
</StackPanel>
```

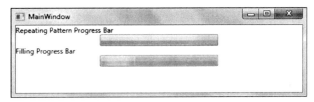

FIGURE 7-16 Repeating and progressively filling *ProgressBar* controls in action.

ScrollViewer

Supported By	
WPF	Yes
Silverlight	Yes

When you design any user interface you need to consider the possible screen resolution, window size and screen size of the devices on which users will access your applications. Often, you will encounter use cases where you need to display content using vertical and horizontal scroll bars, letting users scroll through the content that must appear within an area smaller than the content itself.

The *System.Windows.Controls.ScrollViewer* control provides such a capability. You use it when the content display control (such as a *Grid*) does not have the ability to display scrollbars.

Some of the key properties of the *ScrollViewer* control are:

- **HorizontalScrollBarVisibility** *and* **VerticalScrollBarVisibility**   These dependency properties control whether the horizontal and vertical scrollbars are visible (*true*) or not (*false*).

- **ViewportHeight** *and* **ViewportWidth**   These dependency properties define the height and width of the viewport within which the *ScrollViewer* displays content.

- **ScrollableHeight** *and* **ScrollableWidth**   These dependency properties define the vertical and horizontal size of the content.

- **ComputedHorizontalScrollBarVisibility** *and* **ComputedVerticalScrollBarVisibility**   These dependency properties determine whether the horizontal and vertical scrollbar are currently visible (*true* value) or not (*false* value).

- **HorizontalOffset** *and* **VerticalOffset**   These dependency properties define the horizontal and vertical distance (respectively) between the content and the scrollbars. The default value is *0*.

The following XAML code snippet demonstrates a *Grid* control containing a *Border* control in each cell with alternating black and white background colors. The *Grid* control itself is placed within a *ScrollViewer* control with vertical and horizontal scrollbars visible, as shown in Figure 7-17.

```
<StackPanel>
    <ScrollViewer Width="150" Height="150"
        HorizontalScrollBarVisibility="Auto">
```

```
<Grid Background="White" Height="200" Width="200">
    <Grid.RowDefinitions>
        <RowDefinition/>
        <RowDefinition/>
    </Grid.RowDefinitions>
    <Grid.ColumnDefinitions>
        <ColumnDefinition/>
        <ColumnDefinition/>
    </Grid.ColumnDefinitions>
    <Border Grid.Row="0" Grid.Column="0"
        Height="100" Width="100" Background="White"/>
    <Border Grid.Row="0" Grid.Column="1"
        Height="100" Width="100" Background="Black"/>
    <Border Grid.Row="1" Grid.Column="0"
        Height="100" Width="100" Background="Black"/>
    <Border Grid.Row="1" Grid.Column="1"
        Height="100" Width="100" Background="White"/>
        </Grid>
    </ScrollViewer>
</StackPanel>
```

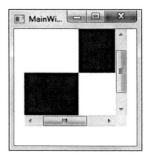

FIGURE 7-17   A *ScrollViewer* control containing a *Grid* with Border controls in each cell.

Summary

This chapter provided an overview of form controls and functional controls. You use *form* controls to provide various types of user interactions with the user interface. For example, form controls include *Button* type controls for initiating actions, and text entry controls for implementing text editing features. *Functional* controls improve the user experience by categorizing information and actions. Functional controls include those that improve usability, such as menus and context menus as well as guidance controls such as tooltips, labels, and text blocks. They also include controls to monitor and control behavior, such as scrollbars, sliders, and progress bars.

PART 4

Content Integration and Animation

CHAPTER 8

Data Binding

In this chapter:

- Data Sources
- Data Binding
- Binding Modes
- Data Templating, Conversion, and Validation
- Creating and Binding to an *ObservableCollection*
- Collection Views
- Hierarchical Binding
- Binding to XML Data
- Summary

Data binding is a process by which applications establish a connection between user interface (UI) elements and data. Using data binding, you can separate the *display* of data from the *manipulation* of data. When the underlying data source used to populate a UI with data undergoes frequent changes, the impact on your application can be huge. The data binding process maintains a connection between the UI and the data such that the impact is minimal.

Data binding can also ensure that whenever bound data changes—either in the UI or elsewhere—the corresponding value will be updated automatically. Most .NET technologies, including Windows Forms and ASP.NET, support data binding. XAML also includes strong support for data binding. In fact, data binding is one of the key capabilities and advantages of XAML. By implementing binding using declarative markup (and occasionally some code), you can ensure better data handling operations in your applications.

Data Sources

To begin working with data, you first need to have data present somewhere. In .NET jargon, a *data source* holds the data that you can use within your application. Examples of such data sources are databases, text files, XML files, object collections, and so forth. You typically connect to the data source or create an instance of it (in case it is a class), and then use the data source to store and retrieve data for your application.

In Visual Studio 2010, you can create a new data source using the Data Source Configuration Wizard.

In addition to databases, Silverlight and WPF applications support the following data source types:

- Service (data from a Web service)
- Object (data from objects in an assembly)
- SharePoint (data from a SharePoint site)

The following sections explore these data source types.

Service

You can use data from a Windows Communication Foundation (WCF) service as a data source. WCF data services consist of patterns and libraries that enable data creation and consumption through the web or an intranet. You use familiar HTTP actions such as *GET*, *PUT*, and *POST* to access and update the data.

Any application that sends HTTP requests and processes responses in the format that a data service understands can work with WCF Data Services.

Object

You can use data from objects in .NET assemblies as data sources. These are classes that define the data. You need to reference the appropriate assemblies in your Silverlight or WPF application.

You can also use the Silverlight Designer in Visual Studio 2010 to add a class as a data source. To do that, from the Choose Your Data Source Type page of the Data Source Configuration Wizard, select Object, and then select the appropriate class.

SharePoint

SharePoint sites can also function as data sources. If you have created a SharePoint List, you can make use of WCF Data Services to retrieve the SharePoint data in the Silverlight application.

In addition to the preceding types, WPF applications also support using a database as a data source.

Database

When employing a database as a data source, you create data objects by using either a *DataSet* or an Entity Data Model.

A *DataSet* is based on a disconnected architecture, and enables data access independent of a data source. The ADO.NET *DataSet* represents a complete collection of data, including tables, constraints, and any relationships among the tables.

Although the most commonly used data sources with *DataSet* are SQL Server databases, you can also use an XML data source, an Access database, an ODBC data source, and so on with a *DataSet*.

An Entity Data Model creates data classes based on the Microsoft ADO.NET Entity Data Framework. Visual Studio 2008 and ADO.NET 3.5 introduced this framework in .NET 4.0 and Visual Studio 2010 enhanced it further.

The ADO.NET Entity Framework is an Object-Relational Mapping (ORM) framework; ORM is a programming approach for converting data between relational databases and object-oriented programming languages. The ADO.NET Entity Framework consists of a data model and a number of design-time and runtime services. Using these, developers can describe the application data and interact with it at a conceptual abstraction level—making it ideal for business applications.

Note You can add an item of type ADO.NET Entity Framework directly to a Silverlight application through the Add New Item dialog box.

More Info Shawn Wildermuth has written an excellent blog post on the pros and cons of various data access strategies in Silverlight at *http://wildermuth.com/2009/09/29/ Choosing_a_Data_Access_Layer_for_Silverlight_3*.

Data Binding

After identifying the data source, you need to establish a link between the business logic and the application UI. In simpler terms, this means creating a link between the data in the data source and your UI elements. Data binding is the process of establishing this link.

Not only are several different kinds of data binding available, but you can also accomplish data binding in different ways.

Four major components are involved in data binding:

- binding target object
- target property
- binding source
- path

The *binding target object* is the object to which you want to bind some data. It's typically a UI element such as *TextBox*, *ListBox*, or *DataGrid*.

The *target property* may display and enable changes to the data. The target property can be any dependency property of a *FrameworkElement*. Silverlight 4 and later versions also support targets that are a *DependencyProperty* of a *DependencyObject* in certain cases:

- The *DependencyObject* is in a *DependencyObjectCollection*.

- The *DependencyObject* is part of a collection that is the value of a *FrameworkElement* property.

- The *DependencyObject* is the value of a property of a *FrameworkElement*.

The *binding source* can be any data source, as explained earlier. The *path* in a data binding expression indicates the path that must be traversed to get to the value in the data source. For example, a binding target object might be a *TextBlock* control. The target property could then be the *Text* property, the binding source could be a collection containing data from a database retrieved through a service, and the path could be the name of the column in the table or the table name.

Figure 8-1 shows an overview of data binding.

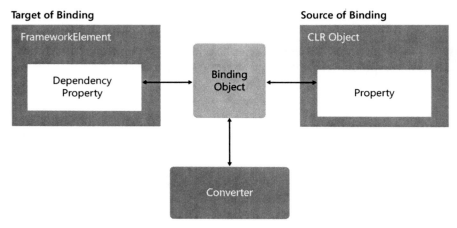

FIGURE 8-1   Data binding overview.

Setting the Binding Source

You can set the binding source in the following ways:

- Using the *DataContext* property

- Using the *Source* property

- Inheriting the *DataContext* property from the parent element

- Using the *ElementName* property

- Using the *RelativeSource* property

- Using the *Ancestor RelativeSource* property

The actual approach you use will depend on your application logic. You will see the details of some of these methods using some actual examples in this chapter.

The *DataContext* Property

The *DataContext* property indicates that any data it binds to is a property on the data item that either it or its parent is set to. Thus, if you have a *Button* defined within a *Grid* and you set the *DataContext* of that *Grid* to an instance of a class named *Toys*, both the *Button* and *Grid* controls can get or set properties from that *DataContext* instance.

Suppose, for example, that you have defined a *Toys* class in MainPage.xaml.cs as follows:

```
public class Toys : List<string>
{
    public string ColorName {get;set;}
}
```

You can now bind the *ColorName* property to a *Button* control in the following manner:

```
<Grid x:Name="LayoutRoot" >
    <Grid.Resources>
        <c:Toys x:Key="myClass" ColorName="Yellow"/>
    </Grid.Resources>
    <Button Background="{Binding ColorName}" DataContext="{StaticResource myClass}"
      Margin="220,140,236,295" Content="Submit"/>
</Grid>
```

Here, the code uses the *DataContext* property of the *Button* along with the *Binding* markup extension to bind the background to the *ColorName* property. The code assumes that you have declared an XML namespace alias named *c* for the current assembly.

The *Source* Property

The following code achieves the same outcome using the *Source* property of the *Binding* object:

```
<Grid x:Name="LayoutRoot" >
    <Grid.Resources>
        <c:Toys x:Key="myClass" ColorName="Yellow"/>
    </Grid.Resources>
    <Button Background="{Binding Path=ColorName, Source={StaticResource myClass}}"
      Margin="220,140,236,295" Content="Submit"/>
</Grid>
```

The difference between the *Source* and the *DataContext* property is that the latter enables all the child elements of the main element to inherit the data source.

Inheriting the *DataContext* Property from the Parent Element

Consider an example where you want to set the *DataContext* on a *Grid* and have all the child elements of the *Grid* inherit that *DataContext*. You can achieve this as follows:

```
<UserControl.Resources>
    <c:Toys x:Key="myClass" ColorName="Yellow"/>
</UserControl.Resources>
```

```
<Grid x:Name="LayoutRoot" DataContext="{StaticResource myClass}" Height="317" Width="358">
    <Grid.RowDefinitions>
        <RowDefinition Height="150" />
        <RowDefinition Height="150" />
            </Grid.RowDefinitions>
    <Grid.ColumnDefinitions>
        <ColumnDefinition Width="174"/>
        <ColumnDefinition Width="172"/>
      </Grid.ColumnDefinitions>
        <Button Background="{Binding ColorName}"  Height="30" Width="120"  Content="Submit"
         Margin="12,52,42,68" Grid.Column="0" x:Name="btn1"/>
        <Button Background="{Binding ColorName}"  Content="Cancel"
         HorizontalAlignment="Right" Height="30" Width="120" Margin="0,52,25,68"
         Grid.Column="1" />
    </Grid>
```

Here, both buttons will have the same background, set through the *ColorName* property, because they inherit the *DataContext* from the *Grid*.

The *ElementName* Property

The following markup shows a simple example of using the *ElementName* property:

```
<Button x:Name="btn1" Background="Pink"  Height="30" Width="120"  Content="Submit"
    Margin="12,52,42,68" Grid.Column="0" />
<Button x:Name="btn2" Background="{Binding ElementName=btn1, Path=Background}"  Content="Cancel"
    HorizontalAlignment="Right" Height="30" Width="120" Margin="0,52,25,68" Grid.Column="1" />
```

Here, the second button will have the same background as the first button because of the binding.

The *RelativeSource* Property

The *RelativeSource* property uses the location of the data source relative to the position of the binding target. The *RelativeSource* property is useful when you specify the binding in a control template or a style.

The general syntax for this property is as follows:

```
<Binding>
  <Binding.RelativeSource>
    <RelativeSource Mode="modeEnumValue"/>
  </Binding.RelativeSource>
</Binding>
- or
<Binding>
  <Binding.RelativeSource>
    <RelativeSource
      Mode="FindAncestor"
      AncestorType="{x:Type typeName}"
      AncestorLevel="intLevel"
    />
  </Binding.RelativeSource>
</Binding>
```

where *modeEnumValue* is one of the following string tokens:

- *Self*   Represents a *RelativeSource* binding source that is created with *Mode* set to *Self*.

- *TemplatedParent*   Represents a *RelativeSource* binding source that is created with *Mode* set to *TemplatedParent*.

- *PreviousData*   Represents a *RelativeSource* binding source that is created with *Mode* set to *PreviousData*.

- *FindAncestor*   Using this string token enters a mode through which a *RelativeSource* specifies an ancestor type and optionally an ancestor level. This is similar to a *RelativeSource* created with its *Mode* property set to *FindAncestor*.

- *typeName*   This string token is an attribute required for *FindAncestor* mode and indicates the name of a type, which fills the *AncestorType* property.

- *intLevel*   This string token is an optional attribute for *FindAncestor* mode, indicating an ancestor level.

Here are a few examples of using *RelativeSource*:

- *{Binding RelativeSource={RelativeSource Self}}* will bind to a target element.

- *{Binding RelativeSource={RelativeSource Self}, Path=Color}* will bind to the *Color* property of a target element.

- *{Binding RelativeSource={RelativeSource FindAncestor, AncestorType={x:Type Window}}, Path=Title}* will bind to the title of the parent window.

- *{Binding RelativeSource={RelativeSource FindAncestor, AncestorType={x:Type ItemsControl}, AncestorLevel=2}, Path=Name}* will bind to the name of the second parent of type *ItemsControl*.

- *{Binding RelativeSource={RelativeSource TemplateParent}, Path=Name}* is the same as *{TemplateBinding Name}* and will bind to the *Name* property of the element to which the template is applied.

Ancestor *RelativeSource*

This is a feature of XAML supported by both Silverlight 5 and WPF that lets you bind to a property of a parent control.

To implement this feature, you first use *{Binding.RelativeSource}* to specify the source in the tree, and then use the *AncestorType* property to specify the type of parent control to bind to, and if necessary, the *AncestorLevel* property to specify how far that parent control is from the current control.

The following markup demonstrates a simple example of using *FindAncestor* and *AncestorType*:

```
<TextBlock Text="{Binding Path=Title, RelativeSource= {RelativeSource FindAncestor,
  AncestorType=navigation:Page}}"/>
```

In that example, the XAML code displays the title of the page in a *TextBlock* control that you place at the top of a page.

The following XAML code shows a series of *TextBlock* controls binding to the same *Tag* property of a *Grid*:

```
<Grid Tag="RelativeSource Demonstration">
    <Grid.RowDefinitions>
        <RowDefinition Height="80" />
        <RowDefinition Height="80" />
        <RowDefinition Height="80" />
    </Grid.RowDefinitions>
    <Grid.ColumnDefinitions>
        <ColumnDefinition />
    </Grid.ColumnDefinitions>
    <TextBlock Text="{Binding Tag, RelativeSource={RelativeSource
      AncestorType=Grid}}"
      Grid.Row="0" Grid.Column="0"
      Foreground="Orange" />
    <TextBlock Text="{Binding Tag, RelativeSource={RelativeSource
      AncestorType=Grid, AncestorLevel=1}}"
      Grid.Row="1" Grid.Column="0"
      Foreground="BlueViolet" />
    <TextBlock Text="{Binding Tag,
     RelativeSource={RelativeSource AncestorType=Grid,
     AncestorLevel=1}}"
      Grid.Row="2" Grid.Column="0"
      Foreground="Magenta" />
</Grid>
```

Figure 8-2 shows the outcome of the markup.

FIGURE 8-2 Using Ancestor *RelativeSource*.

 Note *Source, RelativeSource*, and *ElementName* are mutually exclusive in a binding. After you set one of these attributes, setting either of the other two in a binding results in an exception.

MultiBinding

In addition to binding to single values, you can also implement MultiBinding. MultiBinding is a form of binding that enables you to bind to multiple items but return a single new value by using a converter. This is done by using the *MultiBinding* element in XAML. The simplest example that you can create in WPF to implement MultiBinding is as follows:

```
<StackPanel>
    <TextBlock Height="35" Width="166">
        <TextBlock.Text>
            <MultiBinding StringFormat="Mr {0} is a {1}.">
                <Binding Path="Name" />
                <Binding Path="JobTitle" />
            </MultiBinding>
        </TextBlock.Text>
    </TextBlock>
</StackPanel>
```

The preceding XAML binds a single *TextBlock* to two different items. This would not have been possible before the MultiBinding feature.

> **Note** MultiBinding in WPF is fairly easy, but the process is a little more complex in Silverlight. For more information on MultiBinding in Silverlight, visit Colin Eberhadt's blog, which has a detailed article on this topic along with sample source code, at *http://www.scottlogic.co.uk/blog/colin/2009/06/silverlight-multibindings-how-to-attached-mutiple-bindings-to-a-single-property/*.

Binding to Data from a Database

Binding in Windows Forms and WPF can be fairly direct, but in Silverlight-based Web applications, you must access such data through a service. You can use a WCF service, a WCF Data service, or RIA services to accomplish this.

> **More info** For more information about WCF RIA services and WCF SOAP services, see *http://www.silverlight.net/learn/advanced-techniques/wcf-ria-services/get-started-with-wcf-ria-services* and *http://blog.tonysneed.com/2010/04/13/wcf-data-services-versus-wcf-soap-services/*.

Consider this example to bind a *DataGrid* in a Silverlight application. Assume that you have a Silverlight application named Silverlight_and_Data. For the sake of simplicity, the details of the application are left out here. You may implement a Silverlight Model-View-ViewModel (MVVM) application and then include data binding features in it. MVVM is a framework—a pattern for clean separation of business logic, data, and UI elements.

More Info If you are not familiar with MVVM, the following links will help you understand the concept:

http://www.codeproject.com/KB/silverlight/IssueVisionForSilverlight.aspx

http://weblogs.asp.net/kashyapa/archive/2010/01/01/mvvm-sample-applications-index.aspx

http://alexburtsev.wordpress.com/2011/03/05/mvvm-pattern-in-silverlight-and-wpf/

For now, let's continue with the simple application, by following these steps:

1. Drag and drop a *DataGrid* onto the design area of MainPage.xaml using the ToolBox. Configure the new *DataGrid* as follows:

```
<sdk:DataGrid Name="dgCustomers" AutoGenerateColumns="True" Margin="15,44,45,161"
ItemsSource="{Binding}"/>
```

2. Open Server Explorer and add a new data connection, as shown in Figure 8-3.

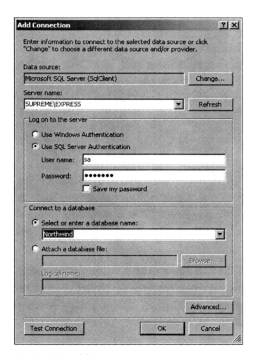

FIGURE 8-3 Adding a new connection.

The Northwind database shown in Figure 8-3 is a sample database for SQL Server. You can download it from the samples provided with this book.

3. Select the Silverlight_and_Data.Web project in Solution Explorer, and add a new item to the application using the Add New Item dialog box.

4. Select the ADO.NET Entity Data Model item, and then rename it **NorthwindModel.edmx,** as shown in Figure 8-4.

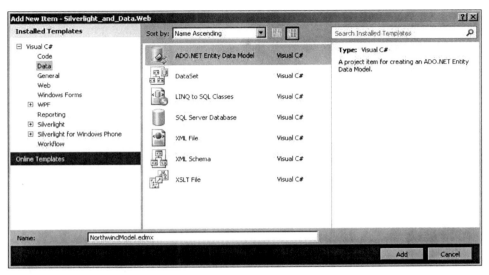

FIGURE 8-4 Adding an Entity Data Model.

5. In the Entity Data Model Wizard, select Generate from the database. Select appropriate connection details, as shown in Figure 8-5. Choose the Customers table in the Choose Your Database Objects section and click Finish.

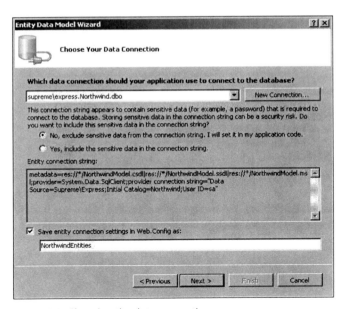

FIGURE 8-5 Choosing the data connection.

6. Select the Silverlight_and_Data.Web project in the Solution Explorer, and then add a new Silverlight-enabled WCF Service item to the application using the Add New Item dialog box.

7. Name the service **NorthwindService,** as shown in Figure 8-6.

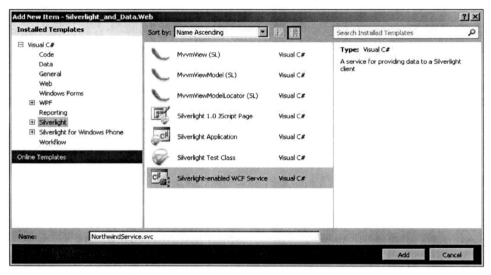

FIGURE 8-6 Creating a WCF service.

8. Add the following code to the NorthwindService.svc.cs file:

```
[ServiceContract(Namespace = "")]
[AspNetCompatibilityRequirements(RequirementsMode = AspNetCompatibilityRequirementsMode.
Allowed)]
public class NorthwindService
{
    [OperationContract]
    public List<Customer> GetCustomers()
    {
        NorthwindEntities ncontext = new NorthwindEntities();
        var customers = from customer in ncontext.Customers
                        select customer;
        return customers.ToList();
    }
}
```

9. Build the Web application containing the service. Add a service reference named **NorthwindServiceReference** in the Silverlight application to the service, as shown in Figure 8-7.

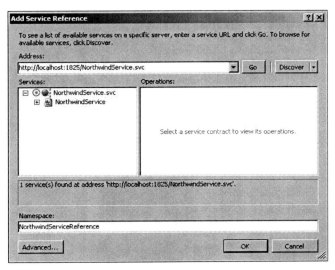

FIGURE 8-7 Adding the service reference.

10. In MainPage.xaml, add the following code:

```
<UserControl xmlns:sdk="http://schemas.microsoft.com/winfx/2006/xaml/presentation/sdk"
x:Class="Silverlight_and_Data.MainPage"
    xmlns="http://schemas.microsoft.com/winfx/2006/xaml/presentation"
    xmlns:x="http://schemas.microsoft.com/winfx/2006/xaml"
    xmlns:d="http://schemas.microsoft.com/expression/blend/2008"
    xmlns:mc="http://schemas.openxmlformats.org/markup-compatibility/2006"
    mc:Ignorable="d"
    >
    <Grid x:Name="LayoutRoot" Background="White" Height="199" Width="466">
      <sdk:DataGrid Name="dgCustomers" AutoGenerateColumns="True" Margin="15,44,45,0"
        ItemsSource="{Binding}" Background="Beige"
      />
    </Grid>
</UserControl>
```

This markup code has specified the target property *ItemsSource* of the UI element *dgCustomers* for data binding. The *Binding* object establishes a binding.

11. In MainPage.xaml.cs add the following code:

```
using Silverlight_and_Data.NorthwindServiceReference;
...
public partial class MainPage : UserControl
{
public MainPage()
{
```

```
        InitializeComponent();
        var client = new NorthwindServiceClient();
        client.GetCustomersCompleted += new
            EventHandler<GetCustomersCompletedEventArgs>
            (client_GetCustomersCompleted);
        client.GetCustomersAsync();
    }
    void client_GetCustomersCompleted(object sender,
        GetCustomersCompletedEventArgs e)
    {
        this.dgCustomers.DataContext = e.Result;
    }
}
```

Figure 8-8 shows the resulting output.

FIGURE 8-8 Output after data binding.

The output from the preceding steps shows an additional column, EntityKey. To remove this column, create an event handler for the *AutoGeneratingColumn* event and add the following code to MainPage.xaml.cs. The code checks each column's property name to see if it matches with the strings *"EntityState"* or *"EntityKey"*. If a match is found, the particular column will not be added:

```
private void dgCustomers_AutoGeneratingColumn(object sender,
DataGridAutoGeneratingColumnEventArgs e)
{
    if ((e.PropertyName == "EntityState") || (e.PropertyName == "EntityKey"))
    {
        e.Cancel = true;
    }
}
```

Also update the XAML to include the event handler:

```
<Grid x:Name="LayoutRoot" Background="White" Height="199" Width="466" >
  <sdk:DataGrid Name="dgCustomers" AutoGenerateColumns="True" Margin="15,44,45,0"
    ItemsSource="{Binding}" Background="Beige"
    AutoGeneratingColumn="dgCustomers_AutoGeneratingColumn"/>
</Grid>
```

Binding Modes

Apart from the default binding, which is one-way, you can also configure binding to be two-way, one-way to source, and so forth. You can do this by specifying the *Mode* property, as shown in Table 8-1.

TABLE 8-1 Binding Modes

Mode	Description
OneWay	This causes changes to the source property to automatically update the target property but the source does not get changed.
TwoWay	This causes changes in the source or target to automatically update the other.
OneWayToSource	This causes changes to the target property to automatically update the source property but the target does not get changed.
OneTime	This causes only the first-time change to the source property to automatically update the target property but the source does not get changed, and subsequent changes do not affect the target property.

Example of Two-Way Binding with *TextBox*

Consider the following example that demonstrates two-way data binding with a *TextBox*. This example creates a *ListBox* containing a set of routes. A *TextBox* control is bound to this *ListBox* using the following code:

```
<TextBox Text="{Binding ElementName=FlightRoutes, Path=SelectedItem.Content, Mode=TwoWay}">
```

Here, the code has specified the binding source, the path to bind to, and the binding mode. Because the binding mode is set to two-way, any changes made to the *TextBox* are automatically reflected in the *ListBox*. As mentioned in Table 8-1, two-way binding means that changes made to the bound control result in updates to the source and vice versa.

The XAML code for this example is:

```
<Grid x:Name="LayoutRoot" Background="White" Height="199" Width="466">
    <Grid.RowDefinitions>
        <RowDefinition Height="150" />
        <RowDefinition Height="150" />
        <RowDefinition Height="150" />
        <RowDefinition Height="150" />
    </Grid.RowDefinitions>
    <Grid.ColumnDefinitions>
        <ColumnDefinition />
    </Grid.ColumnDefinitions>
    <ListBox x:Name="FlightRoutes" Grid.RowSpan="2" Background="Azure" Height="158"
      Margin="0,0,12,142" Width="137">
        <ListBoxItem Content="LA"/>
        <ListBoxItem Content="Mexico"/>
        <ListBoxItem Content="SF"/>
        <ListBoxItem Content="Au"/>
    </ListBox>
```

```
          <TextBox Text="{Binding ElementName=FlightRoutes, Path=SelectedItem.Content, Mode=TwoWay}"
            Background="LightPink" Margin="0,42,12,81" Grid.Row="1" Height="27" Width="137">
          </TextBox>
          <Button Content="Submit" Grid.Row="1" Height="23" HorizontalAlignment="Left"
            Margin="62,107,0,0" Name="btnClick" VerticalAlignment="Top" Width="75" />
      </Grid>
```

Source Updates

When the *Mode* property of a binding is set to *TwoWay* or *OneWayToSource*, the binding will keep
a lookout for changes in the target property and accordingly send the changes to the source. This
process, called *updating the source*, usually takes place whenever the target property undergoes a
change. As a developer, you want better control over what causes an update, rather than relying on a
default mechanism. The *UpdateSourceTrigger* property of the *Binding* class enables you to determine
what causes source updates. This is basically an enumeration.

In WPF, this property has three possible values: *LostFocus*, *PropertyChanged*, and *Explicit*. *LostFocus*
causes the source to update whenever the control in question loses focus. *PropertyChanged* causes
the source to update whenever the property of a control in question changes value. *Explicit* causes
the source to update whenever the application calls the *UpdateSource*() method. Unless you call this
method, the source will not receive any changes.

Different dependency properties have different *UpdateSourceTrigger* values. The default
for most controls is *PropertyChanged*. Though this is good enough for most basic controls, you don't
want to use the same for text boxes or other text fields. For this reason, the default *UpdateSource-
Trigger* value of the *Text* property is *LostFocus* and not *PropertyChanged*.

Silverlight supports only two values: *Default* and *Explicit*. A simple example of updating the source
using the *Explicit* value of *UpdateSourceTrigger* is shown here:

```
<TextBox x:Name="textBox1" Text="{Binding Path=Text, ElementName=textBox2, Mode=TwoWay,
UpdateSourceTrigger=Explicit}" TextChanged="textBox1_TextChanged" Margin="0,117,458,344" />
<TextBox x:Name="textBox2" Margin="0,160,458,302" />
```

Here, as soon as you begin typing in the first text box, the second text box is updated. This is
because of the *UpdateSourceTrigger*. By default, the behavior for *TextBox* is such that the source
updates happen only on the *LostFocus* event.

Data Templating, Conversion, and Validation

Consider a simple example of a *ListBox* bound to the *CompanyName* column of a table named
Customers. The following is the XAML markup for the example:

```
      <Grid Height="383" Width="508">
          <ListBox Height="155" HorizontalAlignment="Left" Margin="12,29,0,0"
            Name="listBox1" VerticalAlignment="Top" Width="202" ItemsSource="{Binding}">
          </ListBox>
          <TextBlock Height="22" HorizontalAlignment="Left" Margin="12,0,0,0"
            Name="textBlock1" Text="Company Name" VerticalAlignment="Top" Width="146" />
      </Grid>
```

The code-behind class logic is as follows:

```
using System;
. . .
using Silverlight_and_Data.NorthwindServiceReference;
namespace Silverlight_and_Data
{
    public partial class MainPage : Page
    {
        public MainPage()
        {
            InitializeComponent();
            var client = new NorthwindServiceClient();
            client.GetCustomersCompleted += new EventHandler<GetCustomersCompletedEventArgs>
(client_GetCustomersCompleted);
            client.GetCustomersAsync();
        }
        void client_GetCustomersCompleted(object sender, GetCustomersCompletedEventArgs e)
        {
            this.DataContext = e.Result;
        }
    }
}
```

Upon executing the application, you will be bewildered to see the series of words Silverlight_and_Data.NorthwindServiceReference.Customer, as shown in Figure 8-9.

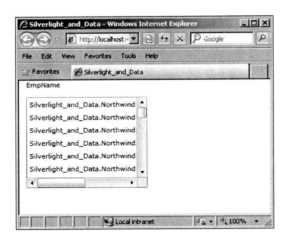

FIGURE 8-9 Output displayed without using templates.

This has happened because there is no template specified to display the data in the *ListBox*. Without a template, the runtime will not know how to render the output in the *ListBox*. In the present example, the *ListBox* by default calls *ToString()* on the objects it is binding to. Hence, the *ListBox* shows a series of strings containing the words Silverlight_and_Data.NorthwindServiceReference.Customer. This is the string representation of each object in the underlying data source.

But what you actually want is the list of company names. You need a means to specify how to render the content.

Data Templating

The *DataTemplate* class enables you to specify a template that will indicate how to render the output for a data object. The MSDN library defines the purpose of the *DataTemplate* class as "Describes the visual structure of a data object." You can use a *DataTemplate* anytime you bind an *ItemsControl* to an entire collection. The *DataTemplate* class also enables you to create visually rich representations of data.

Let's add a *DataTemplate* to the preceding XAML code:

```
<Grid Height="383" Width="508">
  <ListBox Height="155" HorizontalAlignment="Left" Margin="12,29,0,0" Name="listBox1"
    VerticalAlignment="Top" Width="202" ItemsSource="{Binding}">
    <ListBox.ItemTemplate>
      <DataTemplate>
        <TextBlock Text="{Binding Path=CompanyName}"/>
      </DataTemplate>
    </ListBox.ItemTemplate>
  </ListBox>
  <TextBlock Height="22" HorizontalAlignment="Left" Margin="12,0,0,0" Name="textBlock1"
    Text="Company Name" VerticalAlignment="Top" Width="146" />
</Grid>
```

Here, the template specifies that a *TextBlock* that is bound to a target, *CompanyName*, represents each item in the *ListBox*.

Figure 8-10 shows the result of adding this template.

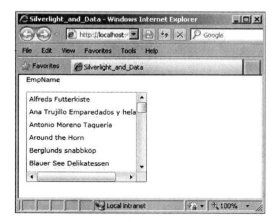

FIGURE 8-10 Output with templates.

The complete XAML code for the example is listed here:

```
<Grid Height="383" Width="508">
  <ListBox Height="155" HorizontalAlignment="Left" Margin="12,29,0,0" Name="listBox1"
    VerticalAlignment="Top" Width="202" ItemsSource="{Binding}">
```

```
    <ListBox.ItemTemplate>
      <DataTemplate>
        <TextBlock Text="{Binding Path=CompanyName}"/>
      </DataTemplate>
    </ListBox.ItemTemplate>
  </ListBox>
  <TextBlock Height="22" HorizontalAlignment="Left" Margin="12,0,0,0" Name="textBlock1"
    Text="Company Name" VerticalAlignment="Top" Width="146" />
</Grid>
```

Instead of defining the template inline as shown in the preceding example, you can also define the template as a resource:

```
<Grid Height="383" Width="508">
  <Grid.Resources>
    <DataTemplate>
      <TextBlock Text="{Binding Path=CompanyName}"/>
    </DataTemplate>
  </Grid.Resources>
  <ListBox Height="155" HorizontalAlignment="Left" Margin="12,29,0,0" Name="listBox1"
    VerticalAlignment="Top" Width="202" ItemTemplate="{StaticResource NameTemplate}">
  </ListBox>
  <TextBlock Height="22" HorizontalAlignment="Left" Margin="12,0,0,0" Name="textBlock1"
    Text="CompanyName" VerticalAlignment="Top" Width="146" />
</Grid>
```

The output in both of the cases would be the same. The advantage of declaring the template as a resource is that it now becomes reusable and you can now apply it to other controls as well.

Data Conversion

Occasionally you may come across situations where the data you are binding to is in a different format from the way you want it to be displayed. In such a case, you would use data value converters. Converters are a provision in WPF and Silverlight to help you bind to data present in one form and display it in a totally different format. Also, data binding mechanisms in Silverlight are far less powerful than those in WPF. To find a workaround for this, you need to create and implement many converters.

You can create custom converters by deriving from the *IValueConverter* interface located in the *System.Windows.Data* namespace. This interface defines two methods: *Convert()* and *ConvertBack()*. When a value that is being rendered from a binding source to a binding target is to be converted, the XAML binding engine calls the *Convert()* method, returns the converted value, and passes the returned data to the target.

In simpler words, whenever you pass data from the source, XAML binding engine calls *Convert()* and returns the converted value. When data is passed from the target, the binding engine calls *ConvertBack()* and passes the returned data to the source.

Consider a scenario where you want to bind an *Image* control to images based on content you choose in a *ComboBox* control. You can implement a custom converter to convert the string returned by the *ComboBox* control to an image. The following markup and code demonstrate how to do this:

```
<StackPanel>
        <StackPanel.Resources>
            <local:TextToImageConverter x:Key="boolToImage" />
        </StackPanel.Resources>
        <ComboBox x:Name="pictureName" Height="33" Width="158">
            <ComboBoxItem Content="Sunset" />
            <ComboBoxItem Content="Winter" />
            <ComboBoxItem />
        </ComboBox>
        <Image Margin="8" Width="191" Height="196"
        VerticalAlignment="Top" HorizontalAlignment="Center"
        Source="{Binding ElementName=pictureName, Path=SelectedItem.Content,
          Converter={StaticResource boolToImage}}" />
</StackPanel>
```

The markup creates a *ComboBox* control with a few sample items. When you select one of its items, it causes the *Image* control to update its *Source*. The *Source* of an *Image* control takes an image—hence you will create a converter that returns an image.

The code for the example is as follows:

```
public class TextToImageConverter : IValueConverter
{
    public object Convert(object value, Type targetType, object parameter,
        CultureInfo culture)
    {
        var text = value.ToString();
        Uri uri;
        try
        {
            switch (text)
            {
                case "Sunset":
                    uri = new Uri("Images/Sunset.jpg", UriKind.Relative); break;
                case "Winter":
                    uri = new Uri("Images/Winter.jpg", UriKind.Relative); break;
                default:
                    uri = new Uri("Images/Blue Hills.jpg", UriKind.Relative);
                break;
            }
            return new BitmapImage(uri);
        }
        catch (Exception ex)
        {
            MessageBox.Show(ex.Message);
            MessageBox.Show(ex.StackTrace);
            return "";
        }
    }
```

```
    public object ConvertBack(object value, Type targetType, object parameter,
      CultureInfo culture)
    {
        throw new NotImplementedException();
    }
```

As you can observe, the *TextToImageConverter* class inherits *IValueConverter*, and *Convert()* and *ConvertBack()* methods are implemented. The *Convert()* method contains the logic for the conversion, which in this case involves a switch-case block that checks for the value passed in and accordingly returns an appropriate URI. A *try...catch* block enclosing the entire block of code captures any exceptions that may possibly occur at runtime.

Note that you don't always need to explicitly implement converters; many inbuilt converters are available with WPF that you use for simple conversions, such as *DefaultValueConverter*, *ObjectTarget Converter*, and *SystemConvertConverter*. These are all internal types defined in the *MS.Internal.Data* namespace.

Data Validation

So far you have seen how to create data sources, bind to data, and create templates to customize the data presentation. But one important aspect in data access is yet to be explored: data validation. Validating user input data is a crucial operation in data handling, especially in CRUD (Create, Read, Update, Delete) tasks. Validation is essential in numerous cases. Numeric data may have to be validated for ranges, alphabetic data may need to be validated for correctness, and so forth.

You will now discover what provisions Silverlight has for data validation. The *Binding* class has a property called *ValidationRules* that you can use to associate your validation rules with *Binding* or *MultiBinding* objects. To specify the value for this property, you can either derive from the *ValidationRule* class or use one of the two built-in classes: *ExceptionValidationRule* or *DataError ValidationRule*. The *ExceptionValidationRule* class catches any exceptions that are thrown when you are trying to update the source, whereas the *DataErrorValidationRule* catches errors thrown if your source implements the *IDataErrorInfo* interface.

Instead of using the *DataErrorValidationRule* class, you can also set the *ValidateOnDataErrors* property of the *Binding* object to true.

For now, let's just see a basic example. Include the following code in your application to indicate that your validation rule is based on any exceptions that may be thrown while updating the source:

```
<Binding.ValidationRules>
    <ExceptionValidationRule></ExceptionValidationRule>
</Binding.ValidationRules>
```

The application will consist of a *TextBox* control data bound to a column HireDate in the Employee table. The following example will raise validation errors if the date format is not correct:

```
<Window x:Class="DataValidation.MainWindow"
        xmlns="http://schemas.microsoft.com/winfx/2006/xaml/presentation"
        xmlns:x="http://schemas.microsoft.com/winfx/2006/xaml"
```

```
             Title="MainWindow" Height="250" Width="432">
        <Grid Height="215" Width="385">
            <TextBox Name="hiredate" Margin="0,29,145,163"
              HorizontalAlignment="Right" Width="140">
                <TextBox.Text>
                    <Binding Path="HireDate" UpdateSourceTrigger="LostFocus">
                        <Binding.ValidationRules>
                            <ExceptionValidationRule></ExceptionValidationRule>
                        </Binding.ValidationRules>
                    </Binding>
                </TextBox.Text>
            </TextBox>
            <Button Content="Submit" Height="23" HorizontalAlignment="Left"
              Margin="165,58,0,0" Name="button1" VerticalAlignment="Top" Width="75" />
            <TextBlock Height="23" HorizontalAlignment="Left" Margin="20,30,0,0"
              Name="textBlock1" Text="Enter HireDate:" VerticalAlignment="Top" Width="77" />
        </Grid>
    </Window>
```

Silverlight has no *Validation.ErrorTemplate;* hence you will need to use some other means to indicate that an exception has occurred.

Creating and Binding to an *ObservableCollection*

When using an *ItemsControl* such as a *ListBox* or *TreeView* to display a collection of data, you need to bind to the collection and enumerate through its elements.

A collection implementing the *IEnumerable* interface is eligible for binding to an *ItemsControl*. The *ObservableCollection* class enables you to easily bind to collections and also provides notifications whenever you add, remove, or refresh items in the collection. Both WPF and Silverlight support this class. It is defined in the *System.Collections.ObjectModel* namespace and implements the *INotifyCollectionChanged* interface.

For example, to bind to a collection of cities, you can use the following XAML markup and code:

XAML Markup:
```
<Grid x:Name="LayoutRoot">
        <Grid.Resources>
           <local:CityList x:Key="CityListData"/>
                <DataTemplate x:Key="test">
                    <TextBlock Text="{Binding Path=Name}"/>
                </DataTemplate>
        </Grid.Resources>
        <ListBox Width="200"
          ItemsSource="{Binding Source={StaticResource CityListData}}"
          ItemTemplate="{StaticResource test}" Margin="220,0,220,356" />
</Grid>
```

Code:
```
using System.Collections.ObjectModel;

namespace ObservableDemo
```

```
{
public partial class MainPage : UserControl
{
    public MainPage()
    {
        CityList cities = new CityList();
        InitializeComponent();
    }
}

public class CityList : ObservableCollection<City>
{
    public CityList()
        : base()
    {
        Add(new City() {Name = "Savannah" });
        Add(new City() {Name = "Des Moines" });
        Add(new City(){Name="Houston"});
        Add(new City(){Name="Phoenix"});
        Add(new City(){Name="Tempe"});
    }
}

public class City
{
    public string Name { get; set; }
}
}
```

This example generates a *ListBox* with the list of cities specified in the class. At a later stage, even if you add 100 or even 1,000 cities, the XAML markup remains unchanged and the binding renders the data successfully.

Collection Views

After binding to a collection of data, you can sort, filter, or group the data using a collection view. A collection view is like a layer on top of a binding source collection, enabling you to navigate and display the source collection based on sort, filter, and group queries, without having to change the underlying source collection itself.

If a source collection implements the *INotifyCollectionChanged* interface, the changes raised by the *CollectionChanged* event are propagated to the views. A source collection can have multiple views associated with it.

Sorting and Grouping Using a *CollectionView*

Although WPF supports several *CollectionView* classes such as *ListCollectionView* and Binding *ListCollectionView*, Silverlight supports grouping functionality only through the *PagedCollectionView* class.

The following example demonstrates how to sort and group bound data in a collection using a *CollectionViewSource* and a *PagedCollectionView,* respectively. The markup adds the *SortDescription* to the *SortDescriptions* collection of the *CollectionViewSource* and specifies the property name on which to sort—in this case, *Name*:

```xml
<UserControl x:Class="CollectionsDemo.MainPage"
    xmlns="http://schemas.microsoft.com/winfx/2006/xaml/presentation"
    xmlns:x="http://schemas.microsoft.com/winfx/2006/xaml"
    xmlns:d="http://schemas.microsoft.com/expression/blend/2008"
    xmlns:mc="http://schemas.openxmlformats.org/markup-compatibility/2006"
    xmlns:scm="clr-namespace:System.ComponentModel;assembly=System.Windows"
    xmlns:dat="clr-namespace:System.Windows.Data;assembly=System.Windows"
    xmlns:local="clr-namespace:CollectionsDemo"
    mc:Ignorable="d"
    d:DesignHeight="300" d:DesignWidth="400"
>
<Grid x:Name="LayoutRoot">
    <Grid.Resources>
        <local:Employees x:Key="emps"/>
        <CollectionViewSource Source="{StaticResource emps}" x:Key="cvs">
            <CollectionViewSource.SortDescriptions>
                <scm:SortDescription PropertyName="Name"/>
            </CollectionViewSource.SortDescriptions>
        </CollectionViewSource>
    </Grid.Resources>
    <sdk:DataGrid Name="dgEmps" ItemsSource="{Binding}">
        <sdk:DataGrid.RowGroupHeaderStyles>
            <!--Define style for groups at the top level -->
            <Style TargetType="sdk:DataGridRowGroupHeader">
                <Setter Property="PropertyNameVisibility" Value="Collapsed" />
                <Setter Property="Background" Value="BurlyWood" />
                <Setter Property="SublevelIndent" Value="25" />
            </Style>
            <!--Define style for groups below the top level -->
            <Style TargetType="sdk:DataGridRowGroupHeader">
                <Setter Property="Background" Value="#44225566" />
            </Style>
        </sdk:DataGrid.RowGroupHeaderStyles>
    </sdk:DataGrid>
</Grid>
</UserControl>
```

The following code creates the *Employee* and *Employees* classes:

```csharp
public partial class MainPage : UserControl
{
    public MainPage()
    {
        Employees emps = new Employees();
        InitializeComponent();
        PagedCollectionView pg = new PagedCollectionView(emps);
        pg.GroupDescriptions.Add(new PropertyGroupDescription("Designation"));
        dgEmps.DataContext = pg;
    }
```

```
}
public class Employees : ObservableCollection<Employee>
{
    public Employees()
        : base()
    {
        Add(new Employee() { Name = "John Evans", Designation = "Manager" });
        Add(new Employee() { Name = "Dylan Miller", Designation = "Accountant" });
        Add(new Employee() { Name = "David Bristol", Designation = "Manager" });
        Add(new Employee() { Name = "Oliver Kiel", Designation = "Programmer" });
        Add(new Employee() { Name = "Jill Shrader", Designation = "Programmer" });
        Add(new Employee() { Name = "Prakash Paramasivam", Designation = "Programmer" });
    }
}
public class Employee
{
    public string Name { get; set; }
    public string Designation { get; set; }
}
```

The code creates a *PropertyGroupDescription* object and passes the name of the property based on which grouping will take place. Then add the *PropertyGroupDescription* to the *GroupDescriptions* collection of *PagedCollectionView*.

On executing, the output will be similar to Figure 8-11. As you can see, the employee details are grouped by designation and sorted within each designation.

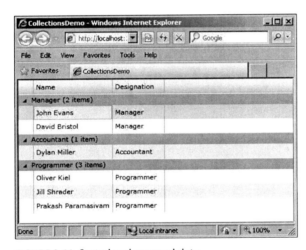

FIGURE 8-11 Sorted and grouped data.

Similarly, you can also filter the data using the *Filter* property of the *PagedCollectionView* class. You need to remove existing filters, if any, and create a callback method that accepts a parameter of type *Object*. Assign the callback method to the *PagedCollectionView.Filter* property.

```
. . .
pg.Filter = new Predicate<object>(PerformFilter);


. . .
}
//Callback method
private bool PerformFilter(object o)
{
    //it is not a case sensitive search
    Employee emp = o as Employee;
    if (emp != null)
    {
        if(emp.Designation=="Manager")
        {
            return true;
        }
        else
        {
            return false;
        }
    }
    return false;
}
```

This filters the data to show only the rows that have Designation as Manager.

Hierarchical Binding

A master-detail relationship is where one table or entity acts like a master or parent table or entity and the other acts like a detail or child table or child entity. Typically, the master and detail tables or entities will have a one-many relationship among them, with the master containing unique records and the child containing details pertaining to those records. One of the simplest examples is that of employees and departments in an organization. A department can have many employees, but an employee typically belongs only to one department. Thus, the department is a classic example of a master while the employee table or entity forms the child. Binding to data in master-detail form is a little more complex when compared to binding regular data.

You will now explore this through some examples. The first example uses the *HierarchicalData Template* to bind to master-detail data.

Using *HierarchicalDataTemplate*

Consider the tables Orders and Order Details in the Northwind database. They have a common column, Order ID. The Orders table contains unique orders. The Order Details can contain more than an instance of an order, and specifies the details of each order, such as the product ID, order date, and so forth.

The XAML code for constructing and binding the *TreeView* instance is as follows:

```
<UserControl x:Class="TreeViewDemo.MainPage"
    xmlns:sdk="http://schemas.microsoft.com/winfx/2006/xaml/presentation/sdk"
    xmlns="http://schemas.microsoft.com/winfx/2006/xaml/presentation"
    xmlns:x="http://schemas.microsoft.com/winfx/2006/xaml"
    xmlns:d="http://schemas.microsoft.com/expression/blend/2008"
    xmlns:mc="http://schemas.openxmlformats.org/markup-compatibility/2006"
    mc:Ignorable="d"
    d:DesignHeight="600" d:DesignWidth="400">
    <UserControl.Resources>
        <sdk:HierarchicalDataTemplate x:Key="ChildTemplate">
            <TextBlock FontStyle="Italic" Text="{Binding ProductID}"/>
        </sdk:HierarchicalDataTemplate>
        <sdk:HierarchicalDataTemplate x:Key="MasterTemplate"
          ItemsSource="{Binding Order_Details}"
          ItemTemplate="{StaticResource ChildTemplate}">
            <TextBlock Text="{Binding OrderID}" Margin="5,0"/>
        </sdk:HierarchicalDataTemplate>
    </UserControl.Resources>
    <Grid>
        <sdk:TreeView Margin="10,10,21,175" Name="TreeView1"
          ItemTemplate="{StaticResource MasterTemplate}"
          Background="Beige" ItemsSource="{Binding}" />
        <Button Content="Button" Height="23" HorizontalAlignment="Left"
          Margin="136,441,0,0" Name="button1" VerticalAlignment="Top" Width="75" />
    </Grid>
</UserControl>
```

Observe that the markup specifies the *HierarchicalDataTemplate*. This template presents data that has multiple items and a header. Typically, you use this template to specify a data template for controls that derive from *HeaderedItemsControl*.

In WPF and Silverlight, the following three controls inherit from *HeaderedItemsControl*: *MenuItem*, *ToolBar*, and *TreeViewItem*.

The following markup binds a *TextBlock* to the ProductID column:

```
<sdk:HierarchicalDataTemplate x:Key="ChildTemplate">
    <TextBlock FontStyle="Italic" Text="{Binding ProductID}"/>
</sdk:HierarchicalDataTemplate>
```

The following markup binds a *TextBlock* to the OrderID column in the Order_Details table. The *ItemTemplate* of *HierarchicalDataTemplate* is set to the previously defined resource *ChildTemplate*:

```
<sdk:HierarchicalDataTemplate x:Key="MasterTemplate" ItemsSource="{Binding Order_Details}"
ItemTemplate="{StaticResource ChildTemplate}">
    <TextBlock Text="{Binding OrderID}" Margin="5,0"/>
</sdk:HierarchicalDataTemplate>
```

Finally, the markup sets the *TreeView's ItemTemplate* to the resource, *MasterTemplate*:

```
<sdk:TreeView Margin="10,10,21,175" Name="TreeView1" ItemTemplate="{StaticResource
MasterTemplate}" Background="Beige" ItemsSource="{Binding}" />
```

In the code-behind, write the following:

```csharp
// Add the service reference manually
using TreeViewDemo.NorthwindServiceReference;

namespace TreeViewDemo
{
public partial class MainPage : UserControl
{
public MainPage()
{
    try
    {
        InitializeComponent();
        // Create an instance of the Service class.
        var client = new NorthwindServiceClient();
        client.GetDataCompleted += new EventHandler<GetDataCompletedEventArgs>
(client_GetDataCompleted);
        client.GetDataAsync();
    }
    catch (Exception ex)
    {
        MessageBox.Show(ex.StackTrace);
        MessageBox.Show(ex.Message);
    }
}
void client_GetDataCompleted(object sender, GetDataCompletedEventArgs e)
{
    var lst = e.Result;
    MessageBox.Show(lst.Count.ToString());
    try
    {
        this.TreeView1.DataContext = lst;
        this.TreeView1.ItemsSource = lst;
    }
    catch (Exception ex)
    {
        MessageBox.Show(ex.Message.ToString());
        MessageBox.Show(ex.StackTrace.ToString());
    }
}
}
}
```

The code for the service NorthwindService.svc.cs is as follows:

```csharp
public class NorthwindService
{
    [OperationContract]
    public List<orders2> GetData()
    {
        NorthwindEntities ne = new NorthwindEntities();
        return ne.orders2.Include("orderdetails2").ToList ();
    }
}
```

The output will show a series of Order IDs. When you expand the Order IDs, you can see the Product IDs, as shown in Figure 8-12.

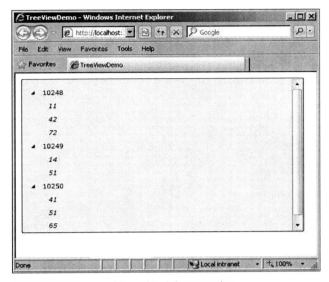

FIGURE 8-12 Using a hierarchical data template.

Using *ObservableCollection* for Hierarchical Binding

The second example will make use of the *ObservableCollection* class to bind to master-detail data. Consider the scenario of departments and employees described earlier. You will define two classes, *Dept* and *Employee*, each having a string property, *Name*. The *Dept* class will also have a property representing an *ObservableCollection* of employees. This establishes a master-detail kind of relationship between the two. Then you define the class *DeptList* as an *ObservableCollection* of departments. For the sake of this example, the code includes some dummy data such as Dept 1, Dept 2, Emp 1, Emp 2, and so forth. The code-behind for the example is as follows:

```
using System.Collections.ObjectModel;
namespace ObsCollMasterDetail
{
    public partial class MainPage : UserControl
    {
        DeptList dept = new DeptList();
        public MainPage()
        {
            InitializeComponent();
        }
    }
    public class Employee
    {
        public string Name { get; set; }
    }
    public class Dept
    {
```

```
        public string Name { get; set; }
        public ObservableCollection<Employee> Employees { get; set; }
    }
    public class DeptList : ObservableCollection<Dept>
    {
        public DeptList()
        {
            for (int i = 1; i < 3; i++)
            {
                Dept dept = new Dept()
                {
                    Name = "Dept " + i,
                    Employees = new ObservableCollection<Employee>()
                };
                for (int j = 1; j < 5; j++)
                {
                    Employee emp = new Employee
                    {
                        Name = String.Format("Emp " + j)
                    };

                    dept.Employees.Add(emp);
                }
                this.Add(dept);
            }
        }
    }
}
```

Here's the XAML markup:

```xml
<UserControl x:Class="ObsCollMasterDetail.MainPage"
  xmlns="http://schemas.microsoft.com/winfx/2006/xaml/presentation"
  xmlns:x="http://schemas.microsoft.com/winfx/2006/xaml"
  xmlns:local="clr-namespace:ObsCollMasterDetail">
    <UserControl.Resources>
        <local:DeptList x:Key="DeptData"/>
        <CollectionViewSource x:Name="Depts" Source="{StaticResource DeptData}"/>
        <CollectionViewSource x:Name="Employees"
      Source="{Binding Employees, Source={StaticResource Depts}}"/>
    </UserControl.Resources>
    <StackPanel x:Name="LayoutRoot" Orientation="Horizontal" Margin="5"
      DataContext="{Binding Source={StaticResource Depts}}">
        <StackPanel Margin="5">
            <TextBlock Text="All Depts" Margin="3" FontWeight="Bold"/>
            <ListBox ItemsSource="{Binding}" DisplayMemberPath="Name"/>
        </StackPanel>
        <StackPanel Margin="5">
            <TextBlock Text="{Binding Name}" Margin="3" FontWeight="Bold"/>
            <ListBox ItemsSource="{Binding Employees}"
              DisplayMemberPath="Name"/>
        </StackPanel>
    </StackPanel>
</UserControl>
```

In the XAML markup, you bind to the *Dept* and *Employee* classes using the *CollectionViewSource* class, which is a proxy for a *CollectionView* class, or any class that you derive from *CollectionView*.

When you execute the application, you will see the output shown in Figure 8-13.

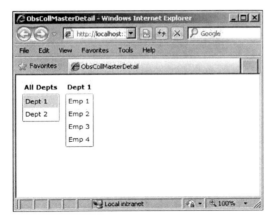

FIGURE 8-13 Using an *ObservableCollection*.

Binding to XML Data

WPF provides support for *XmlDataProvider*, which enables you to easily bind to XML data. With hardly any code and only declarative markup, you can bind to elements from an external XML file.

Consider the following XML file:

```xml
<?xml version="1.0" encoding="utf-8" ?>
<Employees xmlns="">
  <Employee>
    <Name>Jonah Baker</Name>
    <Address>155, Sunshine Apts, 6th Street, Virginia</Address>
    <Designation>Manager</Designation>
  </Employee>
  <Employee>
    <Name>Kyle Patrick</Name>
    <Address>Gordon Bungalows, Behind Lake Tahoe, USA</Address>
    <Designation>Manager</Designation>
  </Employee>
  <Employee>
    <Name>Azhar Umman</Name>
    <Address>707, 5th Floor, StreetSide Western Building, Harrington Road, NYC</Address>
    <Designation>Manager</Designation>
  </Employee>
</Employees>
```

You can now use the *XmlDataProvider* class to display this XML data in a *DataGrid* using the following markup:

```
<Window x:Class="TestXML.MainWindow"
        xmlns="http://schemas.microsoft.com/winfx/2006/xaml/presentation"
        xmlns:x="http://schemas.microsoft.com/winfx/2006/xaml"
        Title="MainWindow" Height="350" Width="525">
    <Window.Resources>
        <XmlDataProvider x:Key="EmployeeData" Source="sample.xml" XPath="/Employees/Employee" />
    </Window.Resources>
<Grid>
    <DataGrid  ItemsSource="{Binding Source={StaticResource EmployeeData}}"
      AutoGenerateColumns="False">
        <DataGrid.Columns>
            <DataGridTextColumn Header="Name" Binding="{Binding XPath=Name}"/>
            <DataGridTextColumn Header="Address" Binding="{Binding XPath=Address}"/>
            <DataGridTextColumn Header="Designation" Binding="{Binding XPath=Designation}"/>
        </DataGrid.Columns>
    </DataGrid>
</Grid>
 </Window>
```

Silverlight does not support the *XmlDataProvider* class. Chapter 4, "Markup Extensions and Other Features," will demonstrate how to implement a custom markup extension to bind to XML data in a Silverlight application.

Note Silverlight also supports additional data-specific controls such as *DataForm* (defined in the Silverlight Toolkit), *DataPager, ValidationError,* and *ValidationSummary.* You can learn about these controls at:

http://msdn.microsoft.com/en-us/library/system.windows.controls.datapager%28VS.95%29.aspx

http://www.silverlight.net/content/samples/sl4/toolkitcontrolsamples/run/default.html

http://msdn.microsoft.com/en-us/library/system.windows.controls.validationsummary%28VS.95%29.aspx

http://msdn.microsoft.com/en-us/library/system.windows.controls.validationerror%28v=VS.95%29.aspx

Summary

This chapter discussed data binding to various kinds of data sources, as well as different binding approaches that you can take. You also explored how to bind to collections and to sort, group, and filter data. Finally, you saw how to validate data and how to implement converters to display bound data in the format you want.

CHAPTER 9

Media, Graphics, and Animation

In this chapter:

■ Media

■ Graphics

■ 3-D Graphics

■ Animations and Storyboards

■ Summary

One key defining feature of a rich application is its ability to render graphics and animations. With multimedia applications becoming the norm these days rather than an exception, rich and interactive applications must also provide strong support for working with various kinds of media such as audio and video. Toward this end, XAML includes several features that enable you to use media, graphics, and animation in your applications.

Media

XAML provides strong support for media such as images, audio, and video.

Images

The simplest media that you can display in a XAML page is an image. An image can take the form of an icon, a picture, a photograph, and so forth. WPF supports native image formats such as .bmp, .gif, .ico, .jpeg/.jpg, .png, .wdp, and .tiff; Silverlight supports only .jpeg and .png formats.

The following basic example demonstrates the use of the *Image* control to display a .jpg file:

```
<UserControl x:Class="MediaApp.MainPage"
    xmlns="http://schemas.microsoft.com/winfx/2006/xaml/presentation"
    xmlns:x="http://schemas.microsoft.com/winfx/2006/xaml"
    xmlns:d="http://schemas.microsoft.com/expression/blend/2008"
    xmlns:mc="http://schemas.openxmlformats.org/markup-compatibility/2006"
    mc:Ignorable="d" >
    <Grid x:Name="LayoutRoot"  Height="300" Width="400">
        <Image Source="Water Lilies.jpg" Stretch="Fill" Margin="197,0,0,129"></Image>
```

```
        </Grid>
</UserControl>
```

In XAML, you can use the *ImageBrush* to paint using an *Image*. Any area that takes a brush qualifies for use with the *ImageBrush* element. In XAML graphics, a brush is similar to the concept of a brush in real life—it is used to paint an object with a color. You will see more about brushes later in the chapter.

The following example uses the *ImageBrush*:

```
<UserControl x:Class="MediaApp1.MainPage"
    xmlns="http://schemas.microsoft.com/winfx/2006/xaml/presentation"
    xmlns:x="http://schemas.microsoft.com/winfx/2006/xaml"
    xmlns:d="http://schemas.microsoft.com/expression/blend/2008"
    xmlns:mc="http://schemas.openxmlformats.org/markup-compatibility/2006"
    mc:Ignorable="d">
    <Grid x:Name="LayoutRoot"  Height="300" Width="400">
        <Grid.Background>
            <ImageBrush ImageSource="Water Lilies.jpg"></ImageBrush>
        </Grid.Background>
    </Grid>
</UserControl>
```

Here, the background of the *Grid* is painted with an *ImageBrush*, which is set to an image named Water Lilies.jpg. Thus, you will see a *Grid* with a picture instead of a standard color.

Audio and Video

A *MediaElement* is a control representing a rectangular region on a Silverlight or WPF user interface that can contain audio or video on its surface. The *MediaElement* control allows you to specify event handlers for mouse and keyboard events. You can either specify a URL for the media element or you can add it as an item to the project.

Media types supported by Silverlight and WPF include:

- Advanced Stream Redirector (ASX) playlist file format

- Windows Media Audio 7 (WMA 7)

- Windows Media Audio 8 (WMA 8)

- Windows Media Audio 9 (WMA 9)

- ISO/MPEG Layer-3 compliant data stream input (MP3)

- Windows Media Video 7 (WMV 1)

- Windows Media Video 8 (WMV 2)

- Windows Media Video 9 (WMV 3)

- Windows Media Video Advanced Profile, non-VC1 (WMVA)

You will now create a Silverlight application that demonstrates the media capabilities of XAML. Name the application **MediaApp2** and add an existing .wmv file to the project. For the purpose of this example, assume the filename is FlyingPlanes.wmv.

1. Modify the default XAML code of *Page.xaml,* as shown here:

```
<UserControl x:Class="MediaApp2.MainPage"
    xmlns="http://schemas.microsoft.com/winfx/2006/xaml/presentation"
    xmlns:x="http://schemas.microsoft.com/winfx/2006/xaml"
    xmlns:d="http://schemas.microsoft.com/expression/blend/2008"
    xmlns:mc="http://schemas.openxmlformats.org/markup-compatibility/2006"
    mc:Ignorable="d"
    d:DesignHeight="640" d:DesignWidth="480">
    <Grid x:Name="LayoutRoot" Background="Bisque" Height="300" Width="400">
        <Grid.ColumnDefinitions>
            <ColumnDefinition Width="400" />
        </Grid.ColumnDefinitions>
        <Grid.RowDefinitions>
            <RowDefinition Height="Auto" />
            <RowDefinition Height="Auto" />
            <RowDefinition Height="Auto" />
        </Grid.RowDefinitions>
    </Grid>
</UserControl>
```

The preceding code will create a *Grid* with a bisque background, one column, and two rows.

2. Drag a *MediaElement* between the *<Grid>* tags after the *</GridRowDefinitions>* tags.

3. Modify the properties of *MediaElement,* as shown here:

```
<UserControl x:Class="MediaApp2.MainPage"
    xmlns="http://schemas.microsoft.com/winfx/2006/xaml/presentation"
    xmlns:x="http://schemas.microsoft.com/winfx/2006/xaml"
    xmlns:d="http://schemas.microsoft.com/expression/blend/2008"
    xmlns:mc="http://schemas.openxmlformats.org/markup-compatibility/2006"
    mc:Ignorable="d"
    d:DesignHeight="640" d:DesignWidth="480">
  <Grid x:Name="LayoutRoot" Background="Bisque" Height="300" Width="400">
            <Grid.ColumnDefinitions>
                <ColumnDefinition Width="400" />
            </Grid.ColumnDefinitions>
            <Grid.RowDefinitions>
                <RowDefinition Height="Auto" />
                <RowDefinition Height="Auto" />
                <RowDefinition Height="Auto" />
            </Grid.RowDefinitions>
        <MediaElement x:Name="myvideo" Source="FlyingPlanes.wmv" AutoPlay="True"
          IsMuted="True" Stretch="Uniform"/>
      </Grid>
</UserControl>
```

The video will play as soon as the page is loaded. Thus, you display a video using pure XAML markup.

Similarly, you can play an audio file, such as .mp3, or .avi, using the *MediaElement*:

```
<UserControl x:Class="MediaApp3.MainPage"
    xmlns="http://schemas.microsoft.com/winfx/2006/xaml/presentation"
    xmlns:x="http://schemas.microsoft.com/winfx/2006/xaml"
    xmlns:d="http://schemas.microsoft.com/expression/blend/2008"
    xmlns:mc="http://schemas.openxmlformats.org/markup-compatibility/2006"
    mc:Ignorable="d"
    d:DesignHeight="300" d:DesignWidth="400">
        <Grid x:Name="LayoutRoot" Background="Bisque" Height="300" Width="400">
            <Grid.ColumnDefinitions>
                <ColumnDefinition Width="400" />
            </Grid.ColumnDefinitions>
            <Grid.RowDefinitions>
                <RowDefinition Height="Auto" />
                <RowDefinition Height="Auto" />
                <RowDefinition Height="Auto" />
            </Grid.RowDefinitions>
        <MediaElement x:Name="MySong" Source="01-Summer Haze.mp3" AutoPlay="False"
            Volume="2" Stretch="Uniform"/>
        <Button Content="Play Me" Click="Button_Click" Margin="157,129,150,127"
            Grid.Row="3"></Button>
        </Grid>
</UserControl>
```

The *System.Windows.Controls* namespace defines the *MediaElement* class. The commonly used properties and methods of *MediaElement* class are listed in Table 9-1.

TABLE 9-1 Properties and Methods of the *MediaElement* Class

Name	Description
AudioStreamCount	Gets the number of audio streams available in the current media file.
AudioStreamIndex	Retrieves or sets the index of the audio stream that plays along with the video component. The set of audio streams is built at runtime and represents all audio streams available within the media file.
AudioStreamCount	Retrieves the number of audio streams available in the current media file.
AutoPlay	Retrieves or specifies a value that indicates whether media will begin playback automatically when the *Source* property is set.
BufferingProgress	Retrieves a value that indicates the current buffering progress.
BufferingTime	Retrieves or specifies the amount of time to buffer.
CanPause	Retrieves a value indicating if media can be paused if you call the *Pause* method.
CurrentState	Retrieves the status of the *MediaElement*.
IsMuted	Retrieves or specifies a value indicating whether the audio is muted.
Source	Retrieves or specifies a media source on *MediaElement*.
Stretch	Retrieves or specifies a *Stretch* value that describes how *MediaElement* fills the destination rectangle.
Volume	Retrieves or specifies the media's volume.

Table 9-2 lists the states of the *MediaElement* Class.

TABLE 9-2 States of *MediaElement* Class

Value	Description
Buffering	Indicates that *MediaElement* is loading the media for playback.
Closed	Indicates that *MediaElement* contains no media; *MediaElement* displays a transparent frame.
Opening	Indicates that *MediaElement* is validating and attempting to open the URI specified by its *Source* property.
Paused	Indicates that *MediaElement* does not advance its position. If *MediaElement* was playing video, it continues to display the current frame.
Playing	Indicates that *MediaElement* is playing the media specified by its source property. Its position advances forward.
Stopped	Indicates that *MediaElement* contains media, but it is not playing or paused. Its position is 0 and does not advance.

Graphics

Consider that you are developing an application that depicts various element of physics or biology. You need to be able to display graphical objects and manipulate them—perhaps showing them in animated form. Obviously, the standard XAML *UIElements*, such as *TextBlock* and *Button*, fall short for such an application. This is where XAML's graphical capabilities come into focus. XAML lets you draw and paint various forms of graphics, including shapes and geometries.

You use *Shape* and *Geometry* to render two-dimensional (2-D) objects. Although the two have much in common, there are important differences between the two sets of drawing objects. The chapter covers these differences in a later section.

Shapes are UI elements, so you can place them inside panels and most controls. The *System.Windows.Shapes* namespace defines shape elements. Some of the commonly used shapes are *Ellipse, Rectangle, Line, Polygon, Polyline,* and *Path*. Table 9-3 lists some of the attributes common to all shape elements.

TABLE 9-3 Attributes Common to All *Shape* Elements

Property Name	Data Type	Description
Fill	*Brush*	Describes how you fill the shape's interior. The default is *null*.
Height	*Double*	Describes the height of the element.

Property Name	Data Type	Description
Stroke	Brush	Describes how you draw the outline of the shape. The default is *null*.
StrokeDashCap	Enumeration	Describes how the ends of a dash look like. Possible values are: ■ *Flat* No line cap. ■ *Round* The line is capped with a semicircle equal in diameter to the line thickness. ■ *Square* The line is capped with a square whose sides are equal in length to the line thickness. ■ *Triangle* The line is capped with a triangle equal in height to the line thickness. The default is *Flat*.
StrokeDashOffset	Double	Describes the distance in the dash pattern at which the dash will start.
StrokeEndLineCap	Enumeration	Describes the shape used at the end of the element's stroke. Possible values are: ■ *Flat* ■ *Round* ■ *Square* ■ *Triangle* The default is *Flat*.
StrokeLineJoin	Enumeration	Sets the type that joins vertices of a shape's outline. Must be one of the following: ■ *Bevel* Indicates beveled vertices (non-perpendicular) ■ *Miter* Indicates normal angular vertices ■ *Round* Indicates rounded vertices
StrokeThickness	Double	Sets the width of the shape's outline.
Width	Double	Describes the width of the element.
Opacity	Double	The transparency factor for *Shape*.

Ellipse

The following XAML markup snippet demonstrates how to draw an ellipse:

```
<Grid x:Name="LayoutRoot" Background="LemonChiffon">
        <Ellipse Fill="BlueViolet" Width="170" Height="83" ></Ellipse>
</Grid>
```

You can further customize the preceding snippet to show an orange border with a thickness of 5:

```
<Grid x:Name="LayoutRoot" Background="LemonChiffon">
    <Ellipse Fill="BlueViolet" Width="170" Height="83" Stroke="Orange" StrokeThickness="5">
    </Ellipse>
</Grid>
```

A creative use of the *Ellipse* element is to include it within the content of another *UIElement*. The following markup shows how to do this with a *Button*:

```
<Button Height="80" Width="100" Background="blue">
    <Button.Content>
```

```
            <Ellipse Fill="Orange" Width="70" Height="50"></Ellipse>
        </Button.Content>
</Button>
```

Rectangle

The following XAML markup snippet demonstrates how to draw a rectangle, and also shows the use of the *Stroke* and *StrokeThickness* properties:

```
<Grid x:Name="LayoutRoot" Background="LemonChiffon">
        <Rectangle Fill="BlueViolet" Width="170" Height="83" Stroke="Orange"
         StrokeThickness="5">
        </Rectangle>
 </Grid>
```

Rounded Rectangle

Although there is no specific element named *RoundedRectangle*, you can easily draw one by using the *RadiusX* and *RadiusY* properties of the *Rectangle* element. The following XAML markup snippet demonstrates how to create a rounded rectangle:

```
<Grid x:Name="LayoutRoot" Background="LemonChiffon">
        <Rectangle Fill="BlueViolet" Width="170" Height="83" Stroke="Orange"
        StrokeThickness="5" RadiusX="7"  RadiusY="7">
        </Rectangle>
</Grid>
```

Polygon

The *Polygon* element enables you to draw polygonal shapes. It takes a *Points* attribute that takes a series of points. The last set of points should connect back to the first. For example, the following markup draws a triangle with a pastel shade of red:

```
<Polygon Points="100,150 300,150 200,50 100,150"
    Fill="Red" Opacity="0.4" Stroke="Black" StrokeThickness="4">
</Polygon>
```

The *Stroke* property indicates the color of the stroke used to draw the shape. *StrokeThickness* indicates the thickness of the brush used to draw the strokes. Finally, the *Opacity* sets opacity level to 0.4, thus rendering a lighter shade of red.

Polyline

The *Polyline* element is similar to *Polygon* except that the last points need not connect back to the first. The following XAML markup snippet demonstrates how to create a polyline:

```
<Polyline
    Points="100,150 300,150 200,50 80,80"
    Stroke="Black"
```

```
StrokeThickness="2" Fill="Red" />
```

The markup produces the output shown in Figure 9-1.

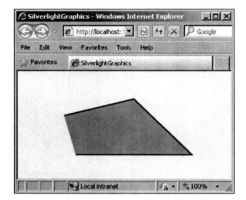

FIGURE 9-1 Creating a polyline.

The following code draws the letter N:

```
<Polyline Points="50, 150 50, 50 120, 140 120, 40 "
StrokeThickness="10"
Canvas.Left="75" Canvas.Top="50" Stroke="Purple" >
  </Polyline>
```

The markup produces the output shown in Figure 9-2.

FIGURE 9-2 Another example of a polyline.

The following markup demonstrates use of the *StrokeEndLineCap* property:

```
<Grid x:Name="LayoutRoot" Width="433" Height="300">
      <Grid.ColumnDefinitions>
          <ColumnDefinition Width="400" />
      </Grid.ColumnDefinitions>
      <Grid.RowDefinitions>
```

```
            <RowDefinition Height="Auto" />
            <RowDefinition Height="Auto" />
            <RowDefinition Height="Auto" />
            <RowDefinition Height="Auto" />
            <RowDefinition Height="Auto" />
            <RowDefinition Height="9" />
            <RowDefinition Height="55" />
            <RowDefinition Height="8" />
            <RowDefinition Height="21" />
            <RowDefinition Height="53" />
            <RowDefinition Height="102*" />
    </Grid.RowDefinitions>
    <Polyline Stroke="Orange" StrokeThickness="12" StrokeEndLineCap="Flat"
        Points="5,10 20,0 30,20 50,10 90,10" Grid.Row="3" Grid.Column="0" />
    <Polyline Stroke="Orange" StrokeThickness="12" StrokeEndLineCap="Round"
        Points="5,10 20,0 30,20 50,10 90,10" Grid.Row="4" Margin="0,11,0,53"
        Grid.RowSpan="3" />
    <Polyline Stroke="Orange" StrokeThickness="12" StrokeEndLineCap="Square"
        Points="5,10 20,0 30,20 50,10 90,10" Grid.Row="6" Margin="-12,41,12,0"
        Grid.RowSpan="5" />
    <Polyline Stroke="Orange" StrokeThickness="12" StrokeEndLineCap="Triangle"
        Points="5,10 20,0 30,20 50,10 90,10" Grid.Row="9" />
</Grid>
```

The outcome of this markup is shown in Figure 9-3.

FIGURE 9-3 Using the *StrokeEndLineCap* property with *Polyline*.

Path

You use the *Path* element to draw a series of graphic elements such as curves and lines. Silverlight and WPF support a powerful and complex mini-language to describe geometric paths using XAML.

The XAML path syntax consists of an optional *FillRule* value and one or more figure descriptions.

```
<Path>
    <object property ="[fillRule] figureDescription[ figureDescription]*" ... />
</Path>
```

Table 9-4 lists the various elements comprising the *Path* markup mini-language.

TABLE 9-4 Elements Available in the *Path* Markup Mini-Language

Term	Description
fillRule	States whether the path uses the *EvenOdd* or *NonZero* fill rule value: ■ The *EvenOdd* rule checks whether a point is inside the fill region by drawing a line from that point to infinity in any direction and counting the all the path segments within the given shape that the line crosses. If this number is odd, the point is inside; otherwise, the point is outside. ■ The *NonZero* rule checks whether a point is in the fill region of the path by drawing a line from that point to infinity in any direction and then checking the places where a segment of the shape crosses the line. If the result is zero, the point is outside the path. Otherwise, it is inside. F0 specifies the *EvenOdd* fill rule. F1 specifies the *NonZero* fill rule. The default behavior is *EvenOdd*.
figureDescription	A figure composed of a move command, draw commands, and an optional close command: *moveCommand drawCommands [closeCommand]*
moveCommand	A move command that specifies the start point of the figure.
drawCommands	One or more draw commands that describe the figure's contents.
closeCommand	An optional close command that closes the figure.

The important elements from the table are:

- **Move Command** You specify a move command with the letter *m,* which signifies a *move to* operation.

- **Draw Commands** A draw command can consist of several shape commands. You can use one of the following shape commands: line, horizontal line, vertical line, cubic Bezier curve, quadratic Bezier curve, smooth cubic Bezier curve, smooth quadratic Bezier curve, and elliptical arc.

You enter each command by using either an uppercase letter or a lowercase letter: Uppercase letters denote absolute values, and lowercase letters denote relative values. The control points for a segment are relative to the end point of the preceding segment.

For example, you use *v* and *h* to indicate a vertical line or a horizontal line, respectively.

Here's a simple example of using the *Path* element:

```
<Path Stroke="Navy" StrokeThickness="3" Data="M 90,90 v 150 h 175" />
```

This markup moves to the point 90, 90; draws a vertical line from 90 to 150; and then draws a horizontal line to 175. The outcome will be similar to Figure 9-4.

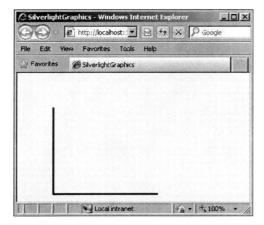

FIGURE 9-4 Using the *Path* element.

The following markup draws a quadratic Bezier curve:

```
<Path Stroke="Red"
            StrokeThickness="3" Data="M 10, 40 q 10,40 70,30" />
```

The markup produces output similar to Figure 9-5.

FIGURE 9-5 Drawing a Bezier curve with the *Path* element.

Geometries

The *Path* class includes a single property, *Data*, that accepts a *Geometry* object that defines one or more shapes the path includes. *Geometry* is an abstract class, so you cannot create *Geometry* objects directly; instead, you use one of the derived classes from the *System.Windows.Media* namespace to create the objects. Table 9-5 describes these classes.

TABLE 9-5 Derived Classes in the *System.Windows.Media* Namespace

Name	Description
LineGeometry	The geometry equivalent of the *Line* shape, representing a straight line
RectangleGeometry	The geometry equivalent of the *Rectangle* shape, representing a rectangle
EllipseGeometry	The geometry equivalent of the *Ellipse* shape, representing an ellipse
GeometryGroup	Adds any number of Geometry objects to a single path, using the *EvenOdd* or *NonZero* fill rule to determine what regions to fill
PathGeometry	The geometry equivalent of *Path,* representing a more complex figure composed of arcs, curves, and lines

The *LineGeometry, RectangleGeometry*, and *EllipseGeometry* classes map directly to the *Line, Rectangle*, and *Ellipse* shapes. The following markup demonstrates the use of the *EllipseGeometry* element:

```
<Path Fill="Green" Stroke="Red" StrokeThickness="3" Margin="88,108,-88,-108">
    <Path.Data>
        <EllipseGeometry RadiusX="55" RadiusY="40"/>
    </Path.Data>
</Path>
```

Brushes

In XAML, you use *Brush* objects to paint the *Stroke* (edge) and *Fill* (interior) of a shape element. The *System.Windows.Media* namespace defines several brushes:

- *SolidColorBrush*

- *ImageBrush*

- *LinearGradientBrush*

- *RadialGradientBrush*

- *VideoBrush*

All of these brushes support object element syntax. In addition, *SolidColorBrush* supports attribute syntax as well. Even though the other brushes cannot use attribute syntax, you can specify properties through binding references.

The *SolidColorBrush*, as its name suggests, paints a region with a solid color. The following markup demonstrates using a *SolidColorBrush* with attribute syntax. It also demonstrates how to customize the *Opacity* property to render a lighter shade of the specified color:

```
<Rectangle Height="40" Width="40">
        <Rectangle.Fill>
            <SolidColorBrush Color="Red" Opacity="0.7">
            </SolidColorBrush>
        </Rectangle.Fill>
</Rectangle>
```

Figure 9-6 shows the rectangle inside the *UserControl*.

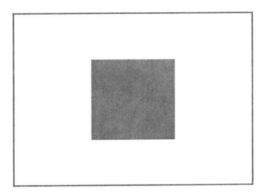

FIGURE 9-6 Using *SolidColorBrush*.

You use *ImageBrush* to paint a shape element with an image instead of a color. You already saw an example that uses *ImageBrush* earlier in this chapter.

LinearGradientBrush lets you paint a region with linear gradients. The following markup demonstrates how to use a *LinearGradientBrush*:

```
<Rectangle Margin="192,39,328,483">
        <Rectangle.Fill>
            <LinearGradientBrush StartPoint="0,0" EndPoint="1,1">
                <GradientStop Color="Beige" Offset="0.09" />
                <GradientStop Color="Green" Offset="0.45" />
                <GradientStop Color="Yellow" Offset="0.75" />
                <GradientStop Color="Navy" Offset="1.0" />
            </LinearGradientBrush>
        </Rectangle.Fill>
</Rectangle>
```

Figure 9-7 shows the result of the markup with each gradient section demarcated by appropriate labels to aid in understanding.

GradientStop 1
Color Beige
Offset 0.09

GradientStop 2
Color Green
Offset 0.45

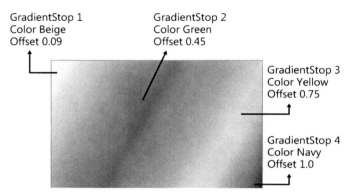

GradientStop 3
Color Yellow
Offset 0.75

GradientStop 4
Color Navy
Offset 1.0

FIGURE 9-7 Using *LinearGradientBrush*.

You use the *RadialGradientBrush* to paint a region with radial gradients. The following markup demonstrates using the *RadialGradientBrush*:

```
<Rectangle Margin="27,20,228,282">
    <Rectangle.Fill>
        <RadialGradientBrush GradientOrigin="0.5,0.5" Center="0.5,0.5"
          RadiusX="0.5" RadiusY="0.5">
            <GradientStop Color="Crimson" Offset="0.5" />
            <GradientStop Color="LightGray" Offset="0.75" />
            <GradientStop Color="Red" Offset="1" />
        </RadialGradientBrush>
    </Rectangle.Fill>
</Rectangle>
```

Figure 9-8 shows the brush in action.

FIGURE 9-8 Using *RadialGradientBrush*.

You use *VideoBrush* to paint a region or shape with video content. *VideoBrush* makes use of a *MediaElement* to render the video content. The following markup demonstrates the use of *VideoBrush*:

```
<Grid x:Name="LayoutRoot">
    <Grid.Resources>
        <MediaElement x:Name="myvideo" Source="WindowsMedia.wmv" AutoPlay="True"
```

```
          IsMuted="True" />
   </Grid.Resources>
   <Rectangle Margin="27,20,56,196">
       <Rectangle.Fill>
            <VideoBrush SourceName="myvideo" Stretch="UniformToFill" />
       </Rectangle.Fill>
   </Rectangle>
</Grid>
```

The video format must be one of the supported formats.

> **More Info** For more information on *VideoBrush* and the relationship between *MediaElement* and *VideoBrush*, see *http://msdn.microsoft.com/en-us/library/cc189009%28v=vs.95%29.aspx*.

Transforms

You can use the two-dimensional *Transform* classes in Silverlight to rotate, scale, skew, and move (translate) objects. The transform classes are:

- *RotateTransform*
- *ScaleTransform*
- *SkewTransform*

The following sections show these classes in action.

RotateTransform

RotateTransform applies a transformation that rotates a UI element by a specified angle. The following example applies a transform that rotates a rectangle:

```
<Rectangle Margin="124,15,-16,216" Fill="LightGoldenrodYellow">
         <Rectangle.RenderTransform>
             <RotateTransform Angle="45" ></RotateTransform>
         </Rectangle.RenderTransform>
</Rectangle>
```

Figure 9-9 shows what the rotated rectangle looks like.

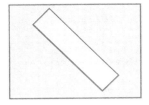

FIGURE 9-9 Using *RotateTransform*.

The properties of the *RotateTransform* class are as follows:

- **Angle**   Retrieves or assigns the angle in degrees of the clockwise rotation

- **CenterX**   Retrieves or assigns the x-coordinate of the rotation center point

- **CenterY**   Retrieves or assigns the y-coordinate of the rotation center point

ScaleTransform

A *ScaleTransform* applies a transformation that scales a *UIElement* up or down by specified *ScaleX* and *ScaleY* amounts. The following markup demonstrates how to scale a rectangle using *ScaleTransform*:

```
<Rectangle Margin="82,85,78,193" Fill="LightGoldenrodYellow">
        <Rectangle.RenderTransform>
            <ScaleTransform ScaleX="2" ScaleY="2" />
        </Rectangle.RenderTransform>
</Rectangle>
```

SkewTransform

A *SkewTransform* skews a *UIElement* by the specified *AngleX* and *AngleY* amounts. The following markup demonstrates how to skew a rectangle using *SkewTransform*:

```
<Rectangle Margin="82,85,78,193" Fill="Blue">
        <Rectangle.RenderTransform>
            <SkewTransform AngleX="25" AngleY="15 " />
        </Rectangle.RenderTransform>
</Rectangle>
```

Complex Transformations

You aren't limited to the three types of transforms described in the preceding sections. You can create more complex transformations using additional classes that Silverlight provides, which are listed in Table 9-6.

TABLE 9-6 Silverlight Classes for Creating Complex Transformations

Class	Description
CompositeTransform	Use this class to apply multiple transforms to the same object.
TransformGroup	You can also use this class to apply multiple transforms; however, the CompositeTransform class is the preferred way of doing this—unless you want to apply the transforms in a specific order or wish to apply different center points for the different transforms.
MatrixTransform	Use this class to create custom transformations that you cannot achieve through the other Transform classes. When you use a MatrixTransform, you manipulate a matrix directly.

3-D Graphics

Having seen how to create and render 2-D graphics objects, you will now explore how to render 3-D graphics objects in XAML.

WPF and Silverlight each implement 3-D graphics in their own way. First you'll see how to work with 3-D graphics in WPF.

3-D Graphics in WPF

As depicted in Figure 9-10, the coordinate system in 3-D is different from that in 2-D.

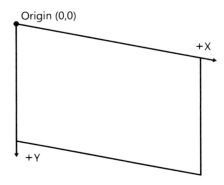

Coordinate System in 2-D

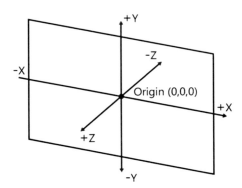

FIGURE 9-10 Coordinate system in 2-D and in 3-D.

To create 3-D graphics, you need four components: a *model*, a *material*, a *camera*, and a *light source*. A model in 3-D is similar to a drawing in 2-D. A material in 3-D is similar to a brush in 2-D.

You use *Model3D*-derived classes to create the models. These classes include *Material*-derived classes for the materials, *Camera*-derived classes to represent the camera in the scene, and *Light*-derived classes to represent the lighting for the scene.

Model3D is an abstract class defined in the *System.Windows.Media.Media3D* namespace. It contains the following classes: *GeometryModel3D*, *Light*, and *Model3DGroup*. Of these, *Geometry-Model3D* is most commonly used in WPF graphics. You use the *ModelVisual3D* class to render *Model3D* objects.

Material is also an abstract class defined in the *System.Windows.Media.Media3D*. WPF graphics commonly use the following types of materials:

- **EmissiveMaterial** Using this class, you can add color to an existing *Material* equal to the color of the *EmissiveMaterial*'s brush.

- **DiffuseMaterial** Using this class, you can apply a *SolidBrush* or *TileBrush* to the 3-D model.

- **SpecularMaterial** Using this material adds highlight-like effects or illuminating effects.

The various types of light are:

- **AmbientLight** Represents a *Light* object that applies light to objects evenly

- **DirectionalLight** Represents a *Light* object that projects its effect in a direction specified by a *Vector3D* object

- **PointLight** Represents a *Light* object that has a specified position in space, and projects its light in all directions

- **SpotLight** Represents a *Light* object that projects its effect in a cone-shaped area in a particular direction

To display 3-D graphics in your applications, you use the *Viewport3D* control, which is similar to the *MediaElement* and *Image* controls. The *Viewport3D* class inherits from *FrameworkElement*.

Viewport3D includes standard properties such as *Height*, *Width*, and so forth. The *Camera* property stores one or more *Visual3D*-derived objects.

The following XAML syntax illustrates the hierarchy of *Viewport3D* objects:

```
<Viewport3D>
    <ModelVisual3D>
      <ModelVisual3D.Content>
        . . .
      <Viewport3D.Camera>
        . . .
      </Viewport3D.Camera>
        </ModelVisual3D.Content>
      <ModelVisual3D>
</Viewport3D>
```

Using this kind of syntax, you will define the 3-D models, materials, lighting, and camera for your 3-D scene.

You can use any *Camera*-derived class as a camera in your 3-D scene. However, you can only use one camera with a *Viewport3D*. If you want to use more than one camera to display your scene, you must create a *Viewport3D* for each camera.

The various camera types are described in the following sections.

PerspectiveCamera

For most scenes, you use the *PerspectiveCamera* (which is the camera that *Viewport3D* uses by default if you do not specify a camera). This provides perspective, because objects that you draw closer to this camera appear larger than objects you draw in the distance. Table 9-7 lists the properties of *PerspectiveCamera*.

TABLE 9-7 Properties of *PerspectiveCamera*

Property	Description
FieldOfView	You use this property to adjust the zoom of the camera in degrees. The *default* value is 45.
LookDirection	You use this property to set the direction that the camera is looking as vector. You set this value by using a Vector3D structure.
Position	You use this property to place the camera in your scene. You set this value as a Point3D structure.
UpDirection	You use this property to change how the camera is oriented. You set this value by using a Vector3D structure. The default value is 0,1,0, which states that the top of the camera is pointing positive Y.

OrthographicCamera

When you use *OrthographicCamera* and draw two elements that are the same size, *OrthographicCamera* renders them in the same size, no matter how near or far away from the camera you place them.

The properties of *OrthographicCamera* are similar to *PerspectiveCamera*, except that *Orthographic-Camera* does not have a *FieldOfView* property—it has a *Width* property that you use to set the width of the viewing box.

MatrixCamera

MatrixCamera gives you the freedom to calculate your own view and projection matrices.

Defining Shapes

You use the *GeometryModel3D* and *Model3DGroup* classes to define the shape of your 3-D objects.

The *Model3DGroup* class enables you to build several models through the *GeometryModel3D* classes and combine them into a single *Viewport3D*. The following XAML code example illustrates the hierarchy of *Model3DGroup* and *GeometryModel3D* objects:

```
<Viewport3D ...>
    <ModelVisual3D>
        <ModelVisual3D.Content>
            <Model3DGroup>
                <GeometryModel3D>
                    <GeometryModel3D.Geometry>
                        <MeshGeometry3D .../>
...
```

Geometry3D is abstract and has only one descendant, called *MeshGeometry3D*. You use a mesh as a foundation to define the geometry of your model. A *mesh* is a representation of a surface described through triangles. Thus, you build all your models in WPF by using triangles. Using one or more *Point3D* instances, you define the position of all the points in your 3-D scene. Then you use the *Positions* and *TriangleIndices* properties of the *MeshGeometry3D* class to make triangles that represent your model.

When defining these values in XAML, you can use a simplified notation, as shown in the following code example:

```
<MeshGeometry3D
    Positions="1 0 -3, 0 1 -3, -1 0 -3"
    TriangleIndices="0 1 2" />
```

The *Positions* property in this example defines three points, with the X, Y, and Z locations separated by spaces and the points separated by commas. The *TriangleIndices* property specifies the order in which to join the array of points defined in the *Positions* property to create a single triangle.

Here's a complete example of using these properties to render a triangle:

```
<Window x:Class="WpfApplication1.MainWindow"
        xmlns="http://schemas.microsoft.com/winfx/2006/xaml/presentation"
        xmlns:x="http://schemas.microsoft.com/winfx/2006/xaml"
        Title="Window4" Height="300" Width="300">
    <Grid>
        <Viewport3D>
            <ModelVisual3D>
                <ModelVisual3D.Content>
                    <Model3DGroup>
                        <GeometryModel3D>
                            <GeometryModel3D.Geometry>
                                <MeshGeometry3D
                                        Positions="1 0 -3, 0 1 -3, -1 0 -3"
                                        TriangleIndices="0 1 2" />
                            </GeometryModel3D.Geometry>
                            <GeometryModel3D.Material>
                                <DiffuseMaterial Brush="Fuchsia"/>
                            </GeometryModel3D.Material>
                        </GeometryModel3D>
                        <DirectionalLight Color="White"  Direction="2,-1,-9" />
                    </Model3DGroup>
                </ModelVisual3D.Content>
            </ModelVisual3D>
            <Viewport3D.Camera>
                    <PerspectiveCamera Position="-1,1,3" UpDirection="1,0,1" />
            </Viewport3D.Camera>
        </Viewport3D>
    </Grid>
</Window>
```

The *Viewport3D* object contains everything required to render the triangle. In simple terms, you can think of each object in the code as follows:

- **Viewport3D**   Represents a container containing elements that will generate 3-D graphics

- **Camera**   Represents a camera that will render the scene

- **ModelVisual3D**   Represents a 3-D object within *Viewport*, which can be either a light or a geometry

- **DirectionalLight**   Represents a light shining in a particular direction

- **GeometryModel3D**   Represents a 3-D geometrical object

- **MeshGeometry3D**   Represents the set of triangles that defines a 3-D object

- **DiffuseMaterial**   Represents a material used to render a 3-D object, such as a brush

Figure 9-11 shows the outcome of the example.

FIGURE 9-11 Creating a 3-D triangle in Silverlight.

Here's another example, which renders a 3-D cube:

```
<Viewport3D Margin="0,0,0,30">
    <Viewport3D.Camera>
        <PerspectiveCamera Position="-40,40,40" LookDirection="40,-40,-40 "
                UpDirection="0,0,1" />
    </Viewport3D.Camera>
    <ModelVisual3D>
        <ModelVisual3D.Content>
            <Model3DGroup>
                <DirectionalLight Color="Yellow"  Direction="2,-1,-9" />
                <GeometryModel3D>
                    <GeometryModel3D.Geometry>
                        <MeshGeometry3D Positions="0,0,0 10,0,0 10,10,0 0,10,0 0,0,10
                            10,0,10 10,10,10 0,10,10"
                            TriangleIndices="0 1 3 1 2 3  0 4 3 4 7 3  4 6 7 4 5 6
                                             0 4 1 1 4 5  1 2 6 6 5 2  2 3 7 7 6 2"/>
                    </GeometryModel3D.Geometry>
                    <GeometryModel3D.Material>
                        <DiffuseMaterial Brush="Yellow"/>
                    </GeometryModel3D.Material>
```

```
            </GeometryModel3D>
          </Model3DGroup>
        </ModelVisual3D.Content>
      </ModelVisual3D>
</Viewport3D>
```

Figure 9-12 shows the resultant outcome.

FIGURE 9-12 Creating a 3-D cube.

For more complex 3-D objects, you need to create comprehensive meshes. The effort to create such meshes, camera properties, and so forth can be quite huge. Fortunately, you can find some ready-to-use 3-D models on the web. For example, a number of models are available at *http://archive3d.net/.*

You can download the desired model in .3ds (3D Studio Max) format, which you can then convert to XAML using a third-party tool. Several popular tools are available for converting a .3ds model to XAML, including:

■ Zam3D from electricrain (*http://www.erain.com/products/zam3d/DefaultPDC.asp*)

■ Deep Exploration from Right Hemisphere (*http://www.righthemisphere.com/products/dexp/de_std.html*)

■ Viewer3ds by Andrej Benedik (*http://www.wpf-graphics.com/Viewer3ds.aspx*)

 Note For the examples in this book I used Zam3D to convert models in .3ds format to XAML.

Follow these steps to create an intricate 3-D object:

1. Visit *http://archive3d.net/* and download any good model in .3ds format. For this exercise, download the Cup model from *http://archive3d.net/?a=download&id=41934.*

2. Launch Zam3D.

   Figure 9-13 shows the ZAM3D tool.

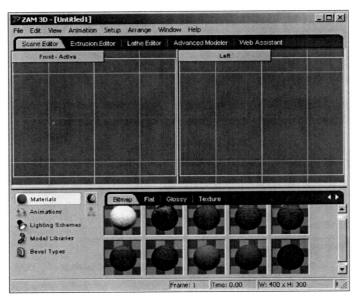

FIGURE 9-13 The ZAM3D tool.

3. From the File menu, select New From 3DS.

4. In the Import 3DS File dialog box, select the .3DS model file you downloaded in Step 1.

5. From the File menu, select Export Scene To XAML.

6. In the Export Options group box, select *Viewport3D* as the Control Type and Export Elements Inline.

7. Copy the generated XAML to a WPF application. Customize any properties such as *LookDirection* or *UpDirection* according to your requirements.

8. Build and execute the application.

Figure 9-14 shows a sample outcome.

FIGURE 9-14 Using WPF 3-D graphics.

Voila! You have rendered an intricate and complex 3-D object with the least possible effort, thanks to the rich set of tools available today.

3-D Graphics in Silverlight

To apply 3-D effects to any Silverlight *UIElement*, you can use perspective transforms. Perspective transforms let you produce an illusion for your objects, making them appear as if they are rotating or moving in a 3-D space.

The *PlaneProjection* class represents a 3-D-like effect on an object. *PlaneProjection* has 12 properties you can use to control the rotation and positioning of an object. Table 9-8 describes these properties.

TABLE 9-8 Properties of *PlaneProjection*

Name	Description
CenterOfRotationX	Specifies or retrieves the x-coordinate of the center of rotation of the object
CenterOfRotationY	Specifies or retrieves the y-coordinate of the center of rotation of the object
CenterOfRotationZ	Specifies or retrieves the z-coordinate of the center of rotation of the object
GlobalOffsetX	Specifies or retrieves the distance by which the object will be translated along the x-axis of the screen
GlobalOffsetY	Specifies or retrieves the distance by which you will translate the object along the y-axis of the screen
GlobalOffsetZ	Specifies or retrieves the distance by which you will translate the object along the z-axis of the screen
LocalOffsetX	Specifies or retrieves the distance by which you will translate the object along the x-axis of the plane of the object
LocalOffsetY	Specifies or retrieves the distance by which you will translate the object along the y-axis of the plane of the object
LocalOffsetZ	Specifies or retrieves the distance by which you will translate the object along the z-axis of the plane of the object
RotationX	Specifies or retrieves the number of degrees to rotate the object around the x-axis of rotation
RotationY	Specifies or retrieves the number of degrees to rotate the object around the y-axis of rotation
RotationZ	Specifies or retrieves the number of degrees to rotate the object around the z-axis of rotation

The following example renders a 3-D like effect to a *StackPanel* and its contents. Thus, when you see the output, you will experience an illusion of 3-D controls.

```
<Grid x:Name="LayoutRoot">
<StackPanel Margin="262,35,100,265" Background="#FF681010">
    <StackPanel.Projection>
        <PlaneProjection RotationX="-35" RotationY="-35" RotationZ="15" />
    </StackPanel.Projection>
    <ListBox Height="100" Name="listBox1" Width="120" >
```

```
        <ListBoxItem Content="Python" />
        <ListBoxItem Content="Ruby" />
        <ListBoxItem Content="C#" />
        <ListBoxItem Content="Java" />
        <ListBoxItem Content="JavaScript" />
        </ListBox>
    <Button Content="Click" Width="100" Margin="25" />
</StackPanel>
</Grid>
```

Here, the properties *RotationX*, *RotationY*, and *RotationZ* indicate degree of rotation. For example, the *RotationX* property will specify the rotation around the horizontal axis of the object. Based on the value of *RotationX*, the object will either rotate toward you or away from you.

Similarly, you specify the rotation around the vertical axis of the object by using the *RotationY* property.

Figure 9-15 shows the output.

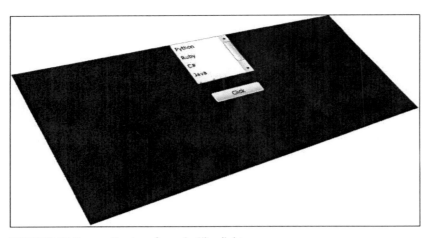

FIGURE 9-15 Perspective transforms in Silverlight.

The following example again similarly renders a 3-D illusion:

```
<Grid x:Name="LayoutRoot">
    <StackPanel Height="150" Background="#FF681010" Width="250">
        <StackPanel.Projection>
            <PlaneProjection RotationX="25" RotationY="5" RotationZ="40"  />
        </StackPanel.Projection>
        <ListBox Height="100" Name="listBox1" Width="120" >
            <ListBoxItem Content="Python" />
            <ListBoxItem Content="Ruby" />
            <ListBoxItem Content="C#" />
            <ListBoxItem Content="Java" />
            <ListBoxItem Content="JavaScript" />
        </ListBox>
        <Button Content="Click" Width="100" Margin="25" />
    </StackPanel>
</Grid>
```

Figure 9-16 shows the output.

FIGURE 9-16 Another example of perspective transforms in Silverlight.

In the next example, you rotate the object, and then—based on the rotation—you apply translations using the *LocalOffsetX* property to translate an object along the X axis of the plane of the object after it has been rotated. Therefore, the rotation of the object determines the direction in which you translate the object:

```
<Grid Background="Gray" x:Name="LayoutRoot">
    <Canvas Grid.Row="1" Margin="20" Width="200" Height="200" Background="Beige">
        <Canvas.Effect>
            <DropShadowEffect />
        </Canvas.Effect>
    </Canvas>
    <Image Grid.Row="1" Margin="20" Width="200" Height="200" Source="Water lilies.jpg">
        <Image.Effect>
            <DropShadowEffect />
        </Image.Effect>
        <Image.Projection>
            <PlaneProjection x:Name="myPlaneProjection" RotationY="65"
    LocalOffsetX="10"/>
        </Image.Projection>
    </Image>
</Grid>
```

As you can see in Figure 9-17, the image is rotated towards you.

FIGURE 9-17 Using the *LocalOffsetX* property.

Pixel Shaders

Pixel-shader effects are effects that you can apply to any user interface element on the Silverlight or WPF UI.

A shader is like a kernel function, executed in parallel for each data element. You can think of a pixel shader as a specialized shader that you execute for each pixel of a bitmap.

A shader is an algorithm compiled and loaded into the Graphics Processor Unit (GPU) that executes once for every pixel in an input image. GPUs are efficient parallel processors; therefore, your algorithm will be executed thousands of pixels at a time.

Pixel shader effects allow you to add effects such as glow, pixel brightness, red eye removal, and shadows to rendered objects. Silverlight and WPF support the use of pixel shader effects.

You can either use the built-in pixel shader effects or custom shader effects. You can add these effects to any *UIElement* using appropriate XAML. You don't need to add any code-behind to use a shader effect.

WPF and Silverlight provide support for several pixel shaders such as *DropShadowEffect, BlurEffect*, and so forth. You can apply only one effect directly to an element at a time. For example, you cannot apply both *BlurEffect* and a *DropShadowEffect* to the same element directly.

The *System.Windows.Media.Effects* namespace defines all the relevant classes for shader effects. Table 9-9 lists a few built-in classes that provide shader effects.

TABLE 9-9 Classes in the *System.Windows.Media.Effects* Namespace

Class Name	Description
Effect	This class acts as a base class for all bitmap effects.
PixelShader	This class acts as a managed wrapper around a High Level Shader Language (HLSL) pixel shader.
BlurEffect	This class represents a blur effect that you can apply to an object.
DropShadowEffect	This class applies a shadow behind a visual object at a slight offset. The offset is determined by mimicking a casting shadow from an imaginary light source.
ShaderEffect	This class provides a custom bitmap effect by using a *PixelShader*.

As listed in Table 9-10, the *DropShadowEffect* class has several important properties that determine characteristics of the drop shadow.

TABLE 9-10 Properties of the *DropShadowEffect* Class

Property Name	Description
Color	Specifies the color of the drop shadow. The default is black.
BlurRadius	Specifies how blurred the shadow is. The default is 5.
Opacity	Specifies how transparent the shadow is. Typical range is between 0 and 1, where 1 means fully opaque and 0 means fully transparent (not visible). The default is 1.

Property Name	Description
ShadowDepth	Specifies how much the shadow will be displaced from the object that is casting the shadow. The default is 5.
Direction	Specifies the direction in which the object casts the shadow. The value is an angle between 0 and 360, with 0 starting on the right hand side and moving counter-clockwise around the object. The default angle is 315.

The following example demonstrates the *DropShadow* effect:

```
<UserControl x:Class="SilverlightGraphics.MainPage"
    xmlns="http://schemas.microsoft.com/winfx/2006/xaml/presentation"
    xmlns:x="http://schemas.microsoft.com/winfx/2006/xaml"
    xmlns:d="http://schemas.microsoft.com/expression/blend/2008"
    xmlns:mc="http://schemas.openxmlformats.org/markup-compatibility/2006"
    mc:Ignorable="d" d:DesignWidth="640" d:DesignHeight="480">
    <Grid x:Name="LayoutRoot">
        <Button Content="DropShadowEffect Demo" Height="30" Width="240"
                Margin="23,23,100,137" Background="AliceBlue">
            <Button.Effect>
                <DropShadowEffect Color="Purple" Direction="270"
                    ShadowDepth="7" BlurRadius="5" Opacity="0.7" >
                </DropShadowEffect>
            </Button.Effect>
        </Button>
    </Grid>
</UserControl>
```

Figure 9-18 shows the output.

FIGURE 9-18 Using *DropShadowEffect*.

Similarly, you can use the *BlurEffect*, which is far easier to use than the previously described effect. For this class, you can just specify the *Radius* property:

```
<UserControl x:Class="ShaderEffects.MainPage"
    xmlns="http://schemas.microsoft.com/winfx/2006/xaml/presentation"
```

```
        xmlns:x="http://schemas.microsoft.com/winfx/2006/xaml"
        xmlns:d="http://schemas.microsoft.com/expression/blend/2008" xmlns:mc="http://schemas.
openxmlformats.org/markup-compatibility/2006"
        mc:Ignorable="d" d:DesignWidth="640" d:DesignHeight="480">
        <Grid x:Name="LayoutRoot">
            <TextBlock Text="BlurEffect Demo" Height="30" Width="100" Margin="23,23,100,137">
                <TextBlock.Effect>
                    <BlurEffect Radius="4" >
                    </BlurEffect>
                    </TextBlock.Effect>

                </TextBlock>
        </Grid>
</UserControl>
```

Figure 9-19 shows the output.

FIGURE 9-19 Using *BlurEffect*.

If you check MSDN for shader samples, you'll find more effects, such as bitmap effects and glow effects. However, these are applicable only to WPF and not supported in Silverlight. By making smart use of the ones that are available in Silverlight, however, you can still work wonders.

Custom Shaders

High Level Shading Language (HLSL) was originally created for DirectX. Using HLSL, you can create programmable shaders for the Direct3D pipeline. The *ShaderEffect* class (mentioned in Table 9-9) provides support for HLSL in Silverlight. Using this feature, you can create pixel shaders that were earlier unavailable in Silverlight or tweak WPF's shaders.

Here's the procedure to create and use a custom shader:

1. Download and install the following tools:

    • Walt Ritscher's Shazzam Shader Editing Tool. Shazzam is a ClickOnce application and provides a cool interface to edit and test HSLS shaders.

- Microsoft DirectX SDK (June 2010) from Microsoft at *http://www.microsoft.com/downloads/ details.aspx?FamilyID=3021d52b-514e-41d3-ad02-438a3ba730ba&displaylang=en.*

2. In Shazzam, specify the path for the fxc.exe file (which is present in Microsoft DirectX SDK).

3. Create a new shader effect file using the File | New Shader File option in Shazzam.

4. Add appropriate code. For example, you could add the following simple code in a shader file named **TestEffect:**

```
sampler2D myImage : register(s0);
// new HLSL shader
float4 main(float2 locationInSource : TEXCOORD) : COLOR
{
     float4 color;
    // get the color of the current pixel
    color = tex2D(myImage , locationInSource.xy);
    color.r = 1;
    color.a=0.25;
    return color;
}
```

5. Compile the shader file by selecting Tools | Compile Shader from the menu.

6. Create a Silverlight library named **EffectsLib.** Delete the default class.

7. Include the compiled (.ps) file in your project, and set its compile type to *Resource.*

8. Copy the C# code generated by Shazzam into a new class file and name it **Effect.cs.**

9. Change the *UriSource* in the code as follows:

```
pixelShader.UriSource = new Uri(
    "/EffectsLib;component/TestEffect.ps", UriKind.Relative);
```

10. Create a new Silverlight application and add a reference to the EffectsLib dll file.

11. Include the namespace and assembly for the library in the XAML code, as shown here:

```
<UserControl x:Class="Effects.MainPage"
    xmlns="http://schemas.microsoft.com/winfx/2006/xaml/presentation"
    xmlns:x="http://schemas.microsoft.com/winfx/2006/xaml"
    xmlns:d="http://schemas.microsoft.com/expression/blend/2008"
    xmlns:mc="http://schemas.openxmlformats.org/markup-compatibility/2006"
    mc:Ignorable="d"
    xmlns:custom="clr-namespace:EffectsLib;assembly= EffectsLib"
    d:DesignHeight="600" d:DesignWidth="400">
```

12. Attach the custom effect class to the element you want in XAML. For example, you can add this effect to a button:

```
<Button.Effect>
    <custom:TestEffect></m:TestEffect>
</Button.Effect>
```

Now you can build and test the application.

Animations and Storyboards

An animation is an action that can change one or more of the properties of an element. For example, when a button is clicked, you might want to change its background color to a darker hue, and then, when the mouse button is released, change the color back to its original color. Or you might want to render a continually moving ellipse. You can achieve all such actions through animations in XAML.

 Note Animations only *temporarily* change the property values of elements—the change isn't permanent.

Though you can create animations directly in C# code, in XAML, you create animations through a *storyboard*. A storyboard in XAML is a resource that contains a collection of animations, each of which targets a specific property of a specific control. A storyboard may even contain other storyboard objects—that is, you can have nested storyboard objects. You typically use nested storyboards to organize rich animation sequences.

You can start, stop, or pause storyboards by using triggers that you set on objects or by using event handlers.

Although Silverlight and WPF share the same framework for animations, the same model for defining animations, and even the same storyboard system, Silverlight uses a scaled-down version of the WPF animation system. There are additional differences in the way you create and begin animations programmatically.

To create an animation in Silverlight or WPF, you basically modify the value of a dependency property over a time interval. For example, to make an image grow taller as soon as it is loaded, you could modify its *Height* property in an animation. To make it expand both horizontally and vertically, you could change both the width and height properties of the image.

Likewise, if you wanted to fade out a *UIElement*, you would change the *LinearGradientBrush* that it uses for its background. The core of animations is knowing which properties to modify and in what manner. For example, to make an element appear and disappear over a few seconds, you should use the *Opacity* property rather than the *Visibility* property. To animate the position of an element, you should use *Canvas.Left* or *Canvas.Top*, which requires the least overheard to alter the position.

Table 9-11 shows three of the most common animation types. The *System.Windows.Media. Animation* namespace defines these classes.

TABLE 9-11 Classes in the *System.Windows.Media.Animation* Namespace

Animation Type	Property Type
ColorAnimation	*Color*
DoubleAnimation	*Double*
PointAnimation	*Point*

You set the *From*, *To*, or *By* (instead of *To*), and *Duration* properties of an animation to specify a starting value, an ending value, an ending value relative to the starting value, and the timeline of the animation.

As an example, the following markup renders a bouncing ball animation using the *Ellipse* element, event triggers, and *DoubleAnimation*:

```
<Canvas Width="60" Height="20" Margin="5">
    <Ellipse x:Name="ellipse" Fill="Green" Canvas.Top="100" Canvas.Left="10"
        Width="100" Height="100">
        <Ellipse.Triggers>
            <EventTrigger RoutedEvent="Ellipse.Loaded">
                <BeginStoryboard>
                    <Storyboard>
                        <DoubleAnimation RepeatBehavior="Forever"
                            Storyboard.TargetName="ellipse"
                            Storyboard.TargetProperty="(Canvas.Top)"
                            To="500" Duration="0:0:1"
                            AutoReverse="True" />
                    </Storyboard>
                </BeginStoryboard>
            </EventTrigger>
        </Ellipse.Triggers>
    </Ellipse>
</Canvas>
```

The following example demonstrates *ColorAnimation*. It renders an ellipse that changes color as soon as it is loaded.

```
<Canvas Width="60" Height="20" Margin="5">
    <Ellipse x:Name="ellipse" Fill="Green" Canvas.Top="-146" Canvas.Left="-150"
        Width="100" Height="100">
        <Ellipse.Triggers>
            <EventTrigger RoutedEvent="Ellipse.Loaded">
                <BeginStoryboard>
                    <Storyboard>
                        <ColorAnimation
                            Storyboard.TargetName="ellipse"
                            Storyboard.TargetProperty =
                            "(Ellipse.Fill).(SolidColorBrush.Color)"
                            From="Blue"
                            To="Red" Duration="0:0:2"
                        />
                    </Storyboard>
                </BeginStoryboard>
            </EventTrigger>
        </Ellipse.Triggers>
    </Ellipse>
</Canvas>
```

The following example demonstrates *PointAnimation*. It renders an ellipse that changes its center as soon as it is loaded and then goes back to the earlier position. This action is repeated infinitely:

```
<Canvas Width="450" Height="350">
    <Path>
```

```xml
<Path.Fill>
    <LinearGradientBrush StartPoint="0,0" EndPoint="1,1">
        <GradientStop Color="Beige" Offset="0.09" />
        <GradientStop Color="Green" Offset="0.45" />
        <GradientStop Color="Yellow" Offset="0.75" />
        <GradientStop Color="Navy" Offset="1.0" />
    </LinearGradientBrush>
</Path.Fill>
<Path.Triggers>
    <EventTrigger RoutedEvent="Ellipse.Loaded" >
        <BeginStoryboard>
            <Storyboard x:Name="myStoryboard">
                <PointAnimation
                Storyboard.TargetProperty="Center"
                Storyboard.TargetName="Ellipse1"
                Duration="0:0:1"
                From="100,300"
                To="175,300"
                RepeatBehavior="Forever"
                AutoReverse="True"/>
            </Storyboard>
        </BeginStoryboard>
    </EventTrigger>
</Path.Triggers>
<Path.Data>
    <EllipseGeometry x:Name="Ellipse1"
    Center="200,100" RadiusX="75" RadiusY="75" />
</Path.Data>
    </Path>
</Canvas>
```

Using Expression Blend for Storyboards and Animations

As you've seen so far, you can create storyboards and animations directly in XAML, but an alternative approach is to use Microsoft Expression Blend to create storyboards.

You can use the following steps to create storyboards in the Blend IDE using the Storyboard Picker:

1. Assume that you have created a new Silverlight application in Blend. Add a *Button* control to it.

2. Launch the Storyboard Picker by clicking the plus (+) symbol and selecting the New option, as shown in Figure 9-20.

FIGURE 9-20 Launching the Storyboard Picker in Blend.

3. In the Create Storyboard Resource dialog box, leave the default name as is.

4. Open the newly created Storyboard by selecting Open A Storyboard from the Object and Timeline drop-down menu (see Figure 9-21).

FIGURE 9-21 Creating a new storyboard in Blend.

5. Select the Properties pane for the button and after scrolling to the Transform property group, choose the Skew option, and skew the button. Figure 9-22 shows this setting in action.

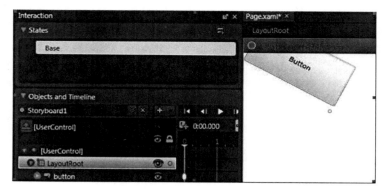

FIGURE 9-22 Recording an animation.

6. Click Base to stop recording. When you view the XAML, you will find that all the lengthy lines of animation are auto-generated. All you need to do now is build and execute your application to view the animation in action.

Now you can see how much easier Expression Blend makes it for you.

Types of Animations

Silverlight and WPF support the following types of animations, each of which uses a different strategy for varying a property value:

- **Linear interpolation**   Also called *From/To/By* animations, they enable the property value to vary in a smooth and continuous manner for the duration of the animation. *DoubleAnimation*, *PointAnimation*, and *ColorAnimation* are examples of this type of animation. You already saw these classes earlier.

- **Key-frame animation**   In general animation terminology, a keyframe is an object in animation that sets the starting and ending points of any transition. A sequence of keyframes defines which movement you will see, whereas the position of the keyframes on the animation defines the timing of the movement. These kinds of animations animate an object between a series of values by using key-frame objects. Key-frame animations are more powerful than the conventional From/To/By animations because they enable you to provide any number of target values. In this kind of animation, values can jump abruptly from one value to another, or they can combine jumps. *ColorAnimationUsingKeyFrames*, *DoubleAnimationUsingKeyFrames*, *PointAnimationUsingKeyFrames*, and *ObjectAnimationUsingKeyFrames* are examples of key-frame animations.

Table 9-12 lists the three most common types of keyframes.

TABLE 9-12 Types of Keyframes

Type	Example
Linear	*<LinearDoubleKeyFrame KeyTime="00:01:01" Value="140"/>*
Spline	*<SplineDoubleKeyFrame KeyTime="00:01:01" Value="140"/>*
Discrete	*<DiscreteDoubleKeyFrame KeyTime="00:01:01" Value="140"/>*

The following markup shows how to create key-frame animations. It renders a rectangle, animates it vertically, and simulates a bounce movement. The markup makes use of event triggers to begin the animations:

```
<Grid x:Name="LayoutRoot" Background="LightGray" >
    <Grid.Triggers>
        <EventTrigger RoutedEvent="Grid.Loaded">
            <TriggerActionCollection>
                <BeginStoryboard>
                    <Storyboard x:Name="Storyboard1"
                        RepeatBehavior="Forever">
                        <DoubleAnimationUsingKeyFrames AutoReverse="True"
                          Storyboard.TargetName="box"
                          Storyboard.TargetProperty=
                          "(UIElement.RenderTransform).(TransformGroup.Children)[3].
                            (TranslateTransform.Y)"
                            BeginTime="00:00:00">
                            <SplineDoubleKeyFrame KeyTime="00:00:01" Value="200"/>
                            <SplineDoubleKeyFrame KeyTime="00:00:02" Value="300"/>
                            <SplineDoubleKeyFrame KeyTime="00:00:03" Value="290"/>
                            <SplineDoubleKeyFrame KeyTime="00:00:03.5" Value="316"/>
                        </DoubleAnimationUsingKeyFrames>
                        <DoubleAnimationUsingKeyFrames AutoReverse="True"
                          Storyboard.TargetName="box"
                          Storyboard.TargetProperty=
                          "(UIElement.RenderTransform).(TransformGroup.Children)[0].
                          (ScaleTransform.ScaleY)"
                          BeginTime="00:00:00">
                            <SplineDoubleKeyFrame KeyTime="00:00:03" Value="1"/>
                            <SplineDoubleKeyFrame KeyTime="00:00:03.5" Value="0.5"/>
                        </DoubleAnimationUsingKeyFrames>
```

```
              </Storyboard>
            </BeginStoryboard>
          </TriggerActionCollection>
        </EventTrigger>
    </Grid.Triggers>
    <Rectangle x:Name="box"
            VerticalAlignment="Top"
            Margin="0,20,0,0"
            Height="100" Width="100"
            Fill="LightSeaGreen"
            RenderTransformOrigin="0.5,0.5">
        <Rectangle.RenderTransform>
            <TransformGroup>
                <ScaleTransform/>
                <SkewTransform/>
                <RotateTransform/>
                <TranslateTransform/>
            </TransformGroup>
        </Rectangle.RenderTransform>
    </Rectangle>
</Grid>
```

The following markup shows how to use *DoubleAnimationUsingKeyFrames* and *LinearDouble KeyFrame*:

```
<Canvas>
    <Canvas.Resources>
        <Storyboard x:Name="Storyboard1">
            <DoubleAnimationUsingKeyFrames Storyboard.TargetName="Rectangle"
              Storyboard.TargetProperty=
              "(UIElement.RenderTransform).(TransformGroup.Children)[3].
              (TranslateTransform.X)" BeginTime="00:00:00">
                <LinearDoubleKeyFrame KeyTime="00:00:00.5" Value="100"/>
                <LinearDoubleKeyFrame KeyTime="00:00:01" Value="426"/>
                <LinearDoubleKeyFrame KeyTime="00:00:01.5" Value="153"/>
                <LinearDoubleKeyFrame KeyTime="00:00:02" Value="13"/>
            </DoubleAnimationUsingKeyFrames>
            <DoubleAnimationUsingKeyFrames Storyboard.TargetName="Rectangle"
              Storyboard.TargetProperty="(UIElement.RenderTransform).
              (TransformGroup.Children)[3].(TranslateTransform.Y)" BeginTime="00:00:00">
                <LinearDoubleKeyFrame KeyTime="00:00:00.5" Value="-11"/>
                <LinearDoubleKeyFrame KeyTime="00:00:01" Value="55"/>
                <LinearDoubleKeyFrame KeyTime="00:00:01.5" Value="305"/>
                <LinearDoubleKeyFrame KeyTime="00:00:02" Value="84"/>
            </DoubleAnimationUsingKeyFrames>
        </Storyboard>
    </Canvas.Resources>
    <Canvas x:Name="LayoutRoot" Background="White" >
        <Rectangle Height="100" Width="163" Fill="Blue" Canvas.Top="54" Canvas.Left="46"
            RenderTransformOrigin="0.1,0.1" x:Name="Rectangle">
            <Rectangle.RenderTransform>
                <TransformGroup>
                    <ScaleTransform/>
                    <SkewTransform/>
                    <RotateTransform/>
                    <TranslateTransform/>
```

```
        </TransformGroup>
      </Rectangle.RenderTransform>
    </Rectangle>
  </Canvas>
</Canvas>
```

Because the preceding code does not use any triggers, you will need to launch the storyboard in the code-behind, as follows:

```
public Page()
{
  InitializeComponent();
      Storyboard1.Begin();
}
```

To create a keyframe-based animation in Expression Blend, you create a storyboard, and in the storyboard, you set keyframes on a timeline to mark property changes:

1. Open an existing application in Blend and open the file Page.xaml in design view.

2. Select the timeline from the Storyboard Picker by clicking the Open a Storyboard button under Objects and Timeline and then select a storyboard.

Working with Storyboards

You can set properties on storyboards to make them automatically reverse or repeat when they reach the end of their last timeline. You can also begin, stop, pause, and resume a storyboard; however, you can't do all this through XAML alone. You need to use a small amount of code to accomplish this task.

The following markup shows how you can begin, stop, pause, and resume a storyboard. It animates a *TextBlock* to behave like a scrolling marquee:

```
<Canvas x:Name="LayoutRoot" Height="480" Width="640" Background="LavenderBlush">
    <Canvas.Resources>
        <Storyboard x:Name="SB">
          <DoubleAnimation Storyboard.TargetProperty="(Canvas.Left)"
            Storyboard.TargetName="tblk"
            Duration="0:0:5"
            From="10"
            To="350"
            RepeatBehavior="Forever" />
        </Storyboard>
    </Canvas.Resources>
    <TextBlock x:Name="tblk" Canvas.Left="10" Canvas.Top="10"
        Text="Demonstrating how to control storyboards" FontWeight="Bold" FontSize="12"/>
    <StackPanel Orientation="Horizontal" Canvas.Left="10" Canvas.Top="265">
        <Button Click="Begin"
          Width="54" Height="30" Margin="2" Content="Begin" />
        <Button Click="Pause"
          Width="54" Height="30" Margin="2" Content="Pause" />
        <Button Click="Resume"
          Width="54" Height="30" Margin="2" Content="Resume" />
        <Button Click="Stop"
          Width="54" Height="30" Margin="2" Content="Stop" />
```

```
        </StackPanel>
    </Canvas>
```

The code-behind for accomplishing the start, pause, resume, and stop actions is straightforward, and looks like this:

```
private void Begin(object sender, RoutedEventArgs e)
{
    SB.Begin();
}
private void Pause(object sender, RoutedEventArgs e)
{
    SB.Pause();
}
private void Resume(object sender, RoutedEventArgs e)
{
    SB.Resume();
}
private void Stop(object sender, RoutedEventArgs e)
{
    SB.Stop();
}
```

Defining Storyboards in Styles

You can also use storyboards within styles and then apply that style to a *UIElement*. The following markup in a WPF application creates a style with two storyboards that use *DoubleAnimations*. It then applies that style to a *Button* element. No code-behind is involved—you can accomplish everything through XAML:

```
<Grid x:Name="LayoutRoot">
    <Grid.Resources>
        <Style x:Key="ButtonStyle" TargetType="{x:Type Button}">
            <Style.Resources>
                <Storyboard x:Key="OnMouseEnterSB">
                    <DoubleAnimation BeginTime="00:00:00"
                        Storyboard.TargetProperty="(UIElement.RenderTransform).
                        (ScaleTransform.ScaleX)" To="4" />
                </Storyboard>
                <Storyboard x:Key="OnMouseLeaveSB">
                    <DoubleAnimation BeginTime="00:00:00"
                        Storyboard.TargetProperty="(UIElement.RenderTransform).
                        (ScaleTransform.ScaleX)" To="1" />
                </Storyboard>
            </Style.Resources>
            <Style.Triggers>
                <EventTrigger RoutedEvent="Mouse.MouseLeave">
                    <RemoveStoryboard BeginStoryboardName="OnMouseEnterSB_BeginSB"/>
                    <BeginStoryboard x:Name="OnMouseLeaveSB_BeginSB"
                        Storyboard="{StaticResource OnMouseLeaveSB}"/>
                </EventTrigger>
                <EventTrigger RoutedEvent="Mouse.MouseEnter">
                    <BeginStoryboard x:Name="OnMouseEnterSB_BeginSB"
                        Storyboard="{StaticResource OnMouseEnterSB}"/>
```

```
                          <RemoveStoryboard BeginStoryboardName="OnMouseLeaveSB_BeginSB"/>
                      </EventTrigger>
                  </Style.Triggers>
                  <Setter Property="RenderTransform">
                      <Setter.Value>
                          <ScaleTransform/>
                      </Setter.Value>
                  </Setter>
              </Style>
          </Grid.Resources>
          <Button Style="{StaticResource ButtonStyle}" Content="OK" Height="40" Width="40"/>
      </Grid>
```

The output shows a button that expands horizontally when the mouse enters its area and reverts to its normal width when the mouse leaves the button area.

You can define global storyboards for an application so that you can use them across any of the pages. This is useful if you want to play a consistent animation sequence on multiple pages in an application. For example, whenever a user clicks a button on any page, the button should expand and then shrink in a span of 1.5 seconds.

You can achieve this by placing the requisite animation in App.xaml and then using that animation wherever that animation needs to be played.

For example, you could place the following markup in App.xaml:

```
<Application.Resources>
    <Storyboard x:Key="GrowButton">
    <DoubleAnimation Storyboard.TargetProperty="Width" Duration="0:0:1"
    From="100"
    To="300"/>
    </Storyboard>
</Application.Resources>
```

In the MainPage.xaml, you could write:

```
<Button x:Name="okbutton" Content="OK" Height="100" Width="100" MouseEnter="
okbutton_MouseEnter" MouseLeave=" okbutton_MouseLeave"/>
```

And to reference the Storyboard in code, you can use the following:

```
private void okbutton_MouseEnter(object sender, MouseEventArgs e)
{
    sb = Application.Current.Resources["GrowButton"] as Storyboard;
    Storyboard.SetTarget(sb, okbutton);
    sb.Begin();
}
```

Easing Functions

So far, you explored how you could create animations through elaborately written XAML markup or by using a design tool like Expression Blend. But what if you don't want to use either? In such a scenario, you use prebuilt animation easing functions. Animation easing requires less effort as compared to creating key frames for animations. Easing functions use mathematical formulas to render the animations.

Silverlight supports several easing functions such as *ElasticEase*, *BounceEase*, *CircleEase*, *BackEase*, and so forth. Table 9-13 offers brief descriptions of some of these functions.

TABLE 9-13 Easing Functions

Easing Function	Description
BackEase	Retracts the motion of an animation slightly before it begins to animate in the path indicated.
BounceEase	Creates a bouncing effect.
CircleEase	Creates an animation that accelerates and/or decelerates using a circular function.
CubicEase	Creates an animation that accelerates and/or decelerates using the formula $f(t) = t3$.
ElasticEase	Creates an animation that resembles a spring oscillating back and forth until it comes to rest.
ExponentialEase	Creates an animation that accelerates and/or decelerates using an exponential formula.
PowerEase	Creates an animation that accelerates and/or decelerates using the formula $f(t) = tp$ where p is equal to the *Power* property.

You use the *EasingMode* property to change the behavior of the easing function. The three possible values you can give for *EasingMode* are:

- **EaseIn**   Interpolation follows the mathematical formula associated with the easing function.

- **EaseOut**   Interpolation follows 100-percent interpolation minus the output of the formula associated with the easing function.

- **EaseInOut**   Interpolation uses *EaseIn* for the first half of the animation and *EaseOut* for the second half.

The following markup demonstrates an example of *BounceEase* and bounces an ellipse when loaded:

```
<Grid x:Name="LayoutRoot" Background="White">
<Ellipse x:Name="ellipse" Fill="Green" Canvas.Top="-146" Canvas.Left="-150"  Width="100"
Height="100" Margin="120,92,420,288" >
    <Ellipse.Triggers>
        <EventTrigger RoutedEvent="Ellipse.Loaded">
            <BeginStoryboard>
                <Storyboard x:Name="myStoryboard" AutoReverse="True">
                    <DoubleAnimation From="25" To="150" Duration="00:00:2"
                        Storyboard.TargetName="ellipse"
                        Storyboard.TargetProperty="Height">
                      <DoubleAnimation.EasingFunction>
                          <BounceEase Bounces="2" EasingMode="EaseOut"
                      Bounciness="2" />
                      </DoubleAnimation.EasingFunction>
```

```
                    </DoubleAnimation>
                  </Storyboard>
                </BeginStoryboard>
              </EventTrigger>
            </Ellipse.Triggers>
          </Ellipse>
</Grid>
```

The following markup shows how to achieve the same animation effect by applying easing functions to key-frame animations:

```
<Grid x:Name="LayoutRoot" Background="White">
      <Ellipse x:Name="ellipse" Fill="Green" Canvas.Top="-146" Canvas.Left="-150"
          Width="100" Height="100" Margin="120,92,420,288" >
          <Ellipse.Triggers>
              <EventTrigger RoutedEvent="Ellipse.Loaded">
                <BeginStoryboard>
                    <Storyboard x:Name="myStoryboard">
                     <DoubleAnimationUsingKeyFrames
                        Storyboard.TargetProperty="Height"
                        Storyboard.TargetName="ellipse">
                         <EasingDoubleKeyFrame Value="25" KeyTime="00:00:02">
                           <EasingDoubleKeyFrame.EasingFunction>
                             <CubicEase EasingMode="EaseOut"/>
                           </EasingDoubleKeyFrame.EasingFunction>
                         </EasingDoubleKeyFrame>
                         <EasingDoubleKeyFrame Value="150"
                             KeyTime="00:00:06">
                           <EasingDoubleKeyFrame.EasingFunction>
                             <BounceEase Bounces="5" EasingMode="EaseOut"/>
                           </EasingDoubleKeyFrame.EasingFunction>
                         </EasingDoubleKeyFrame>
                     </DoubleAnimationUsingKeyFrames>
                    </Storyboard>
                </BeginStoryboard>
              </EventTrigger>
          </Ellipse.Triggers>
        </Ellipse>
    </Grid>
```

Summary

This chapter described how to use various types of media in WPF and Silverlight applications. The chapter defined the purpose of *MediaElement* and illustrated its use with examples. The chapter also explored 2-D and 3-D graphics in detail and demonstrated their use with a number of examples. Then the chapter explained animations and storyboards and discussed how to use them.

Appendixes

Major Namespaces and Classes

This appendix shows the most commonly used namespaces and classes in Windows Presentation Foundation (WPF) and Silverlight, along with a breakdown of the controls and functionality that each namespace provides. Because there are significant differences between the two technologies, they are separated into different sections in this appendix.

Commonly Used Namespaces and Classes in WPF

This section shows namespaces and classes commonly used in WPF development.

System.Windows.Controls Namespace

This namespace defines controls or elements that you can use in XAML. A few of the commonly used classes are listed in the following table.

Class Name	Description
Border	Draws a border and/or background around another element.
Button	This is a standard Windows button control.
Calendar	This control lets users select a date through a calendar display.
Canvas	This container control lets you position child elements using coordinates that are relative to the *Canvas* area.
CheckBox	This control displays options or choices that a user can select or clear.
ComboBox	This selection control displays a *TextBox* combined with a *ListBox*, so users can either select items from a list or type in a new value.
ComboBoxItem	This class represents each selectable item inside a *ComboBox*.
DataGrid	This control displays data in a grid.
DataGridColumn	This class represents each column in a *DataGrid* control.
DataGridRow	This class represents each row in a *DataGrid* control.
DatePicker	This control lets users choose a date by either typing the date text into a text field or by selecting a date from a drop-down *Calendar* control.
FlowDocumentReader	This control lets you view flowed content. It supports several different viewing modes.
Grid	This container control consists of columns and rows that can hold child elements.

Class Name	Description
GridSplitter	This control that reallocates space between the rows or columns of a *Grid* control.
GroupBox	This control is a container with a border and header text.
Image	This control displays an image.
ItemsControl	This control is suited for presenting a collection of items.
Label	This control displays a text label. It is often used as the label for another control.
ListBox	This selection control contains a list of selectable items.
ListBoxItem	This class represents each selectable item in a *ListBox*.
ListView	This control displays a list of data items.
ListViewItem	This class represents each item in a *ListView* control.
MediaElement	This control contains media elements such as audio and video.
Page	This class encapsulates a page of content to which you can navigate. A *Page* can be hosted by a browser, a *NavigationWindow*, and a *Frame*.
Panel	Provides a base class for all *Panel* elements.
ProgressBar	Indicates the progress of a task.
RadioButton	This control allows users to select a single option from a group of choices when combined with other *RadioButton* controls.
RichTextBox	This rich editing control operates on *FlowDocument* objects.
StackPanel	Arranges child elements into a single stack, either vertically or horizontally.
TabControl	This control holds one or more tab pages represented by *TabPage* objects.
TextBlock	This is a lightweight control that displays small amounts of text or flow content.
TextBox	This control enables users to view or edit unformatted text.
UserControl	Provides a simple way to create a custom control.

System.Windows.Data Namespace

This namespace defines classes that support data binding in XAML. A few of the commonly used classes are listed in the following table.

Class Name	Description
Binding	Provides access to define a binding, which connects the properties of WPF elements and any data source.
CollectionView	A view for tasks such as grouping, sorting, and so forth to be performed on a data collection.
CollectionViewSource	The XAML proxy of a *CollectionView* class.
MultiBinding	Defines a collection of *Binding* objects, which are attached to a single target property.
ObjectDataProvider	Enables you to use an object as a binding source.

Class Name	Description
PriorityBinding	Defines a collection of *Binding* objects that are attached to a single target property. This property obtains its value from the first binding in the collection that produces a value successfully.
PropertyGroupDescription	Defines the grouping of items based on the name of a property.
RelativeSource	Implements a markup extension describing the location of the binding source relative to the position of the binding target.
XmlDataProvider	Enables you to bind to XML data.

System.Windows.Shapes Namespace

This namespace defines a set of shapes that you can use in XAML. A few of the commonly used classes are listed in the following table.

Class Name	Description
Ellipse	Enables you to draw an ellipse.
Line	Enables you to draw a straight line between two points.
Path	Enables you to draw a series of connected lines and curves.
Polygon	Enables you to draw a polygon, which is a connected series of lines that form a closed shape.
Polyline	Enables you to draw a series of connected straight lines.
Rectangle	Enables you to draw a rectangle.

System.Windows.Media Namespace

This namespace defines types that enable content integration. This could include media such as audio, video, images, and graphics. A few of the commonly used classes are listed in the following table. Note that most of these classes make use of linear interpolation.

Class	Description
ArcSegment	Creates an elliptical arc between two points.
BezierSegment	Creates a cubic Bezier curve that is drawn between two points.
EllipseGeometry	Creates the geometry of a circle or ellipse.
FontFamily	Creates a family of related fonts.
GeometryDrawing	Enables you to draw a *Geometry* using the specified *Brush* and *Pen*.
GeometryGroup	Creates a composite geometry, composed of other *Geometry* objects.
GradientStop	Defines the color and position of an individual transition point in a gradient.
GradientStopCollection	Creates a collection of *GradientStop* objects which you access through an index.
ImageBrush	Paints an area with an image.
ImageDrawing	Enables you to draw an image within a region defined by a *Rect*.

Class	Description
LinearGradientBrush	Paints an area with a linear gradient.
LineGeometry	Creates the geometry of a line.
MediaPlayer	Provides media playback for drawings.
PathGeometry	Creates a complex shape consisting of various shapes such as curves, arcs, ellipses, lines, and so forth.
Pen	Defines how a shape is outlined.
RadialGradientBrush	Paints an area with a radial gradient.
RectangleGeometry	Defines a two-dimensional rectangle.
RenderCapability	Enables WPF applications to query for the current rendering tier for their associated *Dispatcher* object and to register for notification of changes.
RotateTransform	Rotates an object in the clockwise direction around a given point in a 2-D x-y coordinate system.
ScaleTransform	Scales an object in the 2-D x-y coordinate system.
SkewTransform	Enables you to skew an object.
SolidColorBrush	Paints an area with a solid color.
TileBrush	Paints a region by using one or more tiles.
TranslateTransform	Enables you to move an object in the two-dimensional x-y coordinate system.

System.Windows.Media.Animation Namespace

This namespace defines types that support animations. A few of the commonly used classes are listed in the following table.

Class	Description
BeginStoryboard	Begins a *Storyboard* and allocates the animations to the various targeted objects and properties.
BounceEase	An easing function that creates an animated effect such as a bouncing object.
CircleEase	An easing function that creates an animation that increases or decreases speed using a circular function.
ColorAnimation	Enables you to animate the value of a *Color* property between two target color values over a specified *Duration*.
DecimalAnimation	Enables you to animate the value of a *Decimal* property between two target decimal values over a specified *Duration*.
DoubleAnimation	Enables you to animate the value of a *Double* property between two target double values over a specified *Duration*.
DoubleAnimationUsing KeyFrames	Enables you to animate the value of a *Double* property along a set of *KeyFrames*.
ElasticEase	An easing function that creates an elastic-like animation which looks similar to a spring moving back and forth until it comes to rest.
Int16Animation	Enables you to animate the value of an *Int16* property between two target integer values over a specified *Duration*.

Class	Description
Int32Animation	Enables you to animate the value of an *Int32* property between two target integer values over a specified *Duration*.
LinearDoubleKeyFrame	Enables you to animate from the *Double* value of the preceding key frame to its own *Value*.
LinearInt16KeyFrame	Enables you to animate from the *Int16* value of the preceding key frame to its own *Value*.
LinearInt32KeyFrame	Enables you to animate from the *Int32* value of the preceding key frame to its own *Value*.
LinearInt64KeyFrame	Enables you to animate from the *Int64* value of the preceding key frame to its own *Value*.
LinearPointKeyFrame	Enables you to animate from the *Point* value of the preceding key frame to its own *Value* using linear interpolation.
PauseStoryboard	Pauses a *Storyboard*.
Point3DAnimation	Enables you to animate the value of a *Point3D* property using linear interpolation between two values.
PointAnimation	Enables you to animate the value of a *Point* property between two target values using linear interpolation over a specified *Duration*.
ResumeStoryboard	Resumes a paused *Storyboard*.
StopStoryboard	Stops a *Storyboard*.
Storyboard	Contains object and property targeting information for child animations.

Commonly Used Namespaces and Classes in Silverlight

Because the Silverlight namespaces and classes differ from those in WPF, this section of the appendix lists them separately.

System.Windows.Controls Namespace

This namespace contains classes to create UI controls for an application. Some of the controls defined in this namespace are available with the Silverlight runtime; others are available only in the Silverlight SDK. When you use a control from the Silverlight SDK, you must add a reference to the appropriate assembly. You must also include the XML namespace mapping in XAML. For example, when adding an *AutoCompleteBox* control manually, you must also add a reference to the *System.Windows. Controls.Input* assembly and include the mapping in XAML. However, when you drag the control from the toolbox, Visual Studio adds the reference and namespace mappings automatically.

The following table lists some of most commonly used classes in this namespace.

Class	Description
AutoCompleteBox	A control that accepts or displays text and provides suggestions based on the input in the text box
Border	A control that draws a border around an object
Button	A button control
Calendar	A control that enables you to select a date through a calendar display
Canvas	A container control in which you can position child elements by using coordinates relative to the Canvas area
CheckBox	A control that a user can select or clear
ChildWindow	Provides a window that you can display over a parent window
ComboBox	A container control in which you can position child elements by using coordinates relative to the *Canvas* area
ComboBoxItem	A selectable item contained in a *ComboBox* control
DataGrid	Displays data in a customizable grid
DataGridColumn	A *DataGrid* column
DataGridRow	A *DataGrid* row
DataGridTextColumn	A *DataGrid* column that can contain text
DatePicker	Enables a user to choose a date by either typing it into a text field or by using a drop-down *Calendar* control
Grid	Creates a flexible grid area consisting of columns and rows
HyperlinkButton	A button control that displays a hyperlink
Image	Displays an image in the .jpeg or .png file formats
Label	Displays a caption or other text such as a validation error indicator for an associated control
ListBox	A selection control containing a list of selectable items
MediaElement	An object that contains audio, video, or both
Page	Encapsulates a page having content and is hosted by a browser, a *NavigationWindow*, or a *Frame*
Panel	The base class for all *Panel* elements
PasswordBox	A control that enables you to enter passwords
ProgressBar	A control that indicates the progress of a task
RadioButton	Enables you to provide a group of options from which a user can select one
RichTextBox	A rich-text editing control that supports content such as formatted text
SaveFileDialog	Enables the user to specify options for saving a file through a dialog box
StackPanel	Arranges child elements into a single stack in a vertical or horizontal fashion
TabControl	A control that contains one or more tab pages represented by *TabPage* objects
TextBlock	A control intended to be lightweight that displays small amounts of text or flow content

Class	Description
TextBox	A control enabling a user to view or edit unformatted text
ToolTip	A control that displays information for an element using a small pop-up window
TreeView	A control that displays hierarchical data in a tree structure
TreeViewItem	Provides a hierarchical item for the *TreeView* control that can be selected
UserControl	Provides the base class for defining a new control that encapsulates related existing controls and provides its own logic

System.Windows.Data Namespace

This namespace contains classes that provide support for implementing data binding. Two of the commonly used classes are listed in the following table.

Class	Description
Binding	Defines a binding that connects the properties of binding targets and data sources
RelativeSource	Implements a markup extension describing the location of the binding source relative to the position of the binding target

System.Windows.Documents Namespace

This namespace contains types with text content and document support in Silverlight. A few of the commonly used classes are listed in the following table.

Class Name	Description
Block	Provides a base for all content elements that are present at block level
Bold	Provides an inline-level content element that causes content to render in bold format
FontSource	A set of one or more fonts created from a stream
Glyphs	Renders letters, characters, or symbols in a specific font and style
Hyperlink	Facilitates hosting of hyperlinks
Inline	Supports inline flow content element behavior
Italic	Causes content to render with an italic font style
LineBreak	Causes a new line to begin in content when rendered in a text container
Paragraph	A block-level content element that groups content into a paragraph
Run	A separate section of content that may be formatted or unformatted text
Section	A block-level element that groups other *Block* elements
Span	Groups other *Inline* content elements

System.Windows.Media Namespace

This namespace defines types that enable content integration. This could include media such as audio, video, images, and drawn graphics. A few of the commonly used classes are listed in the following table. Note that most of these classes make use of linear interpolation.

Class	Description
ArcSegment	An elliptical arc between two points
BezierSegment	Creates a cubic Bezier curve that is drawn between two points
DoubleCollection	An ordered collection of *Double* values
FontFamily	Creates a family of related fonts
GeometryCollection	Creates a collection of *Geometry* objects
GeometryGroup	Creates a composite geometry, composed of other *Geometry* objects
GradientStop	Describes the color and position of an individual transition point in a gradient
GradientStopCollection	Creates a collection of *GradientStop* objects that you can individually access through an index
ImageBrush	Fills an area with an image
ImageSource	Provides an object source type for *Source* and *ImageSource*
LinearGradientBrush	Fills an area with a linear gradient
LineGeometry	Creates the geometry of a line
LineSegment	Creates a line between two points, which can be part of a *PathFigure* within *Path* data
PathGeometry	Creates a complex shape consisting of shapes such as curves, arcs, ellipses, lines, and so forth
PathSegment	Creates a segment of a *PathFigure* object
PathSegmentCollection	Creates a collection of *PathSegment* objects that you can individually access by index
PlaneProjection	Creates a perspective transform (a 3-D-like effect) on an object
PointCollection	Creates a collection of *Point* values that can be individually accessed by index
RadialGradientBrush	Fills an area with a radial gradient
RectangleGeometry	Describes a two-dimensional rectangular geometry
RotateTransform	Enables you to rotate an object in the clockwise direction around a given point in a two-dimensional x-y coordinate system
ScaleTransform	Enables you to resize an object in the two-dimensional x-y coordinate system
SkewTransform	Enables you to skew an objec
SolidColorBrush	Fills an area with a solid color
TransformCollection	Creates a collection of *Transform* objects that you can individually access through an index

Class	Description
TransformGroup	Creates a composite *Transform* composed of other *Transform* objects
TranslateTransform	Enables you to move or relocate an object in the two-dimensional x-y coordinate system
VideoBrush	Fills an area with video content

System.Windows.Media.Effects Namespace

This namespace provides types that you can use to apply visual effects. A few of the commonly used classes are listed in the following table.

Class	Description
BlurEffect	Creates an effect that simulates looking at the object through an out-of-focus lens
DropShadowEffect	Creates an effect that renders a shadow behind a visual object with a minor offset
PixelShader	Creates an effect using a HLSL pixel shader
ShaderEffect	Creates a custom bitmap effect using a pixel shader

XAML Editors and Tools

Visual Studio 2010 and/or Expression Blend 4 are commonly used to create and edit XAML markup. In addition to these, there are a number of editors and tools available today that make XAML development a breeze.

Editors

Kaxaml

Kaxaml is a lightweight XAML editor created by Robby Ingebretsen. It provides a split view so that you can see both your XAML and your rendered content. The main Kaxaml website is:

http://www.kaxaml.com/

and you can download it from the following link:

http://www.kaxaml.com/downloads/Kaxaml_1.8.msi

In the words of its creator, Kaxaml is "designed to be a notepad for XAML. It's supposed to be simple and lightweight and make it easy to just try something out. It also has some basic support for IntelliSense and some fun plugins."

Kaxaml supports .NET Framework 4, WPF, and Silverlight.

The Silverlight version of Kaxaml has basic support for Silverlight. The Silverlight support requires Silverlight 4 to be installed.

Requirements

Kaxaml is built using WPF. To use it, you need to have the .NET Framework version 4.0 installed on your computer. If you're running Windows XP, Windows Vista, or Windows 7, you can get it here.

XAML Cruncher

XAML Cruncher was created by Charles Petzold. XAML Cruncher is more or less a Notepad clone, with the addition of a large pane to the right that displays the result of parsing the XAML entered into the text pane.

XAML Cruncher is fast and responsive and automatically re-parses the XAML even as you type. You can download it from the following link:

http://www.charlespetzold.com/wpf/

XamlPad

XamlPad (xamlpad.exe) is a basic visual editor for XAML produced by Microsoft and distributed (sporadically) as part of the Windows SDK.

XamlPad is pretty basic. It significantly lacks any facility to open or save XAML files—you just type your XAML into the text box. It does, however, remember previous content when closed and restarted.

Notable features include the Visual Tree Explorer, which displays the visual tree of your creation. Select an item on this tree and its dependency properties are displayed in the Property Tree Explorer.

As per MSDN, XAMLPad is installed with Visual Studio 2008 and can be found at *Program Files\ Microsoft SDKs\Windows\v6.0A\Bin\XAMLPad*.

XamlPadX

XamlPadX is another fast and lightweight tool, but this one packs a few more features. It was created by Lester Lobo and can be downloaded from his blog.

It features XML syntax highlighting, can collapse tags, and will automatically create closing tags as you type. If your XAML can't be parsed, the error message displayed on the status bar includes a hyperlink to jump straight to the offending code.

Tools

Shazzam

Shazzam is a pixel shader utility for WPF and Silverlight applications. It was created by Walt Ritscher. Shazzam simplifies editing, testing, and learning pixel shader effects.

Shazzam compiles HLSL code, auto-generates C#/VB shader classes, and creates a testing page for each effect. You can download it from the following link:

http://shazzam-tool.com

Ab3d.Reader3ds - 3ds file importer

Ab3d.Reader3ds is a class library used to read 3-D models from .3ds files. You can use it in any WPF application. You can download the tool from the following link:

http://www.wpf-graphics.com/Reader3ds.aspx

XAML Power Toys 3.5

XAML Power Toys is the brainchild of Karl Shifflett and is a Visual Studio 2008 SP1 Add-In or a Visual Studio 2010 Add-In that empowers WPF and Silverlight developers while working in the XAML editor. It provides Line of Business form generation tools, DataForm, DataGrid, Grid tools, and ListView generation. These tools shorten the XAML form layout time.

You can download it from the following link:

http://karlshifflett.wordpress.com/xaml-power-toys/

Aurora XAML Designer

Aurora XAML Designer is a standalone design application that generates the XAML markup required by Visual Studio for developing .NET 4.0 applications. It is intended for use in WPF software applications. Aurora also supports loose XAML files, works in multiple layers and the output is optimized so that the individual graphics can be easily integrated with .NET code-behind.

You can download the tool from the following link:

http://www.dotnetuidevelopment.com/auroraxamldesigner.htm

Index

Symbols

{} (braces), use of in XAML, 95
+ (plus) sign, xvi
| (vertical bar) between menu items, xvi

A

Ab3d.Reader3ds class library, 300
absolute sizing of Grid columns and rows, 146
absolute URLs in Silverlight, 176
AcceptsReturn dependency property, 182
AcceptsTab dependency property, 182
action controls
    ButtonBase class, 172–175
    HyperlinkButton, 176
    RepeatButton, 177
    ToggleButton, 178–181
    types of, 171
Add New Item dialog box, 107
AddOwner() dependency property, 52
ADO.NET Entity Framework, 215
Advanced Stream Redirector (ASX) playlist file
format, 246
alignment properties
    content alignment, 164
    position alignment, 160
AmbientLight object, 262
Ancestor RelativeSource, 219
animation
    bouncing ball example, 276
    controls, 46
    easing functions, 283–285
    EventTrigger class, 82
    Expression Blend for, 15, 277
    namespaces and commonly used classes, 292
    process of, 275–277
    storyboards, 275, 281–283
    types of animation, 278–281
annotation features, 190–193
application and content behavior, controlling and
monitoring
    classes for, 44
    dialog boxes, 44
    RangeBase class
     key properties, 205
     ProgressBar class, 208
     Scrollbar class, 206
     Slider class, 207
applications
    Application.Resources element, 33
    deployment, styles and, 118
    displaying 3-D graphics in, 262
    scope, 129
architecture of WPF vs. Windows Forms, 4
arranging step of the layout system, 130
arrays, creating with markup extensions, 91
artifacts and XAML, 88
Assets folder, creating styles in, 114
ASX playlist file format, 246
attached properties
    accessing, from code-behind, 67
    creating, 65
    defining, using the attribute syntax, 37
    definition and naming conventions, 62
    read/write and read-only properties, defining, 65
    referencing, 35
    syntax, 64
    when to use, 63
attached routed events, 79
attribute syntax
    code to set the value of the Style property using, 88
    of object element properties, 36–39
    vs. property element syntax, for defining styles, 113

About the Authors

 MAMTA DALAL has over 10 years of experience in the IT industry. She is an active contributor to the .NET community and has written several articles on C#, .NET, Silverlight, and WPF on various websites. When not experimenting with technology, she likes to read and write fiction. She is also a travel enthusiast and loves fantasizing about her next trip.

 ASHISH GHODA is the founder and president of Technology Opinion LLC, and an accomplished author with over 15 years of experience in enterprise architecture, application development, and technical and financial management. He is also a director at a Big Four accounting firm and adjunct professor at NJIT and UMUC.

What do you think of this book?

We want to hear from you!
To participate in a brief online survey, please visit:

microsoft.com/learning/booksurvey

Tell us how well this book meets your needs—what works effectively, and what we can do better. Your feedback will help us continually improve our books and learning resources for you.

Thank you in advance for your input!